658.3
Ashby, Frank
Embracing excellence
Prentice Hall

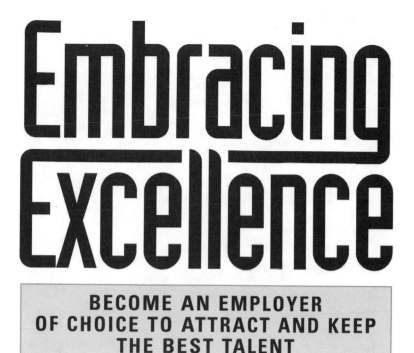

Embracing Excellence

BECOME AN EMPLOYER OF CHOICE TO ATTRACT AND KEEP THE BEST TALENT

FRANKLIN C. ASHBY, Ph.D. • ARTHUR R. PELL, Ph.D.

Prentice
Hall Press

Library of Congress Cataloging-in-Publication Data

Ashby, Franklin C.
    Embracing excellence : become an employer of choice to attract
and keep the best talent / Franklin C. Ashby, Arthur R. Pell.
       p. cm.
    Includes bibliographical references.
    ISBN 0-7352-0263-X
       1. Corporate culture.   2. Employees—Recruiting.   3. Employee retention.
4. Personnel management.   I. Pell, Arthur R.   II. Title.

    HD58.7 .A79695   2001
    658.3—dc21   2001021226

Acquisitions Editor: Luis Gonzalez
Production Editor: Mariann Hutlak
Interior/Design Composition: Inkwell Publishing Services

© 2001 by Prentice Hall

Printed in the United States of America
10 9 8 7 6 5 4 3 2 1

ISBN 0-7352-0263-x

 Paramus, NJ 07652

http://www.phdirect.com

DEDICATION

To our wonderful wives and children, with all our love.

Rita and Erica

Danny, Douglas, and Hillary

About the Authors

Franklin C. Ashby, Ph.D. is chairman and co-founder of *The Leadership Capital Group, LLC* of Princeton, New Jersey, specializing in leadership development, executive and management development, and executive transition. Dr. Ashby is the former chief educational officer of Dale Carnegie & Associates, Inc., the world's largest for-profit adult training organization. He has also served as executive vice president of Manchester Partners International, and president of Manchester Training during his career.

A nationally recognized writer and speaker, Dr. Ashby's recent books include *Revitalize Your Corporate Culture* (Gulf Publishing; 1999) and *Effective Leadership Programs* (ASTD; 1999). His service on boards includes recent terms as chairman of the *Business Advisory Board* at the American Council on Education and member of the *National Commission on Educational Credit and Credentials* in Washington, D.C. He lives with his wife, Rita, and their son, Danny, on Long Island, New York.

Dr. Arthur R. Pell, Senior Vice President of The Leadership Capital Group, is a nationally known author, lecturer and consultant in the human resources field. Among the 47 books he has written are the best selling *The Complete Idiot's Guide to Managing People, The Complete Idiot's Guide to Team Building,* and *The Supervisor's Infobank.* He edited the revised edition of Dale Carnegie's How to Win Friends and Influence People.

In addition to serving on the faculties of New York University, City University of New York and St. John's University, he has conducted public seminars that have been attended by over 300,000 people throughout the United States and Canada. Dr. Pell is listed in *Who's Who in America and Contemporary Authors.* He and his wife, Erica, live in Long Island, New York.

Contents

Acknowledgments   vii

Introduction   viii

1
Corporate Culture——The Key to Employee Retention   1

2
The Qualities and Characteristics of a Great Corporate Culture   21

3
Diagnosing Your Corporate Culture   46

4
How to Find Great People   76

5
Pre-Screening Applicants   112

6
Sharpening Your Interviewing Skills   128

7

Making the Hiring Decision   164

8

You Don't Have to Pay the Most to Get and
Keep the Best   186

9

On-Boarding: Getting the New Employee Off
on the Right Foot   207

10

Why Good People Leave   238

11

Making the Separation Interview
Meaningful   263

12

Leadership—A Key Factor in Retaining Good
People   276

13

Training Well   311

14

Sowing the Seeds for Continued
Success   341

Appendix   362

Index   365

ACKNOWLEDGMENTS

We're very grateful to the many people who have contributed to the development of this manuscript, particularly (in alphabetical order) Pam Bradley, Richard Bradley, Carole Brown, Carmine Fischetti, Dr. Gay Fogarty, Luis Gonzalez, Ron Grant, Dr. Ray Harrison, Kay Harrison, Mariann Hutlak, Jeff Jones, Travis Jones, Grant Lehman, Mike Losey, Carmeane Mackey, Dr. Paul Mackey, Bob McCarty, John Neuman, Dr. Jack Phillips, Patti Phillips, Hon. Mike Pizzi, Molly Shepard, Ron Stone, Dr. Edward Verlander, David Zalik, Andy Ziemins and Peter Ziemins.

Introduction

To win the war for talent, an organization must attract and retain those "A players," the best possible people who can contribute, not only to today's success, but to the organization's long-term prosperity.

Attracting top-level employees has never been more difficult. Keeping those you have is an even greater challenge. In an expanding economy combined with a shrinking labor pool, and a workforce that feels little compunction about changing jobs, companies need to distinguish themselves by developing organizational cultures that enable them to become *employers of choice* — companies that attract and keep the best people.

According to a study made by Aon Consulting in 1999, roughly 25 percent of surveyed employees would change jobs for as little as a 10 percent pay raise and more than half would leave for a 20 percent increase. Pirating people from competitors by offering more money or benefits, or stopping current employees from defecting by making counteroffers has only a short-term value. Companies must reexamine their corporate cultures to uncover the real reasons employees leave and correct any problems before they grow into crises.

Most companies agree that it's tough to fill jobs today and it's becoming more difficult as time goes on. But filling the job is just the beginning. The real challenge is keeping good people once they are hired, trained, and become productive.

It's rare today for a person to join a company after graduating from high school or college and remain there until retirement. Most people have several jobs during their work life. Sometimes the reason for changing jobs is involuntary—the worker is fired, or due to downsizing or reorganization, a job is eliminated. But, quite often the employee leaves voluntarily. For some reason, he or she is not getting from the job what had been hoped for.

Every time a person leaves a job, whether it's voluntary or involuntary, the company suffers. Productivity is curtailed until a replacement can be found and trained—and it's expensive to recruit and select a new employee.

According to the Bureau of Labor Statistics, the average number of years employees stay at their jobs decreased to 3.6 years in 1998 from 3.8 years in 1996. The Bureau of National Affairs reported that in the first quarter of 1999, companies were losing 1.1 percent of their work force every month. This is a 13-year high.

We know turnover is costly. But how costly? Most managers haven't an inkling. Kepner-Tregoe, a management-consulting firm in Princeton, N.J., asked 1,290 managers the cost of losing an employee. Two-thirds couldn't do it.

According to a recent *Wall Street Journal* article, replacing an employee costs roughly one-and-a-half times a year's pay. Both employers and employees report that the loss of workers has led to declines in quality and customer service, resulting in extra marketing costs.

The cost, of course, varies with the type of job and the location of the organization. For example, the cost of replacing a Human Resources manager in the automobile industry was calculated to be over $130,000; the loss of a machinist, $100,000; replacing a store manager in a fast food chain, $20,000.

Cost alone is not the only concern. In today's knowledge-based economy, where often one or two key people have the specialized know-how to create and implement a project, loss of one of them can delay or even stop dead the company's ability to meet its commitments. To avoid the costs incurred with hiring and training new workers, companies are turning to more innovative methods to recruit valuable staff and then retain them for as long as possible.

Just as companies today must "sell" good applicants to accept their job offers, they must provide their good people with incentives to stay. What forms these incentives take vary. Some companies depend on financial deals—salary increases, bonuses, or stock options. Others offer generous benefits or exciting perks. Does this help? Of course, it does—some of the time. But there are limits to how much a company can spend and today's deal may become only the foundation for even greater demands tomorrow. Our research has shown that to attract and retain the best people, these band-aid solutions have only a short-term value. Companies must rethink and revitalize their corporate cultures. They must become *employers of choice*.

Every year *Fortune* magazine lists the 100 best companies to work for—the *employers of choice*. Companies included in this list attract the best candidates for their job openings and maintain a highly stable and productive workforce. An analysis of the financial performance of publicly traded companies in *Fortune's* "100 Best" list showed that these companies performed better in terms of average stock returns than companies that did not make the list and these companies had a lower turnover rate (12.6 percent compared to 26 percent). The study also showed that employees of these firms stayed longer and that these companies received almost twice as many job applications as those that applied for the list, but were not picked. The magic formula that makes a company an employer of choice is the quality of the corporate culture it manifests.

The material in this book stems from over 30 years' experience of the authors and six years of research, studying numerous companies—large and small in a variety of industries—to determine why good employees *really* quit and what might be done to reduce this disruptive and expensive turnover.

WHY GOOD PEOPLE LEAVE

Nothing is as frustrating to a supervisor as having one of the best associates quit. It has often taken months or years to bring that person up to optimum productivity—and now suddenly he leaves. Not only does this disrupt the momentum of the team's work, but also it has negative effects on the other members—unless, of course, the person who quit is universally disliked.

Most companies do try to find out why people decide to leave either through informal chats or formalized separation interviews. You ask the person why he or she quit. Often the answer will be that it's for personal reasons. Carl decided to go back to college; Vicki's chosen to be a full-time mother; Sam's father's illness requires him to take over his business; Jane's spouse is transferred to another city.

Or the answer indicates a career move. Ben has gone as far as he can in your company; Geri is offered more money by another firm; an opportunity arises in a different field—one in which Tom is particularly interested. Hilary's going into her own business.

But often the reason given is not totally true. Yes, Tom did go to an industry in which he has particular interest, but would he have made that decision if he were obtaining job satisfaction in his current job? Geri is leaving for more money. Sure, she would like more money, but perhaps she wouldn't have even looked for a job if she were not unhappy with the supervisor's management style.

Probing for the Real Reasons

Every time someone quits, it's important to determine the true reason. This isn't easy because it may not even be clear to the person who leaves. It may be something deeply imbedded in the culture of the company that subtly has made the person discontented.

People may feel they are not making the progress they had hoped for, that their salary is too low, that working conditions are unsatisfactory, or that the job has become boring. Some are reluctant to divulge the real reason for deciding to quit. This is particularly true if the real cause of discontent lies with the supervisor or other employees. Not only is it embarrassing to tell their boss they don't like him, but they may be concerned about getting a poor reference.

In our research we found that most of the real reasons for discontent lie deep in the culture of the organization. Managers and supervisors tend to reflect that culture in the manner in which they deal with their staff members.

TEST YOUR COMPANY'S RETENTION QUOTA

Examine your personnel practices to determine some of the reasons that your turnover rate is higher than you would like it to be.

Yes No

☐ ☐ Is the company's compensation program (salary plus benefits) at least at a par with competitors for the same types of personnel?

☐ ☐ Do you make employees feel that their work is vital to the company's success?

☐ ☐ Do you provide training to keep your staff at the cutting edge of the technology needed in their work?

☐ ☐ Do you send employees to professional development programs on a regular basis?

☐ ☐ Do you keep in mind employees' personal goals and provide opportunities for them to achieve these goals?

☐ ☐ Do you encourage employees to contribute their ideas and suggestions?

☐ ☐ Do you provide opportunity for employees to assume more responsibility—and pay them accordingly?

☐ ☐ Do employees see the career paths open to them and what steps you are taking to help them move along those paths?

☐ ☐ Do you give both private and public recognition to each person's accomplishments?

☐ ☐ Do you sense a feeling of pride in the work and the company among the employees?

Review your responses. Any "No" answer is an indicator of a problem that may lead to the loss of some of your good employees.

This book will provide readers with the tools needed to examine and revitalize their corporate cultures, and create a climate that will enable their companies to become employers of choice.

WHY THIS BOOK WAS WRITTEN

Our research confirmed that companies throughout the economy have found that retention of employees at all levels is fast becoming one of the most compelling and difficult challenges they face as they enter the first decade of the 21st century.

Our objective was to seek research-based solutions by studying what company practices really work as compared to those that either have superficial value, don't work at all, or worse, have negative effects.

Ignoring the problem, hoping it will go away or that changes in the economy will alleviate it, is self-defeating. Not only will turnover increase, but also morale will suffer, productivity will decrease, and the effect will show up in the bottom line.

Another objective in writing this book is to call attention to the myths and misconceptions that persist in the minds of many managers and by debunking them, compel these managers to take a more realistic look at their policies, procedures, philosophies, and actions.

We will provide guidelines based on our research to help managers develop and strengthen strong leadership and organizational behavior that will build solid relationships between managers and their staffs, creating that spirit of loyalty and commitment that is the essential element of retention.

Most important, this book will encourage the readers to carefully reevaluate the corporate culture that permeates their organizations. Only by identifying how this culture affects the climate in which employees work can the process of making the culture more employee-friendly begin.

HOW THE RESEARCH WAS CONDUCTED

Over the past several years the authors have consulted with many companies on a variety of human resources problems. We learned that quite often our clients had only a vague and often mistaken concept of the nature of the real problem. Even a cursory observation brought out facets that were overlooked by managers. We soon learned that people too close to a situation often miss key points.

To delve more deeply into the situation, we used a variety of techniques including interviews with line supervisors, employee attitude surveys, analyses of performance reviews, and other traditional techniques. Although each approach gave us some information, we found that combining several gave us a more comprehensive view of the company's culture. Indeed, the whole was greater than the sum of its parts.

From this we designed an eclectic tool, the *Organizational MRI (O-MRI),* a holistic diagnostic tool that not only examines specific aspects of a company's problems, but demonstrates how each relates to other phases. How this diagnostic approach is conducted and what information it provides will be discussed in detail in Chapter 3.

The O-MRI not only helped us identify internal problems, but, more important, it provided a three-dimensional picture of the corporate culture. It bared factors that were deeply engrained in that culture, which were the root causes of most of the organization's problems. It was a key first step in revitalizing that culture.

We learned that those companies who had relatively low turnover, who attracted good applicants and built a loyal and supportive work force—in other words, the employers of choice—had a corporate culture that cultivated the talents, interests and strengths of their employees. They were truly "people oriented." Among these companies were Milliken & Co., a prestigious textile firm; Pfizer, the large pharmaceutical company; and General Electric, judged the "most admired company in the world" by a recent *Fortune* magazine survey, and dozens of other companies with fine records of retention. In addition we studied numbers of organizations with heavy turnover and many personnel problems, that prefer to remain anonymous, but from whom we learned a great deal on what companies do wrong.

To focus on the specific aspects of employee retention, we designed a structured separation interview procedure, and trained the clients' managers and H.R. staffs to use it. The separation interview process will be discussed in Chapter 11.

We studied the reports based on these interviews and augmented the information by personally interviewing former employees who had left the companies within the past year. This gave us additional insight into the reasons good people were leaving the companies. What we learned from the MRIs and the separation interviews, supplemented by our years of experience in human resources development, provided us with the data upon which this book is based.

WHAT'S IN THE BOOK?

This book will provide the reader with both a broad look at the subject of keeping your best employees, and specific tools for identifying problems and changing the corporate culture to make your company an "employer of choice."

Chapters 1 and 2 will lay the groundwork for your analysis. You'll learn what employees seek in a company and what features make for a great corporate culture.

In Chapter 3, you'll learn all about the Organizational MRI (O-MRI). You will be shown how each part of the process is applied and will be given the tools to conduct an O-MRI in your company.

Chapters 4 through 8 will review how to attract the employees you want without necessarily having to pay higher salaries than are warranted. Potential problems that lead to high turnover can be avoided if the new hire starts off on the right foot.

In Chapter 9, you will learn the techniques of "on-boarding"—how to help new hires become oriented to the corporate culture.

Chapter 10 will explore the reasons good people leave, examine the facts, explode the myths, and provide solid advice on establishing a workable preventive maintenance program.

Chapter 11 will introduce the structured separation interview, how to conduct it, and how to interpret the information developed.

Chapter 12 is devoted to the role of the supervisor or team leader in keeping employees satisfied without coddling them or sacrificing productivity.

How a solid training and development program can change corporate culture is the focus of Chapter 13. In this section you will learn several techniques for building the soft skills of your staff: leadership, communication, team building, and interpersonal relations.

Chapter 14 will summarize what companies can do to get and keep "A players" by adapting their corporate cultures to meet the needs of the 21st century.

You will find real-life examples illustrating the situations presented. In many cases the company is identified, but in others we have disguised the names of companies and individuals to protect their privacy.

This book is easy to read. You can read it from cover to cover to get an overview. You can read and apply specific sections of the book to your needs. You can use the O-MRI and structured separation interview as presented in the text or adapt them to the specific situations that you face.

Consider this book a challenge to you and to your company. Keep an open mind. Be prepared to see things you and your bosses and colleagues may have intentionally ignored or inadvertently overlooked—and to do something about them. No battles are won by complacency. And it is a battle today to make your company an employer of choice and win the war for talent by attracting and retaining top-level employees.

1

Corporate Culture— The Key to Employee Retention

Finding top-level employees has always been a high priority for companies, but keeping them in this highly competitive work world has become an even greater challenge as we enter the 21st century.

The time has long passed since a young person joined a company early in his or her career and stayed with it until retirement. Today, executive recruiters, Web site notices, attractive help-wanted ads, and word-of-mouth information on who's seeking employees provide a constant temptation for everybody to at least look into positions outside of their current companies.

The increased turnover and loss of key employees has compelled management to take steps to keep their best people from leaving. Some have done this by increasing salary and bonuses or by designing innovative financial incentives. Others have added perks that make the job or the workplace more desirable—and often they work. But, despite these changes, many companies are still faced with a continuing loss of experienced and productive workers.

In our research on this critical matter, we have found that although both financial and nonfinancial incentives do help somewhat, they are not enough. It is like treating an illness with band-aids and aspirin when serious surgery is required.

It all starts with the organizational culture of the company. All companies have such a culture—a corporate way of life followed consciously or subconsciously in the day-to-day activities of the organization. We have found that companies with the highest turnover rates are those in which the corporate culture is one of domination, autocracy and inflexibility. In these companies, no matter what incentives and perks are added, good people will still leave. In companies in which the culture is one of participation, cooperation, and communication, employees are less likely to be tempted to look into other company's offers.

In cases where the culture is one of inhibition and negativism, the culture must be radically changed. Unless top management is totally committed to making a change in the organizational culture, it is more likely than not that nothing of significance will happen. Unfortunately, too many CEOs give lip service to the need for change, but resist any real efforts to shake up their traditional way of doing business. One of the most common comments we hear is: "My boss talks a big game, but when it comes to action, it's business as usual."

> QUOTES AND QUIPS
>
> **"Let us train our minds to desire what the situation demands."**
> **—Seneca,**
> **Roman philosopher**

CREATE A CLIMATE OF UNDERSTANDING AMONG ALL LEVELS OF THE ORGANIZATION

Employees of culture-stagnant companies bemoan the stubborn adherence of their managers to archaic and morale-destroying methods and concepts. Middle-level managers are frustrated when their bosses veto innovative ideas. Rank-and-file workers feel that they are ignored, or worse, looked upon as expendable components instead of contributing participants.

The prevalence of such attitudes was reinforced recently when we conducted two surveys in a number of manufacturing and service companies in various parts of the United States. One survey queried mid-level managers about the major complaints they had about the people who directed their organizations. This was followed by a survey of top managers asking about their complaints about their staffs. The surveys showed that unless and until management fully appreciates how they appear to their subordinates, and employees see how they appear to management, cultural changes cannot even begin to be effected. This knowledge paves the way for planning and implementing a program for a culture change that will be meaningful to all involved. Let's look at the results of both of these surveys.

The Nine Big Complaints Employees Have About Their Managers

1. Gross compensation inequities

Compensation for top managers in most organizations is based on a combination of salary, bonus, stock options and a variety of perks. Their earnings are often considerably more than other employees. Although some people may resent this disparity, it is a generally accepted practice. However, when employees' wages are frozen, bonuses curtailed and people laid off, and senior managers continue to receive high salaries and bonuses, there will be increased dissatisfaction in the company.

This was highly publicized a few years ago when a Fortune-500 industrial conglomerate was faced with increased costs and lower return on investment. It instituted a cost reduction program including downsizing, wage freezes and tightening of expenses throughout the organization. However, the Board of Directors voted to give the CEO a seven figure bonus despite the fact that he was already one of the highest paid executives in the industry. The outcry from employees, customers and the public was so great, the CEO was shamed into declining the bonus.

In less well-known companies, particularly those that are privately held, such inequities are not publicized, but everybody within the organization is aware of them. This often leads to poor morale and the loss of talented people. In one company in the survey, the CEO brought his management staff together and told them that because of a business slow-down, raises for all employees would be eliminated for that year, there would be no bonuses, and the company would cut back on their contributions to the 401K and medical plans. Shortly after this announcement, he persuaded the Board to give him a substantial salary increase and buy him a new Mercedes. He issued an order that employees who travel must select the least expensive way possible. In addition, he limited the amount that these travelers could pay for hotels and meals. However, this rule did not apply to him. Indeed, he upgraded his accommodations to $900-a-night presidential suites and unlimited "entertainment" expenses. You can guess how that affected the morale of that company's employees.

2. A fear-based management style

Many bosses act like "bosses"—they manage by intimidation. Why, in this so-called age of participative management and empowerment, do so many managers still revert to the "I am the boss" mentality? Just as parents who mistreat their children had most likely been mistreated by their parents, it's likely that managers who rule by fear were raised that way by their early bosses. It takes a major change in thinking to overcome this.

> **QUOTES AND QUIPS**
>
> What you *are* stands over you the while, and thunders so I cannot hear what you say to the contrary."
>   **Ralph Waldo Emerson,**
>   **American essayist**

The sad part is that many such managers do not realize that instead of developing loyalty and the desire to cooperate, the result of intimidation is anxiety, indecision and low morale. The survey brought out some of the tactics managers use that cause or aggravate anxiety among their people:

Intolerance of disagreement. The owner of a machine shop prided himself on his knowledge of his field—and he did have considerable expertise in the type of machining the company did. If any of his workers made suggestions on improving a method, which differed from his ideas, he disparaged their concepts and made them feel stupid. Continued disagreements led to termination. He refused to accept that even experienced "experts" don't know everything about an activity. Progressive managers encourage disagreement and learn from it.

Telling an employee you want to see him or her the next day and not explaining what it is about. Has that ever happened to you? I bet you stayed awake most of the night trying to guess what you did wrong—and worrying about how you can defend possible accusations or criticisms. In many cases, all the boss wanted to discuss was some routine matter. The smart manager lets the associate know the subject to be discussed. Not only will this alleviate tension and worry, but will enable him or her to prepare information that may make the meeting go smoothly.

Constantly looking over an employee's shoulder. Certainly, it is occasionally necessary to check a person's work, but a boss who watches every step intimidates most people. People, once trained, should be trusted to do the work properly. More effective is to set control points at strategic intervals. This is usually adequate to assure things are moving along as scheduled.

Eavesdropping on employee's conversations with other workers or worse, listening in on telephone calls, and reading their e-mail. Not only is this an invasion of the employee's privacy, but also it creates a climate of suspicion and fear.

Assuming employees are wrong before getting all the facts. This forces people to take defensive positions on everything they do. People who have to be constantly on the defensive spend more time and energy providing protective measures than getting their work done.

3. Lack of a clear career path

Although not all people are career-oriented, those who look upon their jobs as steps in a growing career are the hope for the future of almost every organization. Of course, no company can or should guarantee employees a certain growth pattern in the company. Those who see opportunities for advancement on the job will likely put out the effort to earn the chance to move ahead.

> QUOTES AND QUIPS
>
> "Fear is an acid which is pumped into one's atmosphere. It causes mental, moral, spiritual asphyxiation, and sometimes death; death to energy and all growth."
> **Horace Fletcher, American author and nutritionist**

Several of the companies in our survey were family-owned businesses and it was generally accepted in those firms that many senior management spots were reserved for family members. This, obviously, limits the potential for advancement to all other employees. In cases like this, a key question looms: How can such companies attract and retain good people? The answer depends on the approach to advancement taken by the powers-that-be. Owners that follow the "blood is thicker than water" concept and restrict most management jobs to family will probably lose their best people. However, there are still good opportunities in many family-owned businesses. Often there are a number of high-level jobs in these organizations that family members cannot or do not want to hold. Non-family members who hold such positions often move up to significant management jobs.

Lack of opportunity is not limited to family businesses. We saw this happen when one of our friends—a bright, creative marketing specialist—was stymied in his career because the company for which he worked promoted people primarily on the basis of seniority. It would have taken him years to move up to a management position for which he was well qualified. He had no choice but to seek another job. By sticking to the archaic promotion policy of seniority, they lost this high-potential employee—and probably many others like him.

To help such high potential employees move ahead in their careers some companies have instituted formal programs called "career pathing." These organizations use techniques such as performance evaluations, psychological testing, assessment centers, counseling sessions and informal meetings with senior executives to evaluate the potential of their employees.

What have these programs accomplished? People who have gone through the programs report that they learned much about themselves. As a result, many of them have undertaken additional training—both within the organization and on their own—to build up their capabilities.

Other companies encourage all managers to cultivate employees' skills and build productivity by providing career counseling and training as part of their regular activities. The HR departments of these companies provide the tools and training that managers need to accomplish this.

The HR department of Motorola, for example, provides career-planning modules for both managers and associates. Chrysler Corporation's HR department has a similar program. Susan McGraw, an HR executive at corporate headquarters explained how it works: "During the first day of supervisory training, managers assess themselves in terms of their own careers and planning. The second day focuses on coaching and facilitation strategies. Nonsupervisory training includes a lot of exercises on self-assessment, value clarification, receiving career feedback and developing career networks."[1] This is followed through with periodic discussions between the manager and the associates concerning progress made and additional steps that should now be undertaken.

Coaching becomes an integral part of the career pathing program. Edward G. Verlander, a prominent management consultant notes: "At the heart of retention is the ability of company management to build a psychological connection with employees so they do not want to leave. They are convinced that by staying, there will be more to gain. While this connection can be gained in many ways, coaching is one of the most effective and beneficial tools to use since it benefits both employees and managers. By its very nature, coaching engages the most basic and important of all human motivations—the desire to learn and grow. If done well, coaching mitigates turnover and helps retention. It gives both the high potential, and the riskiest employee a way to feel trusted, nurtured, valued, and championed. They will learn that even if things in this organization are not perfect (no organization is) and the money may not be the highest they could earn, at least in this company, management looks after its people, fosters growth and development, and gives greater responsibilities, challenges and rewards. And this will tip the balance in favor of staying."

---

[1]Tyler, Kathryn, "Prepare Managers to Become Career Coaches," *HR Magazine*, June 1997, p.100.

4. Tolerance of poor performance

One of the major complaints of those who expend their energies, talents and expertise to do superior work is to see others who just barely get the work done receive the same recognition and rewards as they do.

It is important for people to know what performance standards are expected of them. Unfortunately, too many people interpret "standards" to mean acceptable production and make no effort to do better than "what is expected."

One of the respondents in the survey reported: "In my company the CEO favors the plodding drones, those who come to work a little early and work a little late despite the fact that all they produce is average work. When this was called to his attention, he commented that he'd rather have a 'team of average workers who consistently meet production standards than temperamental stars.'

Over the past four years the company has lost several high achievers who felt frustrated by this accent on mediocrity—and the company's business has lost market share to its more progressive competitors."

Another respondent complained that her CEO withdrew the tuition reimbursement for her MBA program because he felt she should put all of her energies into the job, and the time and effort spent in "unnecessary schooling" was distracting her from her work. When she continued the program at her own expense, he let her know that he was unhappy about it and "it would be reflected in her next performance review." You can bet that when she obtains her degree, she'll be moving to a more enlightened organization.

5. Broken promises

Paul Cullen was the type of businessman who makes a mockery of the term "business ethics." He built his business on the Barnum principle—"There's a sucker born every minute." Making promises he had no intention of keeping was just one of his commonly used practices.

In 1994 he read in a trade journal that the patent on a well-known industrial product was to expire in 1997 and that several companies were tooling up to manufacture what had been the monopoly of the patent holder.

"Why wait three years," Cullen figured. "I'll get a head start." He approached several of the patent holder's engineers and offered them big bonuses and salaries to leave their current jobs and join him. As one of these engineers told me, "it was the kind of an offer you couldn't refuse. I would get a much better starting salary than I was now making, plus a very large bonus once the product was on the market. Three of us left the old company, sold our homes and moved 1000 miles to his facility."

For the next nine months they taught Cullen and his staff all that they had to know to manufacture the product. Now that Cullen no longer needed their expertise, he fired them. He gave them one month's separation pay and no bonus. This exemplified Cullen's concept of management. Achieve your goal even if it involves infringing of patents, breaking promises, or disrupting people's lives.

To a lesser degree, the world of management is strewn with broken promises. There are some companies that promise raises and benefits they have no intention of granting or hint at company cars, country club memberships and other perks that somehow never are realized. Never forget: Unless managers are truthful and loyal to their people, it's hard to expect loyalty in return.

6. Putting personal interests ahead of what's best for the company

Over the years we have observed many situations in which decisions were made by managers who were motivated, not by what was best for the organization, but by the personal interests of the decision maker. Bob H., Executive Vice President and General Manager of the Friendly Finance Company, is one of those managers. A few years ago, the company having outgrown its office space in downtown Atlanta needed to move to larger quarters. Two facilities were under consideration. One was about a mile from the present office in a newly constructed high-rise building; the other a free-standing building in a suburb close to Bob's home. As most business was done by phone and fax, customer accessibility was not a factor. Although the downtown location was much more easily reached by most of the employees, Bob chose the suburban space. Sure, it would be much easier for him to get there, but it caused a great deal of inconvenience to everybody else on the staff.

7. Being treated as second class citizens

In discussing the complaints employees have about their managers, one that came up over and over again as being most annoying was lack of respect. "The boss thinks he is much better than we are and this shows up in the way he talks to us, gives us orders and condescendingly 'listens' to our ideas." A good example of this is Lt. Col. Carl Carlson. When he retired from the army, he was hired to head an administrative department of a large hospital. He never let anybody forget that he had been a lieutenant colonel in the army and insisted that employees call him "Colonel." He treated them as "enlisted personnel." He ran his department like a military unit.

During the first year of his tenure the employees filed seven grievances against him with the Human Resources department, several clerks requested transfers and others quit. Despite counseling by his supervisors and HR staff, he could not accept that his position was not a "superior officer" but a team leader. As a result, he was asked to resign.

Carlson's attitude may have been carried over from his military training, but such behavior is not limited to former officers. Many managers are "rank conscious" and build barriers between themselves and their staffs. Although there are times when the position of authority one has is needed to make decisions, managers should not depend on their rank to run their departments. The best managers have rejected authoritarianism in favor of understanding, diplomacy, and teamwork.

8. Lack of reward for superior work

In our survey, we found many respondents were unhappy with management's lack of appreciation for superior performance— work that is above the standards that have been set for that assignment. As mentioned

earlier in this chapter, many managers will settle for "satisfactory" work. Inasmuch as there is no showing of appreciation, financially or otherwise, for workers who produce more than what is expected, there is no incentive for them to exceed performance standards. This is exacerbated when co-workers put pressure on peers not to exceed quotas "because it makes the rest of us look bad."

Some companies have overcome this by awarding production bonuses to the entire group or team when standards are exceeded. Although financial reward is naturally welcome, even nonfinancial rewards such as team recognition, a team dinner when the project is completed, and similar signs of appreciation can be effective.

One respondent noted that in his company, workers are actually punished for doing more or better work than co-workers. Management feels that to encourage cooperation and team spirit, no one person should be recognized for his or her contribution. Needless to say, such a shortsighted approach inhibits individual creativity and innovative initiatives.

An effective way to assure increased commitment, loyalty and enthusiasm among employees is to give them added compensation in areas where it is not required by law or custom. For example, many companies require employees to work many hours over the normal 40-hour work-week. The law requires that nonexempt employees be paid at overtime rates for this work, but companies do not have to pay supervisors and other exempt personnel extra pay. It's simply part of the job. In cases where excessive overtime is routine, why not give these people some form of added compensation when they put in those extra hours? Sure, it may cost the company a few dollars, but it will pay off in added productivity and high morale.

An example of this was North Atlantic Constructors, a construction company that had to meet a tight deadline to complete a major project. All the employees were working 50 to 60 hours a week. Of course, non-exempt workers were paid time and a half for the excess hours. Although not required by law, North Atlantic opted to give all supervisors and other non-exempt employees additional pay for the time put in after 40 hours. This resulted in a fierce commitment on the part of these men and women toward meeting the deadline.

9. Feeling unappreciated

Pioneer psychologists from William James to Abraham Maslow pointed out the importance to individuals of having their worth recognized and appreciated. This can range from simple feedback from one's boss to elaborate recognition awards and ceremonies.

> **QUOTES AND QUIPS**
>
> **"One way of winning the full support of your staff and assuring their enthusiasm to meet the company's goals is to reward them with more than they expected."**
> **Robert J. McCarty,**
> **Executive coach**

A survey conducted by the Council of Communication Management indicated that recognition for a job well done is the top motivator for employee performance[2]. For feedback to be most effective, it should be face to face and given as soon as possible after the accomplishment. Positive feedback provides immediate acknowledgment that what the employee has done is not just "doing the job," but that the boss and the organization appreciate what has been done.

This follows the principles advocated in *reinforcement theory,* which states that behavior is contingent upon reinforcement. This theory is based on the work of B. F. Skinner and advocated by most behavioralists as the most effective way to motivate and modify behavior.

---

[2]Koch, Jennifer, "Perpetual Thanks: Its Assets," *Personnel Journal,* Jan. 1990, pp. 72-73.

There are times when criticism is needed to correct errors, or to get mediocre workers to meet your standards, but even then, it should be positive and constructive rather than negative and degrading.

Managers should make it a practice to communicate with their associates all of the time—not just to criticize or compliment them. Day-to-day interaction between managers and staff members leads to a smooth flow of activity, an ongoing commentary on both bad and good aspects of their work to reinforce, to improve, and to obtain full commitment to achieving departmental and company goals.

The Seven Big Complaints Managers have about Employees

To obtain the other side of the picture, we also conducted interviews with a number of senior managers to elicit how they perceived employees. Most managers agreed that their people were basically satisfactory, but felt that there were many areas in which they could improve. The following were the seven most commonly mentioned complaints.

1. Poor work habits

Frequently heard in our interviews was the comment that the so-called "work ethic" which at one time permeated American industry has long since passed. Many workers, they said, no longer consider it an obligation to give their full energies and efforts to their jobs. To paraphrase John F. Kennedy, they ask "What can this company do for me?" rather than "What can I do for this company?"

A typical complaint about rank-and-file workers is that they have no interest in their work. They watch the clock, put out just enough production to meet minimum standards and are constantly seeking ways to beat the system. One manager commented that he spends excessive time arguing about and defending himself and his management staff from unfounded gripes and grievances. "One

woman filed six separate charges of sex harassment and discrimination—all of which were found to be groundless—taking an inordinate amount of time and expense. She was looked upon by her
co-workers, who knew the charges to be false, as a side-show."

Another respondent, the CEO of a warehousing and distribution company, reported that her human resources department has
to train new employees, most of whom are recent high school
graduates, in the simple common-sense concepts of coming to
work on time every day, that assigned work must be completed on
schedule, and that a ten-minute break is really only ten minutes in
duration.

This is not limited to hourly workers. Several CEOs complained
about the work habits of some of their first-line and middle-management people. "When I entered the work force in the 1970s," one
executive commented, "my job was the most important thing to
me. I worked long hours, took work home and went anywhere the
company sent me at short notice without complaint. Now, many of
these young MBAs don't have this dedication. I hear things like
'Sure this work is important, but I have family obligations that are
equally important.' With such an attitude how can I expect them to
put out the work that is needed for the company to grow?"

These complaints about work habits and attitudes, justified or
not, must be taken into consideration in managing people with different backgrounds and goals. What appears to be unreasonable to
one person is an accepted principle of others. The successful manager of the early 21st century will have to be perceptive enough to
recognize these differences, to change what should be changed,
and to accept and adjust to what cannot. With a changing culture
in which family values are considered as important as job values,
managers may have to adjust their organizational cultures to con-
form to the larger community culture.

2. They don't care enough about doing quality work

Despite the emphasis being placed on quality and the installation
of Total Quality Management programs in many organizations,
many managers in the survey pointed out that their employees re-

sisted the company's efforts to help them improve the quality of their work. An example of this was exhibited at Collins Electronics. This company manufactures precision electronic parts as a subcontractor to a manufacturer that deals primarily with the U.S. Department of Defense. In order for the payment for their work to be received reasonably fast, the paperwork must be in perfect form. One slight mistake requires redoing the work and delaying payment—sometimes for several months. Despite careful training and reiteration of the importance of accuracy, many clerks do not take the time to check and recheck their work. This leads to a failure to find errors until late in the process or not at all. Charles Collins, the company CEO, blames it on the schools. In his community, he says, teachers pass students even if their work is sub-standard. They are so accustomed to getting away with slovenly work in school, it continues in the workplace.

Companies that have become involved in the Total Quality Management (TQM) movement report that one of their first tasks is to change employees' attitudes about quality. Until they are convinced that poor quality cannot be tolerated, that "slightly off the standard" is not acceptable, the TQM program cannot even be undertaken.

3. Employees spend too much time socializing

"Every time I walk through the office, I see people gabbing with each other. I can't see how any work is ever done." We've heard this complaint over and over, not only in this survey, but also in many other companies with which we have had dealings. Yes, the workplace is a social environment. We spend more time with the people with whom we work than with any other group other than our immediate families. Socializing on the job is normal and should be expected. It serves a valuable purpose. It results in better communications among co-workers. Especially when people work in teams, this social interaction solidifies the team relationship. However, when non-job related socializing interferes with accomplishing goals, managers must step in and bring it to the attention of the offenders.

Even non-business related chatting among employees could serve a positive purpose. It can be an antidote to stress and boredom. Some people find taking a break from the tensions of the job to discuss last night's sporting events or the latest movies or TV shows gives them new energies to resume work.

This was brought home to us when we were given a tour of the assembly department at a plant in which the workers spend their entire shifts putting together small plastic parts. It appeared that the workers seemed to be spending an inordinate amount of time talking and socializing. When this was mentioned to our host, he responded: "The work is tedious and boring, the pay is low and the turnover of new workers is exceedingly high. However, we have found that workers who stay on the job for at least three months tend to remain with the company for years. We attribute this to the social interaction on the job. Once these workers get into the swing of things, they become part of the social group. They all know about the families, activities, romances, troubles and triumphs of each of the others. Despite the boredom of the work, they look forward to each workday—and notice that all of the time that they are talking, their hands are working. Productivity is really good here."

4. Lack of initiative

Several managers in the survey commented: "My employees depend on me to make every decision, to come up with every idea. They're good people. If I tell them what to do and how to do it, I get the work out, but they never suggest anything." Often they added: "Workers either cannot or will not take the initiative to contribute suggestions or to start projects. They must be prodded to do so."

On the other hand, we found quite a number of managers who had the opposite experience. Their associates were not only capable of taking initiative but also sought such opportunities. Why the difference? In most cases, it depended on management. If management from the CEO down the line encouraged workers to take initiative, they would.

Many executives who decried their people's lack of initiative overtly or inadvertently inhibited it. By consistently rejecting ideas, by contending that the employee did not have enough know-how to initiate a project, by dogmatic insistence of following old procedures, they send a clear message: "We do the thinking; you do the work."

5. Poor communication skills

Several managers in the survey reported that many members of their work force do not have good communication skills. They cannot express themselves clearly and concisely in one-to-one conversations and freeze up when required to speak at a meeting. In cases where skill in writing is required, they noted that even many college graduates couldn't write a decent report or a clearly composed letter.

> **TACTICAL TIPS**
>
> Communication skills can be taught. There are some excellent courses available at community colleges, universities and through private training groups to help people learn or improve their techniques of oral and written communication.

This is one of the areas in which training can be of great value. We've seen how relatively short-duration programs can make significant improvements in the techniques and styles of the participants. The time and cost of such programs is insignificant in relation to the results attained.

6. "I can't depend on them"

Several of the executives interviewed felt that lack of dependability was probably a major complaint. One respondent commented: "I can't do everything myself, yet if I delegate it to others, I can never be sure it will be done right and done on time."

Yes, there are some people on whom you just cannot depend. Such people should be restricted to positions where they can be carefully monitored. However, most people can be depended on if they believe you really trust them.

Rosa Gomez, who runs a successful printing shop in El Paso, Texas, learned this the hard way. Gomez prides herself on the quality of her work. "I am a perfectionist," she says "and I expect my people to put out perfect work." To assure that every order was filled with total accuracy, she would spend hours and hours proofing and re-proofing copy. She did not trust anybody else to do this. In 1989 she collapsed at her desk. Her doctor insisted that she take an extended vacation and cut back on her work hours. She refused to take the vacation, but reluctantly delegated some of the proof-reading. To her surprise her people did excellent work. They knew that Gomez needed their help and they lived up to her hopes. A year later, she had enough confidence in their dependability to take her very first extended vacation.

7. They are unwilling to go that extra mile

TACTICAL TIPS
Establish high standards, train people to adhere to those standards, reinforce their successes with praise and have the confidence to allow them to do their jobs without looking over their shoulders.

Several managers reported that workers just won't stretch. They do what they have to do and no more. One manager reported that at 5 P.M., several of his people stopped work even though they had been told that the work had to be completed that night. "I didn't expect them to put in another shift, just another half hour to finish the job, but it never occurred to them to volunteer to stay. Even after I reiterated the need to meet our commitment to the customer and politely asked them to finish the assignment, it was only with reluctance and resentment that it was accomplished."

Of course, there are many people who do put in that extra mile. The survey brought out that most companies have some workers and managers who willingly devote extra time and effort to their jobs, who put reaching company goals and achieving customer satisfaction on the top of their priority list—and the most successful companies have ingrained this attitude in their people.

Yes, there are some people whose attitudes toward their jobs and their employers will always be negative. This may stem from deep-seated factors in their lives or bad experiences with other employers. But, our experience has proven that this is not true of most men and women. Through training, trust and motivation, people can be inspired

QUOTES AND QUIPS
"When work is a pleasure, life is a joy. When work is a duty, life is slavery"   **Maxim Gorky, Russian novelist**

to put out that extra effort and dedication that is the hallmark of successful organizations, and will lead to attracting and retaining "A-players."

SUM AND SUBSTANCE

Companies with the highest turnover rates are those in which the corporate culture is one of domination, autocracy, and inflexibility. In these companies, no matter what incentives and perks are added, good people will still leave. In companies in which the culture is one of participation, cooperation, and communication, employees are less likely to be tempted to look into other companies' offers.

The nine big complaints employees have about their managers are:

1. The difference between manager's compensation and that of the rank and file workers is inequitable.

2. Too many managers manage by fear.

3. The company does not offer clear career paths to employees.

4. Mediocre performance is tolerated, so why bother to do superior work.

5. Making promises that are not kept.

6. Putting the personal interests of a manager above what is best for the entire staff.

7. Treating employees as second-class citizens.

8. Failure to reward superior work.

9. Employees feel unappreciated.

Although most managers do not deal with employees in these ways, those who do must be made aware of their practices and trained to overcome them.

Seven common complaints managers have about their employees are:

1. They have poor work habits.
2. They don't care enough about quality work.
3. They spend too much time socializing.
4. They lack initiative.
5. They have poor communication skills.
6. You can't depend on them.
7. They're unwilling to go that extra mile.

The Qualities and Characteristics of a Great Corporate Culture

Our research has shown that there is a direct relationship between the employee retention rate and the corporate culture of the organizations involved. Organizations that focus on the utilization of the best talents of their employees have much lower turnover rates than those whose emphasis is primarily on productivity.

MANAGEMENT STYLE

Too often the top-level managers of an organization think that keeping their companies at the cutting edge of the technology in their field is enough not only to maintain high productivity, but also to build morale. After all, as one executive told us, people feel good when they work with the very best tools and techniques. This is not always the case.

This was reinforced in our studies when the CEO of a well-known housewares distributing company retained us to analyze the company's training needs. He complained: "I have invested a fortune in computers and automation in my warehouses, but the productivity of my people has not increased proportionately. How can we improve their performance?"

From our analysis we learned that the staff were well trained in the technical aspects of using the new equipment, but were not sold on its benefits to them. Some workers looked upon it as a threat to their security. They were concerned that the computers might replace them. Others felt that it dehumanized them—that judgments usually made by them would now be made by the computer. Still others felt that computers stifled their creativity. They complained that the work became so routine that it was no longer a challenge.

The CEO could not understand this. He believed that the new equipment should help the staff. The equipment would now do much of the routine drudgery. The employees could use their time to do creative things. He failed to realize that elimination of drudgery alone is not enough to foster creativity.

Too often, the perceptions of the CEO and higher levels of management are much different from those of the men and women who do the day-to-day work of the organization. A complete re-thinking must be made of the interrelationships from the top layers to the bottom levels of the company.

> **QUOTES AND QUIPS**
>
> **"Never forget the human angle. It's the people that use the technology that makes it either succeed or fail."**
>
> **Dr. Paul J. Mackey,
> Management consultant**

CULTURAL CHANGE TRANSCENDS ORGANIZATIONAL LEVELS

Everybody in an organization must recognize the need for culture change and be committed to taking the necessary action to make changes. Although the full commitment of the CEO and others in top management is essential, they must enlist the full cooperation of *all* of the people to achieve real success. A climate must be created in which managers and workers alike are encouraged to challenge current practices without fear of reprisal. Establishing an environment in which people are stimulated to think about, develop, and implement new ideas should enhance this.

Complacency can no longer be tolerated. Employees at all levels must be imbued with the desire to improve their performance. The traditional industrial cultures have stifled creativity in people. Deviations from the norms, variations from standard operating procedures, and disagreements with the powers-that-be have traditionally been punished, which led to uncritical acceptance of the status quo. Giving the people who work on a job the opportunity to unleash their creative energies will foster new ideas, more efficient methods, and closer cooperation and interaction among staff members and between departments. This will lead to a new, dynamic, exciting, and productive culture that will enable organizations to survive and thrive as we enter the first part of the new century.

It is not easy for most managers to look at their organization's culture objectively. It has been an integral part of their lives for many, many years. It is natural to resist change; even to fight to keep practices with which one has become comfortable. Some organizations can make this commitment and put it into effect on their own. Sometimes it is desirable to bring in an outside consultant to help in analyzing the organizational culture and suggest and implement appropriate changes. But whether a company uses its own resources or outside experts, everybody concerned must be aware of and committed to the process.

> **TACTICAL TIPS**
>
> Success in changing an organizational culture requires not only the full commitment of top management, but the cooperation of all the people at all levels of the organization. A climate must be created that stimulates people to challenge current practices and to develop and implement new ideas.

THE UNOFFICIAL ORGANIZATIONAL CULTURE

Organizational culture is not limited to what is written in a formal statement. Much of what becomes culture develops slowly and imperceptibly over time and becomes ingrained in the behavior of everybody in the organization. Company executives may have idealistic concepts about the culture of their organizations, but what actually exists may be quite different. The real culture often stems from the *informal organization*—the acts, thoughts and perceptions of the rank-and-file workers, which have evolved from a variety of sources. Let's look at some of them:

Customs

Over the years certain customs develop which may have had value when initiated, but as circumstances change, no longer have any meaning. There's the old Chinese story of a newly appointed military commander who questioned why a sentinel was posted at a certain location. He could find no logical reason for a soldier to be assigned to that place. He was told, "But, Sir, there has always been a sentinel there. He searched the archives and learned that two hundred years ago, the Empress had a rose garden at that spot and ordered that a sentinel be assigned to protect it from intruders. The empress was long dead, the rose garden not even a memory, but the sentinel still guarded the spot.

Many companies still follow old practices and policies that may have served a purpose once, but are no longer useful. Not only does this waste time, money, and energy, but it contributes to low morale and employee turnover.

> **TACTICAL TIPS**
>
> Every policy and practice should be tried for its life periodically. Ask: "Why do we do this?" "Does this practice serve the purpose for which it was established?" "Can we do this better?"

Dominant person

Often an organizational culture is created because of the influence of a dominant person—often a founder or subsequent top manager. His or her personality sets the organizational culture for good or bad. In some companies the top executive must make every decision—important or trivial. This may have started when the company was small and the CEO could keep close tabs on everything, but years later, when this is no longer practical, it still persists, making the organization less flexible than it need be to deal with routine matters.

The experience of White Plastics exemplifies this. When Larry White started this business, he made all decisions and knew what was happening in all aspects of the operation. As the business expanded, he began to lose touch with some of the activities. So that he could keep informed, he required that copies of all correspondence be sent to him every day. Today, forty years later, his current successor still gets a file copy of every letter, FAX, memo, etc. He rarely has time to even glance at them, yet the practice continues. When this was brought to his attention, he refused to change the practice. He commented: "It helped my predecessor and it may come in useful sometime."

Sometimes a dogmatic executive, who must have everything done "my way," has instituted these patterns and no deviations are tolerated. Charles R., the founder of a large dress-manufacturing firm, was such a person. No subordinate manager could make a decision—even on minor matters—without passing it up to Mr. R. —and it worked! His dynamism and expertise in the marketing of dresses brought his company to the pinnacle of the fashion industry. However, it was actually a one-man organization. Creative people were milked for their ideas and then fired; innovators were discouraged from implementing any projects unless Mr. R approved it. Managers tended to be yes-men. People with high potential were frustrated and left the company.

When Mr. R. died, there was no line of succession. The company's culture had discouraged creativity. It discouraged anybody but Mr. R. to participate in decision-making. As a result, there was no competent manager within the organization to replace him. The company went downhill. Only after new ownership and an entirely new organizational culture was developed did the firm begin to move upward again.

Other dynamic leaders set organizational cultures that were more positive. For example, early in his management of IBM, Thomas Watson set a culture which led to the immense growth of the organization. Sam Walton, the founder of Wal-Mart, is another executive who set the tone for his firm's organizational culture, which is still followed today—many years after his death.

The real power centers in the organization

In some organizations customs are inaugurated and perpetuated by informal leaders—men or women who do not have formal authority, but exert influence. Organizational charts are supposed to indicate the chain of command and enable one to see immediately who has the authority in the organization to make decisions. But this is not always so. Often the real power is not indicated. Often there are people whose position on the chart places them at levels well below their true position of influence. They carry significantly more weight than the chart indicates. One has to study the interactions among the management group to really understand the power structure. Here are two examples of how such people have extraordinary influence:

Diane Fiore, administrative assistant to the marketing manager, is shown well down in the hierarchy on her firm's organizational chart, but she is a major power figure in the company. Over the years she has built her position into a clearinghouse for all activities related to marketing. Even her boss is afraid to contradict her. To obtain action, one has to first convince Diane.

José Fernandez, a bilingual clerk, is not even listed on his company's organizational chart. Early in his career, José took upon himself the role of translator and interpreter for Spanish-speaking workers. He became the intermediary between them and others in the company. Because of his success in this role, other employees in the department, regardless of their ethnic background, would go to José when they had to deal with management. He became the informal spokesperson for all the workers. In cases of this sort, the culture will most likely change when the individual leaves the company, but so long as this person wields that power, it cannot be overlooked.

> **TACTICAL TIPS**
>
> Don't rely solely on the organizational chart to determine where the power lies in an organization. Listen to what goes on in the lunchroom and the hallways. Observe the interactions of people to uncover the real power structure.

Unions

When a company has a labor union, much of the organizational culture is dictated by the union contract and the on-going relationship with the union. Unless union cooperation is obtained, little can be done to change the culture of the organization. Unions often resist change to protect the interests of their members.

One of the strongest unions in the United States is the United Automobile Workers. Over the years and through many negotiations, they have established work rules that workers and companies must follow. These are now an integral part of the organizational culture of the Big Three automobile makers. When competition from Japanese carmakers cost the Big Three a significant loss of market share, the organizational culture of American auto manufacturers had to be changed. This could be accomplished only by tough negotiation with the unions.

Although some labor leaders oppose any change which they feel will weaken the union's position, more and more enlightened labor union leaders are moving from an adversarial to a more co-operative philosophy.

Among these leaders is Irving Bluestone, retired vice president of the United Automobile Workers. He proposes a new type of working relationship between management and labor, which he calls the *enterprise compact,* consisting of seven provisions,[1]

1. The union and management agree to pursue mutually established productivity growth targets.

2. Wage and compensation goals are set to be consistent with productivity growth in order to maintain global competitiveness.

3. Price-setting in the company is subject to joint action by union and management.

4. To assure that products and services meet or exceed international standards, quality is a "strikable" issue. Bluestone admits

---

[1]U.S.Dept. of Labor, *State of the Art Symposium,* BLMR 124, 1989.

that using the word "strike" impresses on both sides that survival depends on quality. He believes that this one issue can unite management and labor at every level.

5. Employment security is guaranteed for the workforce. This is likely to be resisted by management who demand flexibility to respond to shrinking market share by cutting jobs. Bluestone points out as an example the Saturn plant in Tennessee, which provides secure employment to 80 percent of their work force—unless catastrophic economic events dictate otherwise as agreed by the union and management.

6. Extra financial rewards are provided through profit and gain sharing throughout the enterprise. Management shares profits in good times with the workers.

7. The union and management agree to joint decision-making throughout the company including labor representation on the board of directors. This provision would abolish the last remnants of the management rights clauses, which assign all matters not directly covered by the contract to management's discretion. These concessions have been part of most collective bargaining agreements. This would give unions a voice in decisions such as pricing, marketing, quality, and everything else that traditionally had been exclusive to management.

Bluestone and others argue that the concept of enterprise compacts will not be readily accepted by either management or labor as both must give up cherished rights, but if we are to meet the challenges of the 21st century, all parties must reexamine their thinking and be prepared to make compromises that will work for the benefit of both management and labor.

Pragmatism

Much of what is defined as an organizational culture develops over time and emanates from practices and customs that have worked in the past and have become part of the company way of life. This is exemplified in the commonly heard expressions: "If it ain't broken, don't fix it" and "Don't tamper with success." On the surface this is true. Why change something that doesn't need changing? If after several trials, we learn from our errors and the result is a viable process or practice, why not stick with it? Quite often we should. Change for the sake of change does not make any more sense than continuing practices just because "we always did it that way."

The longer a company has been in business, the more likely there will be patterns of behavior that are universally practiced. Taking advantage of past experience in dealing with day-to-day matters often gives established companies a competitive edge. *The danger comes from failing to recognize when what has worked well in the past may not be the best approach for the present or the future.* The challenge managers in older companies face is to identify patterns of behavior that have become obsolete and to make necessary changes.

> **TACTICAL TIPS**
>
> Do not assume that what has worked well in the past is the best approach for the present or the future—or that just because an approach isn't new, it is out of date or useless.

The image of the organization

How an organization wishes to be perceived by its owners, its customers, its employees, and the community often influences the development of the culture. Image is not a superficial matter. It is more than just a public relations gimmick. It can set the stage for everything a company does.

Sometimes this image is dictated by a vision determined by the founder. George Merck, founder of the pharmaceutical company that bears his name, projected the image he wanted for his new firm: The company is committed to the ideals of advancing medical science and being of service to humanity. This mission, which has been adhered to by several generations of management, is taken very seriously and has kept the company and its employees focused on this primary goal.

The community

The community in which a company is located often influences its organizational culture. This was demonstrated in the early 1970s, when the Official Airline Guide, then a division of Dun & Bradstreet, was having difficulty obtaining personnel for its expanding operations in a Chicago suburb. To attract the young mothers, who were the main source of clerical workers, OAG developed an organizational culture that would appeal to this market. They were among the first organizations to create a flexible time schedule, to arrange for shared work, and to open their own day-care center. As expected, OAG became known as *the* place to work in the area, resulting in attracting a high-quality workforce and a low rate of absenteeism and turnover.

Companies opening facilities in areas that have different customs and work practices from those they practice at the home base have to accommodate to local customs. When the North Atlantic Constructors, a joint venture of four Midwestern construction companies, opened its New York City office, they established a workday schedule that started at 8 A.M.—the usual starting time in their home areas. They were shocked to learn that virtually all New York City offices opened at 9 A.M. In order to compete for good workers in the city, they had to adjust their working hours to the usual local hours of 9 to 5.

In communities dominated by certain ethnic groups, an organizational culture often is influenced by the customs and practices of that group. Many managers assigned to supervise newly arrived immigrants from Latin America or Asia were unsuccessful in obtaining full commitment and effort from them until they recognized their cultural differences and modified their practices to accommodate to what the workers would accept. American firms opening branches in other countries have had to adapt to the customs of each country rather than attempting to follow the same organizational culture practiced in the United States. For example, companies with facilities in Pakistan, Indonesia, and the Arab countries had to allow for prayer breaks for their devout Moslem employees.

Local customs often are incorporated into organizational culture. For example, in

QUOTES AND QUIPS

"Why not go out on a limb—Isn't that where all the fruit is?"
—Frank Scully,
Business executive

New Orleans, most businesses cease work at Mardi gras even though it is not a formal holiday. In companies whose windows faced the ticker-tape parade route in New York City, the parades took precedence over work.

Government

Many aspects of an organizational culture are superimposed on the company by federal and local governments. There is no choice but to comply. Laws and regulations dictate how companies can conduct their businesses, deal with employees, design and utilize equipment, handle their finances and act and react in every aspect of their activities.

Some of these laws go back for so many years that they are accepted with little thought. Sure, we may be unhappy about maintaining certain records for the IRS or other government agencies, but it has been part of the practices and procedures for so long, it has become an established aspect of a company's way of life.

New laws and rules often require companies to radically change long-established practices. Unfortunately, over the years many companies accepted the premise that certain jobs were limited to men and others to women. Although there were some exceptions, it just wasn't the "correct" thing to hire a woman as a mechanic or a man as a telephone operator or secretary; a woman supervising men was unheard of. In many industrial companies only male college graduates were hired as management trainees or salespeople. As many business contacts were made over golf or dinner at the all-male country club, it was not considered prudent to promote women to management jobs. This was the organizational culture that permeated many companies until civil rights laws and regulations forced companies to change their cultures.

Special situations

Long before Congress and the state legislatures passed laws requiring accommodation in the workplace for the handicapped, Henry Viscardi created a company with a culture based primarily on helping disabled people. Viscardi, who walks on two prosthetic legs, founded a company, Abilities, Inc., which only hires people with physical and/or mental disabilities, trains them, and puts them to work in productive jobs. By obtaining sub-contracts for manufacturing components from other firms, Abilities, Inc. has become a successful operation.

HOW ORGANIZATIONAL CULTURE AFFECTS CONDUCT

The organizational culture, as perceived by employees, dictates how they think about their jobs, perform their functions, and plan for the future. If employees are convinced that the company is truly concerned about quality, they will make every effort to produce quality work. But if employees believe that the management's talk about quality is just lip service, the "quality" program will be ignored or even ridiculed.

For example, when the Metal Fabrication Company introduced its "quality" program, managers gave the employees lectures on the importance of quality and posted this motto on the office and factory bulletin boards: "WE AIM FOR PERFECTION." But they made no substantive changes in their methods and paid no attention to quality improvement suggestions from employees. It didn't take long for the workers to become skeptical about the "quality" program, and some wag added this sentence to the motto: "BUT WE USUALLY MISS." On the other hand, Ford Motor Company's motto, "Quality is Number One" is taken seriously by workers and managers alike. All employees are imbued with the company culture that truly puts a high priority on quality.

> **TACTICAL TIPS**
>
> **Actions speak louder than words. Unless mission statements or mottoes are truly followed by management, employees will not take them seriously.**

Organizational Culture Affects Creativity

We've observed that in the companies that come up with creative ideas, innovative techniques, and new products or services, the organizational culture fosters creativity. New ideas are encouraged, seriously considered, and frequently accepted. Unfortunately, too many companies stifle creativity. The organizational culture is one of complacency: "Don't rock the boat."

High-Tech Industries, a pioneer manufacturer of computer components, provides an illustration of how such complacency can almost destroy an organization. High-Tech led its segment of the industry for many years. Its original products were innovative and made the company a major player in the field. Engineers and technicians were proud to be part of this organization and a strong sense of pride in the organization was ingrained as part of the organizational culture. Management continuously reminded the staff that their loyalty was appreciated.

On the other hand, any criticism of company products, services or practices was considered disloyal. Any dissension—even suggestions for changing current practices—was viewed almost as treason. Innovative ideas by creative engineers were scoffed at if they varied from accepted company practices. Some people left in frustration. Others were complacent with the status quo. They believed that because they always had been the best, they would always lead the field. Even if they felt things could be changed, they were reluctant to do or say anything that would make them appear disloyal. As the industry changed and competitors introduced new concepts, products, and technologies, High Tech began to lose market share. This resulted in the loss of hundreds of jobs and millions of dollars in revenue.

Creativity is fostered by a culture of trust and respect. Gary L., a long-time Human Resources manager, proved this when he left the corporate scene to open his own out-placement service. Gary resolved to practice what he had preached in his HR career. His first step was to carefully select a highly competent staff, and train them thoroughly. Staff members were encouraged to develop their own approaches to solving problems, but had easy access to the expertise of all of the other members of the staff and to Gary. All employees, whether they were on the professional staff or the support group, could come to Gary's office and discuss any problem with him. To supplement this open-door policy, Gary ran periodic meetings in the lunchroom, where—over coffee and pastry—discussions were held about any matters that were brought up. No question or comment was considered too serious or too trivial to be introduced. The respect given to all participants by management and by other participants led to an openness that fostered constructive critiques of practices, introduction of innovative ideas and a spirit of collaboration that helped Gary's firm become one of the leaders in the outplacement field.

> QUOTES AND QUIPS
>
> **"Love is a given. Trust and respect have to be earned."**
> **—Earl Woods to his son, Golfer Tiger Woods**

THE 10 IDENTIFYING FEATURES OF A GREAT ORGANIZATIONAL CULTURE

Some organizations have developed corporate cultures that can serve as a model for most others. Let's look at ten features that have worked to make these companies stand out as employers of choice.

1. An almost-missionary zeal

It is no secret that their respective management teams enthusiastically shared the excitement and dedication of Bill Gates and Sam Walton that permeated their organizations. This same fervor is found in companies of all sizes and throughout all industries

Leading the *FORTUNE* list of the 100 fastest growing companies in America a few years ago was Grow-Biz International, a franchiser of four separate retail chains specializing in new and used goods including PCs, children's clothing, sporting goods, and musical instruments.

Grow-Biz started as a one-store unit selling used sporting equipment. Once the founders, Ron Olson and Jeff Dahlberg, identified that this was a growing market, they began franchising stores. But, the factor that made Grow-Biz the fastest growing company despite the competition of so many other—and better known—franchisers was the excitement and enthusiasm generated by the founders and the franchisees.

Olson and Dahlberg not only had an idea whose time had come, but they chose as franchisees men and women who were in many ways as excited and enthusiastic as they were. Many of these people were former middle-management staffers who had been downsized, reorganized, or frustrated in corporate jobs. The challenge offered by Gro-Biz to give them the chance to run their own stores in an atmosphere that generated a passion for the work was a major factor that brought this relatively new organization to the top of *FORTUNE's* fastest-growing-companies list.

Over the years, countless authors and business consultants have recognized and written about the power of enthusiasm. Author and adult trainer Dale Carnegie, in fact, called it "the little recognized secret of success." He wasn't wrong.

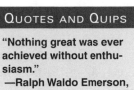

QUOTES AND QUIPS

"Nothing great was ever achieved without enthusiasm."
—Ralph Waldo Emerson, American essayist

2. A sense of pride, sincerity, and cooperation

Not just managers, but all employees of Nordstrom, the Seattle based national retail chain, seem to radiate pride in their company and their jobs. This is projected in the demeanor shown in dealing with each other and particularly with customers. Nordstrom prizes its reputation of going out of its way to serve customers. Countless stories of customer service in action not only circulate within the company, but also have spread throughout the communities it serves. These stories are frequently commented on in business literature. Among the common practices: Employees write "thank you" notes to customers, personally deliver merchandise when the customer needs it faster than the normal delivery time, and exchange merchandise with no-questions asked. Nordstrom's staff members are known to take special pains to assure that every customer leaves every Nordstrom store thoroughly satisfied with both their purchases and the level of professionalism and helpfulness demonstrated by each of the employees with whom he or she had contact.

Another example of an organization with a deep-seated sense of pride and a *one-for-all-all-for-one* spirit is Home Depot, the largest home improvement retailer in America. This special mindset is instilled in employees right from the very start, beginning with an inspirational orientation program at hire right through to regular reinforcements on the job. Has it paid off? You bet! Home Depot has had record-breaking sales volume year after year and steady expansion and new store openings throughout the United States and Canada.

3. An attitude of constructive discontent

Few organizations can ever be complacent about what they do. Complacency can lead to stagnation; in the most severe cases, it can literally destroy a company.

A quick example to help demonstrate the point: Not long ago the manager of a well-known sales organization complained about the high turnover among his salespeople. "We have an excellent screening process, he claimed, so we know we're attracting and selecting top candidates for our jobs. We also give them a solid orientation and training program. Yet, we lose over 50% of our people every year."

Surprising? — Not really. In fact, according to some experts a 50% annual turnover in sales personnel is not at all uncommon. It happens for a variety of reasons, but in the case of this company, it was a classic example of failing to keep pace with changes in the expectations of employees. Among the problems: a badly outdated compensation structure and a failure to recognize that most sales programs today emphasize the building of relationships with customers and the exceeding of expectations. The sales manager's program was based on the "old model" of salesmanship emphasizing memorized "closing techniques" and a highly standardized, inflexible sales presentation. In short, while no doubt excellent in its day, this manager had one major problem: He assumed that what once had been "state-of-the-art" was still so. In this dynamic world, no organization can be content to assume that what worked in the past is still the best way. Every system, every program, every approach must be continuously reevaluated and, where appropriate, adjusted to keep it at the cutting edge of productivity.

4. A value based mind-set and management style

Emphasizing values is not a new phenomenon. As pointed out earlier, Merck & Company, a 100-plus year old organization pronounced these ideals by declaring that Merck is an organization dedicated to the ideals of advancement of medical science and of service to humanity.

These values are never far from the minds of management. Decisions concerning new products, expansion, personnel and every aspect of their activities are made with these values in the forefront. When the CEO of Merck was asked why the company decided to provide a certain drug to Third World countries at no cost and even to pay for its distribution, he responded that not to do so would demoralize Merck scientists, who view seriously Merck's commitment that they are in the business of preserving and improving human life. Indeed, that is why for years, Merck has been looked upon as one of America's most admired companies.

Changing management style is often essential to changing a lack-luster organizational culture to an outstanding one. A good example of this is SurfSoft. Inc., listed as one of the "1998 INC 500 Fastest growing private companies in America."[2]

Chuck Hickey, CEO of SurfSoft, an Internet software consulting company based in Capitola, California, had previously headed Microport Systems, another software firm which had gone bankrupt in the 1980s.

---

[2]Reported in *The INC 500,* 1998, p. 31.

After several years working as a consultant, he decided to try running a business once again. He took control of a company that had two full-time employees and was generating annual revenues of about $500,000. Following the practices he had used at Microport Systems, he quickly grew the company to $1.7 million in sales. But then sales leveled off to $400,000 a month and employee turnover soared to 25 percent.

Just at this time, Hickey read about W. Edwards Deming and was shocked by his concept of management. It read like an indictment of the management practices that Hickey had practiced all of his life. Deming warned against sales quotas; Hickey had sworn by them. Deming stressed collaboration among employees; Hickey prodded his workers to compete. Deming favored continuing training education of workers; Hickey had spurned such benefits.

Faced with this new crisis and fearing a repeat of his Microport failure, Hickey decided to follow Deming's teachings and make a radical change in his organizational culture. He junked all sales quotas, he scrapped his organizational structure and established interdepartmental teams to foster cooperation. Remembering Deming's emphasis on education, he required his management team to read and discuss one business book a month. This resulted in the development of a statement of the company's core values that Hickey says has helped improve morale and productivity.

In March 1997 SurfSoft's monthly sales topped $500,000. Employee turnover had dropped to five percent a year. Revenues were expected to reach $10 million in 1998, up nearly 50 percent from 1997.

5. An emphasis on creativity and innovation

The Research and Development departments of companies often have formal programs for innovation which have paid off in the introduction of new products and methods over the years. Truly creative organizations must budget for long-term growth—not only in R & D, but also in all aspects of its activities. One company that has proven the value of commitment to innovation is Motorola. Each year a significant portion of its earnings are earmarked for future innovations. Here's one example of how this paid off: The company's Research and Development team devoted two years in developing a satellite system to connect calls anywhere in the world, even in remote locations where there is no cellular infrastructure. This will make it possible to reach a person in a canoe, fishing in a remote lake in Alaska or a medical team working with primitive tribes in the rain forests of Brazil.

Chrysler (now DaimlerChrysler) exemplifies how creativity brought the company back to profitability from a long period of depressed sales. They encouraged their designers and engineers to make a radical change in car design. This resulted in the development of the minivan—the first significant change in the look of American cars in decades—opening a new and growing market for Chrysler.

A climate of creativity is not limited to just encouraging employees to be innovative. It must extend to suppliers and other outside sources. When UPS wanted to improve its package tracking capabilities, it called on Motorola to design a more effective system than used by most of its competitors. Using its cellular technology, Motorola came up with an electronic clipboard to send a signature instantly to a central station. As a result, delivery information can be provided almost instantaneously to customers around the world.

6. A focus on building role models, not just leaders

Many men and women are successful leaders in government, industry or other phases of life, but they are not role models for their employees, nor indeed, for the entire world. A leader gets things done—often for good, but sometimes for evil. Stalin, Hitler and Mussolini were leaders. They had great powers of persuasion, but their ultimate end was self-aggrandizement, which ultimately led to the destruction of their followers. In business organizations, there are countless examples of managers who built great empires, but due to their lack of ethical or moral standards, led to the decline or failure of their companies. On the other hand, there are industrial leaders who put ethical standards first, even if it may involve making decisions that result in lower profitability.

One example is Aaron Feuerstein, CEO of Malden Mills, a Lawrence, Massachusetts textile firm. When most textile firms left New England to take advantage of non-union, low-paid labor in the South, Feuerstein determined to stay in Lawrence. "Southern town officials made it clear that we'd be welcome if we didn't bring our liberal Northern ideas with us," he told the *New York Times*. "My grandfather came here from Hungary for political freedom and I was not about to sell my soul for cheap labor."

To succeed in the highly competitive textile field, Feuerstein chose to specialize in producing two specialized fabrics, used in outdoor wear by upscale clothing manufacturers. Malden Mills holds patents on both the fabrics and on the machines used to make them. These items now are sold in 60 countries, and his workforce has tripled over the past ten years. His managerial staff shares his commitment to providing good jobs to people, who in turn produce high-quality merchandise.

But that heroic act was only a prelude to what was to be an even more magnanimous gesture. Just before Christmas in 1995, the Malden Mills plant burned to the ground. Rather than close the facility and lay off the 3000 workers, Feuerstein announced that he would keep all employees on the payroll for a month while he started rebuilding the facility. When the month was over, he extended the pay period for a second month and then a third. He encouraged his employees to contribute ideas to make the new facility even more effective than the destroyed one. By March most of the employees had returned to full-time work. This not only prevented a major catastrophe for his employees, but for the entire community, which depended on Malden as its major employer. This cost Feuerstein several million dollars. One of his employees commented: "Another person would have taken the insurance money and walked away . . . but he was not that type of person."

When Feuerstein was asked by *Parade Magazine,* what set him apart from other CEOs, he responded: "The fundamental difference is that I consider our workers an asset, not an expense. I have a responsibility to the workers, both blue-collar and white-collar. I have an equal responsibility to the community. It would have been unconscionable to put 3000 people on the streets and deliver a deathblow to the cities of Lawrence and Methuen. Maybe on paper our company is worth less on Wall Street, but I can tell you, it's worth more."[3] The heroism of men like Feuerstein provide a role model to guide business leaders as they evaluate their own management thinking.

7. A sense of high expectations and professional standards

Hewlett-Packard has a culture in which all of its people are imbued with the culture of excellence. It started when David Packard and William Hewlett founded the company in 1938 and continues to this day. Everybody is expected to do the very best, to work at the highest level of professional competence. Nothing less is accepted. The result? The company has a well-established history of innovating new ideas and producing superior products.

This concept is not limited to large and well-known organizations. Claudia Gardiner, owner of a small but profitable fabric-designing firm, exemplifies what a smaller firm can do. Gardiner is a stickler for perfection. In her company, which specializes in the design and fabrication of customized fabrics for interior designers, this attitude is instilled in all the employees—from the creative artists to the sewing machine operators. When she screens candidates for employment, she tells them that she only hires the very best people and that working for her will be tough and demanding. Unlike many of her competitors, Gardiner insists on a thorough re-training of all new employees—no matter how experienced they may be— so they recognize and accept the high standards she demands. In short, she gives her staff a fine reputation to live up to. This has resulted in a team of men and women who pride themselves in their work and the work of their colleagues. Each knows that everybody

> ### QUOTES AND QUIPS
>
> **"Excellence is an art won by training and habituation. We do not act rightly because we have virtue or excellence, but we rather have those because we have acted rightly. We are what we repeatedly do. Excellence, then, is not an act but a habit."**
> **—Aristotle**

---

[3]Ryan, Michael, "They Call Their Boss a Hero," *Parade,* September 6, 1996, pp 4-5.

in the group is committed to excellence, to each other and most importantly, to exceeding their customers' expectations.

8. A fair, commensurate compensation and incentive program

Unless people feel they are being fairly compensated for their work, it is difficult to get their full cooperation. Most companies use the traditional mode of compensation: Annual raises are often automatic and based on a set percentage of increase over the previous year's salary. Under such a program, the highest paid people in any grade are those who are the most senior—not necessarily the most productive. This is neither fair nor does it reward competence.

Many types of incentive pay plans have been used, often including some variation of profit sharing. The assumption is that when a part of the workers' income is based on the profits, they will have the incentive to work to maximize those profits. Unfortunately in many profit-sharing plans employees have no idea as to how profits are calculated and often perceive the determination of the amount of profit as an arbitrary decision of management. This may cause more ill will than benefit.

One company, which has made their profit-sharing program meaningful to its employees, is Wal-Mart. It has created an internal culture in which every employee knows each month how well the store, division or plant met its profit, sales, and production goals. Any year in which the anticipated goals are exceeded, one-third of the excess goes to the hourly workers. All Wal-Mart stores give their staffs monthly updates of their profits and this is reflected in the employee's concern for customer satisfaction.

Bill Gates, the creator of Microsoft, and one of the world's wealthiest people, strongly believes in sharing the wealth. His profit sharing and stock option opportunities for employees have made over 2000 of them millionaires. Microsoft staffers know that their personal wealth depends on keeping Microsoft on top, and in most cases, they aim to do their best to assure it.

In order for a culture change to be successful, organizations engaged in this process should carefully reevaluate their compensation systems and adapt them to any changes that are made.

In a survey of 750 midsize and large U.S. employers conducted by Sandra O'Neal, director of the employee pay practices section of the prestigious management consulting firm, Towers Perrin, more than 75 percent of the respondents indicated that they were planning to make major changes in the way they pay their employees. Nearly one quarter of the companies are considering eliminating base pay increases and shifting to a system in which the company sets a total compensation target and uses a variable pay system based on a wide variety of performance measures. O'Neal predicts that this will mean less and less distinction for individual workers and more reliance on a person's ability to perform as a member of a broader team.[4]

Boyett and Conn in their book, *Workplace 2000,* comment that to correct the inequities in compensation systems, more and more companies are adopting a four-part approach:

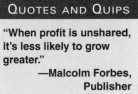

QUOTES AND QUIPS

"When profit is unshared, it's less likely to grow greater."
—Malcolm Forbes,
Publisher

1. Slowing or stopping entirely the growth in base pay

2. Relying more heavily on bonuses tied to group performance

3. Linking base pay to knowledge and skill rather than position

4. Providing expanded opportunities for employees to share in company profits and, in some cases, acquire ownership in the company.[5]

9. A habit of celebrating successes

One of the characteristics of happy organizations, of companies where morale is high and employees are excited about their work

---

[4]Reichheld, Frederick F., *The Loyalty Effect,* Harvard Business School Press, 1996, p. 15.
[5]Boyett, Joseph H. and Conn, Henry P., *Workplace 2000,* New York, Penguin Books, 1991.

is a practice of showing appreciation for accomplishments. This can be expressed in warm, private moments of hearty congratulations by a manager to a subordinate or by team members to each other. Or it can be a public demonstration of an achievement by rallies, parties, dinners or just informal get-togethers.

When festivity and jubilation accompany achievements, it adds to the achievement itself. By enabling everybody to share in the accomplishments of associates, it inspires them to work toward accomplishments of their own.

10. Adhering to the GOLDEN RULE

Perhaps all of the features of a great organizational culture can be summarized in the Golden Rule:

Do unto others as you would have others do unto you.

One of the indicators of a great company is that management truly believes in this rule and carries it into the workplace. Of course, it would be unrealistic to expect that everybody in any organization always follow this practice. Companies are made up of people and people differ. In applying this precept we can only comment that when top management treats its employees, its suppliers, its customers, its shareholders and the public equitably, it enhances the company's reputation as a good company to work for, to deal with, and to patronize.

SUM AND SUBSTANCE

- To survive and thrive in this dynamic world, organizations must not only keep up with the technological changes in their fields, but must adapt their organizational cultures to meet the needs of their staffs, their customers and their community.

- Managers cannot make a culture change alone. Everybody at all levels of the organization must take part in the process.

- The informal organization plays the major role in establishing and perpetuating the organizational culture.

- The employees' perception of the organizational culture dominates their actions in the way they think about and perform their jobs.
- Creativity is fostered by a culture of trust and respect.

Diagnosing Your Corporate Culture

The foundation on which a company's image to its present and prospective employees is based is its company culture—the *way of life* followed consciously or subconsciously in the day-to-day activities of the organization.

Corporate culture is often expressed formally in the company mission statement, and in directives from the executive committee or board of directors. But more often, the true corporate culture is manifested informally. It develops slowly and imperceptibly over time and becomes ingrained in the behavior of everybody in the organization. Company executives may have idealistic concepts about the culture of their organizations, but what actually exists may be quite different. To assure that a company will become an employer of choice, the true corporate culture must be uncovered and, quite often, significantly changed.

Before an organizational culture can be changed, it must be analyzed and assessed. It's necessary to understand the current culture, and to determine what problems exist and how seriously they affect productivity, quality of product or service, morale of the workers and the overall efficacy of the organization.

Too often, managers deceive themselves about the true condition of their organization. Of course, they know the figures: sales volume, market share, production, payroll, and all the tangible statistics. But they delude themselves on such vital information as employee attitudes and morale, the level of the skills of their people, the willingness of their people to cooperate and extend themselves, and the commitment of staff at all levels to company goals.

Perception Is Reality in the Mind of the Perceiver

It's human nature for people to see what they want to see, to hear what they want to hear and to believe what they want to believe. People tend to overlook or even fail to note matters that do not agree with their perceptions. Most of us do not like to be shaken out of our comfort zones. There is a strong tendency to believe whatever is consistent with what already is believed rather than accept new information that is inconsistent with established beliefs.

Each of us tends to accept as truthful information that which is compatible with our own perceptions. To us it is reality. However, in the minds of others, be they superiors, peers, or subordinates, the same information may be perceived totally differently.

Like most consultants, we have witnessed instance after instance where senior executives truly believed that they were respected—even loved—by their people and were literally stunned by the results of employee surveys suggesting that they were very much disliked and considered mean-spirited and even incompetent. The void between one set of perceptions and the other could not have been wider.

Why should this be? The answer is often surprisingly simple. It is difficult, if not impossible, to be totally objective about oneself. People tend to be defensive about their beliefs and perceive their actions as being the best possible course to take. They attribute negative reactions to a lack of understanding or even the incompetence of others. It does not take long for subordinates to recognize that often the perceptions of the boss are different from their own, but because a boss has power over them, they keep their reservations and feelings to themselves—festering inside and perhaps leading to discontent and reluctant obedience.

Often, managers misinterpret the employee's compliance, not recognizing its true cause—fear of contradicting the boss. They perceive the employee's attitude as total agreement with the manager's concepts, actions and attitudes. To these managers this "agreement" is the reality. On the other hand, the men and women who must live with this situation see a different reality. What to the boss is white, to them is black or perhaps shades of gray. It's a totally different reality.

If culture change is to take place, the first step the organization must take is to identify what the perceptions of employees truly are and how they got that way. To accomplish this, the organization must undertake a comprehensive examination similar to the periodic examinations people take to assess their medical condition.

THE ORGANIZATIONAL MRI

Physicians use a variety of techniques to evaluate the health of a patient. Companies must do the same. Just as the doctor takes blood pressure, EKGs, X-rays, temperature and blood tests to obtain basic vital statistics, so the company uses financial, production, sales and other figures to diagnose many aspects of the business. Just as in our bodies, many critical problems may not show up in these routine tests, subtle and incipient conditions exist in an organization that may not be uncovered by traditional business analyses.

In recent times sophisticated diagnostic techniques and equipment have been developed to help uncover these hidden symptoms in our bodies. One of the most useful of these is the MRI, or *Magnetic Resonance Imaging,* which enables the physician to look deep into the body and focus in detail on problem areas by viewing things from various angles.

To enable managers to look deep into their businesses, to learn about the perceptions of employees, to determine how such perceptions affect performance, to analyze subtle details, and to observe actions, reactions, attitudes and viewpoints perhaps not ever explored or even considered, we have designed the *Organizational MRI.* (O-MRI).

Utilizing variations of established evaluative tools and innovative techniques, the Organizational MRI becomes an instrument that can specifically uncover culture-related problems and challenges.

The Holistic Approach

In order to make an accurate diagnosis of an organization, we cannot rely on one- or two-dimensional tools. The O-MRI provides a multi-dimensional view that not only examines a specific aspect of the organization, but shows how it relates to other phases.

Let's take a look at how this was applied at an aircraft parts factory in Wichita, Kansas, at which the number of industrial accidents had increased significantly. Although these injuries were not life-threatening or serious, they caused increases in down-time, lengthy workers' compensation hearings and other time consuming and annoying distractions. The safety specialists who were retained to study the problem corrected some mechanical defects and initiated a safety-training program. This helped for a time, but within a few months, the accident rate began to creep up again.

When consulted about this, we suggested that an O-MRI be conducted. Instead of concentrating primarily on the accident rate, the entire organization was examined. Using the diagnostic tools described later in this chapter, it was found that there was a pattern of discontent and even rebellion in the company. Certain actions on the part of management had destroyed morale, leading to loss of enthusiasm for any actions of management—even a safety program that was designed to keep them from being injured. Only by initiating a holistic diagnosis were the real reasons for the safety problems identified and steps suggested to overcome them.

Delve for Root Causes

The O-MRI seeks the reason for the existence of a problem, not just the overt cause. Its goal is to peel layer after layer off the situation until the underlying reasons are bared.

The ultimate objective of the O-MRI system is to answer one question:

W H Y ?

In many ways, problems are like icebergs. The ostensible cause of the problem is like that part of the iceberg that is above the water line. The real cause lies well below the water line. By continuing to ask "Why?" after each response, the true cause will emerge. This can be illustrated by a conversation that took place between Andy, a member of the consultant's staff and Peter, a machine operator at the aircraft parts company:

Andy: Why did that machine break down?

Peter: The rotor wore out.

Andy: Why did the rotor wear out?

Peter: It wasn't properly lubricated?

Andy: Why wasn't it properly lubricated?

Peter: The oil is too light.

Andy: Why do you use light oil?

Peter: The boss ordered it.

Andy: Why didn't you tell him it was too light?

Peter: He never listens to anything I say.

TACTICAL TIPS
Ask "Why?" Ask "Why?" again. Ask "Why? once more. Continue to ask "Why?" until the root causes are unveiled.

The continuing questioning finally brings out the real problem. If workers perceive that their boss is not interested in what they have to say about the work, it leads to a variety of troubles.

Earning Trust

It's normal for employees to be reluctant to provide meaningful information if they feel that their comments will be reported back to the managers, who, of course, have power over their jobs. Fear that anything they say will be held against them keeps people from telling the whole story.

Even though an outside consultant usually conducts the O-MRI, lower level managers and rank-and-file workers often look upon consultants as tools of top management. "The bosses are paying them, so they probably blab everything we say back to them" is a commonly heard remark.

The O-MRI consultant has to win the confidence of all employees before the process even begins. To do this takes time. Trust cannot be dictated or mandated. It must be earned. One cannot go into a company, announce that a survey is being taken on employee morale and expect cooperation and candor. The consultant must earn people's trust by being consistently trustworthy. This can be accomplished by using proven techniques to facilitate the process.

One approach we have used that works well is to start with a nonthreatening series of workshops in areas that are of some value to the people involved. Some of the workshops that have been used to break the ice are:

- For first-line supervisors and middle management: a workshop on improving supervisory techniques
- For employees at all levels: a workshop on improving communication skills, getting along with others, and building self-confidence.

These programs are given in one- or two-hour sessions once or twice a week for three or four weeks. During these sessions, the consultant gets to know many of the workers as individuals and establishes rapport with enough of them to gain their confidence and remove the stigma that the consultant is solely on the side of management. One of the most important things that the consultant should do when conducting these classes is to identify the informal leaders and make an effort to cultivate them. They are the best source of establishing credibility among the employees.

Once these informal leaders have been identified either through the classes or by other means, a rapport must be devel-

TACTICAL TIPS

Identify and cultivate the informal leaders in the organization. They can be a major source of information and a significant aid in implementing change.

oped with them and other staff members. In short, get to know them as individuals. Get them to talk, not only about the job, but about their personal interests. Get to know them as they really are—as multi-dimensional human beings.

Six Terrific Techniques to Obtain Reliable Information

Over the years through our own trial-and-error approaches and research on the effective methods used by consultants, we have pinpointed six techniques that help encourage candor and provide for a free flow of significant and accurate information from employees. These will be briefly noted below. Details as to how they are used will be discussed later in this chapter.

1. Get them away from the company environment

When people are relaxed, they are much more likely to share ideas, complaints and true feelings. As we know, executives and salespeople often make their best deals on the golf course or over a relaxing meal. Why limit this informality to big deals? Participate in some extracurricular activity with those from whom you need helpful information. Find out about their interests. Join them at the bowling alley, attend a softball tournament or go to lunch or dinner with an informal leader.

Rita Sable, a successful human resources consultant, found that the women employed by her client were reluctant to express their attitudes, observations, and thoughts about the company. She tried to find some way to overcome this resistance. Rita noted that at lunch or dinner in social situations, women often would leave the table together to freshen up, and in that most informal environment, talk about matters dear to their hearts. She decided to use this approach with these women employees. She joined them at their breaks and became

QUOTES AND QUIPS

"To improve your listening skills, challenge yourself to say nothing for the first half-hour next time you have a meal with a group."
Jeffrey Gitomer,
Business writer

a participant in their chitchats. This opened up a channel that enabled her to learn a good deal about how they really felt about the bosses, the company and specific situations

2. Organize focus groups

The concept of focus groups was developed by market researchers to learn about the reactions of typical consumers to a company's product or service. Many consumer product manufacturers have potential customers try out a product and then conduct a focus group to obtain the opinions of its members. Service organizations use focus groups to evaluate the service they are providing. Over the past few years many organizations have used this approach to reveal the true attitudes of employees about their company, their department, their managers and specific aspects of their jobs.

Let's look in as the facilitator of a focus group begins his orientation:

"As you know, I've been working with most of you for several months as part of the company's efforts to improve the quality of the workplace. I've spoken to you individually from time to time. You've been selected as a focus group to discuss one particular situation about which we're concerned—the proposed changes in the health insurance program. You were chosen as typical members of our staff. You represent several departments and range in years of employment from one to twenty-two. You've been given copies of the current plan and the proposed plan to study before this meeting. Our first step is to give you the chance to ask Linda, the benefits manager, questions about the plan. Then we'll ask for your comments and reactions. Please note that the proposed plan hasn't yet been adopted and no decisions will be made until after much further study, beginning with this focus group."

Note that the facilitator identified the matter to be discussed and assured participants that this was not an attempt to sell them on it, but to obtain input. This is essential for a successful focus group experience. Participants must be assured that their ideas and feelings will be considered.

TACTICAL TIPS

Although focus groups are most effective when restricted to a specific area, they can also be used as means of identifying basic problems, which can be explored later in other groups.

Also note that the benefits manager is there to answer questions. However, she will not express her opinions or participate in the discussion in any way other than to elucidate technical aspects of the plan.

The facilitator will be just that—a person who facilitates the discussion, who will keep it on keel and assure that it runs along smoothly and in a reasonable time frame.

3. Conduct confidential employee surveys

Employee attitude surveys have been used for a long time as a means of determining employee morale and locating problem areas. In recent years, these have been refined to make them an even more sophisticated diagnostic tool.

Inasmuch as such surveys should be designed to fit each company's special needs, they should be developed and conducted by organizations geared for that purpose. Getting the most from an employee survey goes beyond just obtaining information. How an attitude survey is used in the O-MRI will be described later in this chapter.

4. Conduct individual employee interviews

Unlike the informal meetings with employees discussed earlier, some consultants prefer to use more formal interviewing techniques. The same series of questions is asked each of the respondents. In addition the interviewer will ask follow-up questions so that the respondent can expand, explain and elucidate when doing so helps clarify an answer.

The advantage of this technique is that it assures that all of the aspects that are being investigated will be covered in a systematic manner. A knowledgeable consultant can design very comprehensive questionnaires that will shorten the time it takes to obtain key information.

Questions are framed that will help in the diagnosis of the situation. Although the questions should be related to the organization's activities, general questions such as the following often help set the stage and lead to more questions in more specific areas:

- What do you like most about working in this organization?
- What do you like least?
- In what way could the organization improve its relations with its employees?
- Describe your supervisor's style of managing.
- How do you relate to this style?
- How effectively do you feel management communicates its ideas to the staff?
- How do you believe you can be a more effective employee?

The main limitation of such a formal tool is that unless the interviewer is very skilled, such interviews tend to become stilted and only routine information is developed. Informal approaches often uncover the hidden areas that formal methods may overlook. These formal interviews provide a means of obtaining the basic information about the organization and should be followed up with informal discussions. If an area of specific concern develops from these questions, it is followed up by immediately asking for more details including specific examples. If some situations are more complex, they should be explored in more depth later, in informal discussions.

5. Conduct 360-degree assessments of key managers

Multi-level assessments have become an increasingly popular approach used to identify how bosses, peers, subordinates and even such outsiders as vendors and customers view a manager. Usually referred to as 360-degree assessments, they have been adopted by such companies as AT & T, Hewlett Packard, Walmart and hundreds of other large and small organizations. According to Tom Pawlak, a principal with the management-consulting firm, Towers Perrin, the use of multi-source feedback is growing rapidly. He predicts it will be the most widely used form of performance appraisal by the end of the decade.[1] How 360-degree assessments are conducted will be described later in this chapter.

People do not see themselves as others see them. They perceive their actions as rational, their ideas as solid, their decisions as meaningful. Traditionally, only one's own manager evaluates performance. This does provide insight into how one's work is perceived by that person, but he or she is not the only person with whom the employee interrelates.

Even more complex is the evaluation of senior managers, who frequently are not evaluated at all. When assessed by peers and subordinates, these executives may learn much about their management style of which they were not aware. Many are shocked to realize that they are perceived by others far differently than they believed. As a result, some have taken steps to change their management styles.

Despite these advantages of multi-source assessments, there are also serious concerns about them. Mary N. Vinson, director of the regulatory relations group at Bell Atlantic-Virginia, is a strong advocate of these programs, but she cautions that there is a downside.

She notes that feedback can hurt, and points out that evaluators aren't always nice or positive. Some people see their role as a feedback provider as an opportunity to criticize others' behavior on the job.

Another flaw concerns conflicting opinions. Who decides who is right? There also may be a question about whether the feedback is truthful. If the evaluator does not like the person being evaluated, the responses might be skewed negatively; if the assessee is a friend, it might be skewed positively. In addition, Ms. Vinson reported that often people rating senior executives thought it was dangerous to be completely truthful. In order to ensure that the 360-degree feedback has a better chance of producing a change, Vinson recommends:

---

[1]*Newsday*, Long Island, NY, March 12, 1996.

- The feedback must be anonymous and confidential.

- To have sufficient knowledge of the person being rated, the appraisers should have worked with the appraisee for at least six months.

- A feedback expert should interpret the feedback.

- Follow-up on improvements made as a result of the assessment should be made about six months later.

- Appraisers should give written descriptions as well as numerical ratings. This enables them to be more specific and the results more meaningful.

- Ensure that the feedback instrument is statistically reliable and valid.

- To avoid "survey fatigue," don't use 360-degree feedback on too many employees at one time.[2]

6. Scheduling a multi-level retreat

Many companies have gathered people away from the workplace for training or for discussions. Combined with recreation and social activities, the relaxed atmosphere lends itself to accomplishing a good deal of creative work. Usually these retreats are restricted to senior managers and the subjects covered involve long-range planning or dealing with specific situations.

A multi-level retreat involves inviting people from various levels of the organization. A theme should be chosen that will give the participants an opportunity to express ideas and ask questions. Discussions should stimulate management to identify where change is desirable or even necessary for the health of the organization. The consultant charged with facilitating the retreat will draw out participants both during the formal sessions and in informal conversations.

---

[2]Vinson, Mary N. "The Pros and Cons of 360-Degree Feedback: Making It Work," *Training & Development,* April 1996, pp.11-12.

The Four Worst Techniques

We all learn from our failures. Here's a look at a handful of approaches that seem to fail more often than they succeed.

1. "Town meetings"

Let's sit in at a "town meeting" in any town in America. There are several important issues on the agenda, but most never reach the floor. Men and women with their own agendas dominate the meeting. They grab the microphones, harangue the audience, and plug their messages until most of the other attendees leave in disgust. It is, at best, a disconcerting, uncomfortable and unproductive experience.

Company "town meetings" may not get that far out of hand, but organizations that have used them find that often they become little more than gripe sessions. Some people with personal agendas tend to dominate the meetings. At one such gathering, for example, a small group of employees attempted to use the meeting as a forum on a grievance, which already had been adjudicated, but not to their satisfaction. This distracted from the objectives of the meeting and not only wasted the time of the majority of participants but soured everybody on the concept of "town meetings."

2. Meetings led by the managers of the attendees

When a boss conducts the meeting, employees are inhibited from telling the whole story. They may fear that dissension from the boss's opinions will be long remembered and may be reflected in their next performance evaluation.

This happened to Douglas T. At a meeting of engineers from various departments of a public utility in Pennsylvania, Douglas voiced his reservations about a program of which his boss was a prime supporter. Douglas reported: "I had told my boss about these reservations in one-to-one discussions so he knew I had doubts about the project. But because I expressed them at an open meeting, he called me disloyal and our relationship has seriously deteriorated."

3. Poorly designed problem-solving teams

Problem-solving teams can be an effective way of identifying and seeking solutions to problems. However, such team activity must be carefully planned and participants thoroughly trained in problem-solving techniques. Unfortunately, this is often not the case. The manager identifies a problem and appoints a "team" to study it. Often, these people come from several departments and have not worked together before. The team members are primarily concerned with how what they say or do will affect their own departments and perhaps their own careers. This results at the minimum in wasted time and often results in more conflict than resolution.

4. Employees interviewed by company managers

In many cases the person assigned to diagnose a problem that involves relationships between a supervisor and his or her people is that very supervisor. In such cases, most people will be afraid to be truthful. Even if the investigator is another supervisor, the fear—although somewhat less—still exists. Such interviews should be conducted by an outsider such as a consultant, or, if a divisional or departmental situation, an executive from the home office.

Often representatives of the Human Resources Department conduct these types of interviews. Unless employees view the H.R. staff as impartial and fair-minded, they will be unwilling to be fully truthful. Using outside consultants or independent survey groups bring the best results.

Conducting the O-MRI

In conducting the O-MRI, it is wise to follow a carefully planned agenda. In this section, the steps that should be taken will be described. To help implement these steps, following this section is a set of step-by-step guidelines.

1. Secure full support of top management

Once the consultant and the client have agreed that an O-MRI is to be conducted, careful preparation must be made. It starts with gaining the full support of top management. Often, the CEO and other senior executives feel that they know all of the problems and call in the consultant to provide solutions, or to impose their pre-conceived solutions on to the lower echelons. In many cases, senior managers are reluctant to really delve too deeply into how lower ranking people perceive things for fear that it may bring out negative aspects of their own managerial styles and actions.

Often managers tell us that they know the problems facing the company and have retained the consultant to persuade others to their way of thinking. First, it must be made clear to all that senior executives are often unaware of significant issues facing an organization. People at lower levels are closer to the problems, and often may see them more clearly.

This point can best be conveyed by commenting on similar situations in other companies. There are many examples of where critical matters were either not known by top management or were perceived by them to be unimportant. It is also essential that executives truly understand how peers, subordinates, customers and others with whom they relate view them. They must accept that if the diagnosis indicates that they are the cause of part of the problem, the solution depends on their willingness to change their behavior. Obviously, this must be done in a diplomatic manner. Top management must be fully in accord. If not, at the minimum, it will result in sulking and reluctant cooperation or, at the maximum, the entire process could be sabotaged.

Once this hurdle is overcome, senior managers should be given an overview of how the O-MRI will proceed. It must be clear that this is a diagnostic process. The objective is to obtain information—not to solve problems. This can be done only if an accurate analysis is accomplished. Point out that the process will include conducting surveys and speaking formally and informally to lower level managers, rank and file employees and perhaps to vendors and customers. There must be clear understanding that the process is nonjudgmental and is concerned only with getting as much information as possible that will bring out facts, feelings, and perceptions about the organization.

It is advisable to have a small team (2 to 4 people) assigned to act as internal coordinators. These people will assist the consultants by acting as the liaison between them and top management. They also provide the necessary links with other managers and employees with whom the consultants will be interacting. This team is usually made up of managers drawn from varying departments such as Production or Operations, Finance, Marketing, Research & Development and Human Resources.

The first step is to work with this team in the design of the program. This cannot be done haphazardly and may take several weeks. The consultant orients the team about the process, and specific aspects are worked out. A time-table is developed. Once this process is established, the program is announced to the entire organization.

> ### QUOTES AND QUIPS
>
> "In all affairs it's a healthy thing now and then to hang a question mark on the things you have long taken for granted."
> —Bertrand Russell, British philosopher

2. The announcement

As virtually everybody in the company will be involved to some extent in the O-MRI, it is essential that they are not only made aware of what is being done, but also that they become part of the process from the beginning.

When the Excelsior Paper Box Company initiated their O-MRI, CEO Douglas Stewart sent a letter to each employee describing briefly why the program was being conducted and the importance of his or her participation. Brief departmental meetings in which the consultant was introduced to the various staff members followed. In both the letter and the meetings, the importance of each person's contribution was emphasized and the confidentiality of all matters related to the process was assured.

The first step, after the announcement, was to gain the confidence of the middle- and lower-level personnel. The consulting team identified the informal leaders and through workshops, off-premises meetings and personal contacts, as described earlier in this chapter, began the process of getting to know them and win their support.

3. The confidential employee survey

Another tool that we use to help uncover situations that may not be easily identified is the confidential employee survey. A carefully designed survey form was prepared. A professional survey organization was retained for this purpose. They designed an instrument that was as specific as possible to the organization's culture and that was easily understood, designed to yield usable data, and distributed in a way to ensure a significant response.

For any attitude survey to be truly meaningful, confidentiality must be stressed. Employees should be convinced that their interests are protected. A cover letter with the questionnaire assuring that no individual employee's answers will be identified was mailed to each employee's home. As a computer was to be used to tabulate the results, questions were formulated so the response would be easily codified and retrieved.

Before the questionnaire was distributed the purpose and methods to be used in the survey were explained to the participants by articles in the company newsletters and bulletins. This was reiterated in a letter sent by a senior executive that accompanied the questionnaire. In addition, face-to-face meetings were held to discuss the questionnaire before distribution.

Before putting the questionnaire in its final form, a small group of employees were selected to review a draft. This enabled the survey team to identify and correct ambiguous questions, and to determine the ease of understanding and responding to the questions.

Once the questionnaires were returned, they were evaluated immediately. A report was prepared that included:

1. Background of the survey
2. The process used to obtain the information
3. A summary of the key points that were learned
4. Recommendations for implementation

The remainder of the report included details on specific aspects of the survey. As a place had been provided in the questionnaire for comments by respondents, these comments were presented in raw form for perusal by management.

The results obtained from the survey were used as the basis for further investigation and as taking-off points for the other approaches that were used in the O-MRI.

To the delight of the survey group and management, a 67% response was received by the deadline, and additional questionnaires trickled in for the next few weeks. Responses were tabulated and key comments studied. The report was examined by the CEO, the O-MRI team and by the consultants.

The survey showed four major problem areas and a variety of lesser ones. The four key areas of concern were:

1. A pervasive sense of insecurity, distrust, fear and resentment
2. Poor internal communications
3. Inequities in compensation
4. Too much internal politics

4. Focus groups

In selecting focus groups to explore these further, it was decided to use peer-based rather than multi-peer groups. A peer-based group consists of people at the same level in the organization. For example: all rank-and-file workers with no managers or supervisors; all first-line supervisors, but no workers or higher level managers, etc. Multi-level groups are drawn from all echelons.

Using peer-level grouping minimizes "us vs. them" inhibitions. Multi-level groups often are useful because of the interactions that can be observed and have a place in the O-MRI. However, because the survey uncovered distrust of management, the use of peer groups was the preferred way to go.

Three of the four focus groups were drawn from rank-and-file workers: two groups from plant personnel and one group from office personnel. The fourth group consisted of first-line supervisors. It was decided not to have a middle-level management group, as there were relatively few people in that category.

TACTICAL TIPS

Focus group participants should be close to the situation being studied, knowledgeable about the subject, and willing to express their ideas.

The eight members of each group were selected from men and women who had shown some signs of serious concerns about the company in the workshops or in early informal discussions. A member of the consulting staff facilitated each focus group.

The meetings started with a brief discussion about the purpose of the group. The leader greeted them and congratulated them on being chosen for this important work. They were assured that their individual comments, concerns and contributions would be kept confidential. Then, the process that would be followed was described in terms similar to this:

"By authorizing this program, the company accepts the fact that there are challenges that are keeping all of us from giving our whole-hearted cooperation to achieving company goals. The survey all of you have participated in has given us an overview of some of these problems. In this focus group, we are going to delve deeper into the situation and identify the real problems and seek their causes. Often what is perceived to be the crux of the problem is only a symptom of something more serious.

"You have been selected for this group because all of you are respected members of the employee staff. When the number of years each of you has been with the company are added up, we find we have over 120 years of tenure in Excelsior Paper represented in this room. You have observed, experienced and were affected by what has happened in this organization over the years. Your input will be extremely important in our efforts to make working for this company a more rewarding endeavor."

Participants were then asked to express their opinions about each of the factors brought out in the survey. The objective was to keep the conversation flowing, to encourage—even urge—the participants to express disagreement, to provide added ideas and, wherever possible, give specific examples illustrating the matters under discussion. The facilitator made no comments on the content, but concentrated on keeping everyone on target, stopping digressions and making sure that the concern was on finding problems, not seeking solutions. If a participant suggested a possible solution, it was pointed out that solution-finding will come later, but at this time all energies should be devoted to seeking the roots, the real causes.

As comments, suggestions, and ideas were brought up, they were listed on a flip chart. This became the tool for the next step, which was to separate the items into categories related to their importance.

Most focus groups usually complete their business in one two-hour session, but it may be extended if needed. The O-MRI team then discussed the information developed by the four groups and plans were made for the next steps.

In some cases, focus groups are also drawn from customers, vendors or other outsiders with whom the company interrelates. The format and technique are the same as with employees, but of course, the matters discussed are geared to the experience the members of the group have had with the organization.

> ## QUOTES AND QUIPS
>
> "Approach each new problem not with a view of finding out what you hope will be there, but to get the truth, the realities that must be grappled with. You may not like what you will find. In that case, you are entitled to try to change it. But do not deceive yourself as to what you do find to be the facts of the situation."
>
> **Bernard M. Baruch, Presidential advisor and financial executive**

5. Interviews with informal leaders

From observations made during the pre-O-MRI workshops and from discussions with supervisors, managers, and employees, several people were identified as being informal leaders. These are men and women who are respected by their peers and often have been spokespersons for them in dealings with management. Their views reflect those of their co-workers and they are usually articulate and willing to express these views to whoever will listen.

The principal consultant or a member of his or her staff should conduct interviews with informal leaders. Because of the need for complete frankness, no representative of management should be present. In the Excelsior Paper O-MRI seven informal leaders were interviewed.

In each case the interviews were conducted away from the premises. The interview with one man, an avid golfer, was combined with a round of golf. The consultant conducted an interview with a woman while she drove to the school to pick up her daughter after band practice. Others were interviewed at lunch or dinner at a local restaurant.

The interviews started with discussions of the results of the questionnaire and what had been learned at the focus groups. As the rapport with the employees increased, quite often they opened up and expressed their feelings about various aspects of the job and the organization. They provided specific examples of both positive and negative practices they had observed, either augmenting what had been learned or adding additional matters. To maintain the integrity of the procedure, the confidentiality of sources was carefully preserved. These results were then discussed with the O-MRI team.

6. 360-degree assessments

As a result of the information thus far obtained, the consultants inferred that one of the most significant problems faced was a basic distrust of management by both rank-and-file workers and lower-echelon supervisors. To verify this and to develop more specific aspects of actual perceptions of these executives, 360-degree assessments of all middle and senior management people were instituted.

To start this process, a comprehensive questionnaire was designed to be completed by the four levels of personnel that each manager usually interacted with:

Superiors. Except for the CEO, (who was also assessed), the person to whom the manager reported and at least one other higher-ranking executive with whom he or she had frequent contact

Peer group members: persons at or close to the same level as the assessee who interface with that person on a regular basis

Others: This depended on the person being assessed. In some cases, it included outside people including vendors or customers. In one case, where the assessee had experienced a high turnover of subordinates, some former employees were interviewed.

Subordinates: personnel who report directly to the assessee. In some cases, people who report to the assessee's subordinates

The written surveys were mailed to each respondent. For those who did not respond, follow-up calls were made and where pertinent, a member of the O-MRI team personally requested the respondent to participate. Results were close to 100 percent. The written surveys were augmented by personal interviews with many of the respondents, who pinpointed specific areas that had to be addressed if the culture change process was to succeed.

7. Multi-level retreats

The participants in a multi-level retreat come from a variety of levels within the organization. Who should these people be? Most companies select representatives from middle- and first-line management. Occasionally, informal leaders from the rank-and-file workers may be included. The participants should reflect a cross-section of the entire organization and should include both long-term employees, who have intimate knowledge of the company, the department and their people, as well as relatively new employees who may look at the company with fresh views, who can contribute their experiences with other organizations where they had been employed.

Why bring this group together? In order for a culture change to take place, all levels must be involved. Senior managers have a broader outlook on company matters, so their input can provide important information. However, depending only on senior executives can be shortsighted. They often do not observe significant facets or are themselves the causes of the problems. Lower level personnel see things in a different light and can be valuable contributors. Also, by including them in the O-MRI, they are assured that the organization is serious about changing its culture and is going about it in a smart and respectful way. This is reinforced when serious consideration is involved in designing the strategy.

> **TACTICAL TIPS**
>
> In order to achieve a full and open discussion among lower echelon staff members, their bosses should not be present at the meeting and they should be assured that their comments will be kept confidential.

The consultant will coordinate the meeting. It will start with a discussion led by the CEO or another senior executive outlining the reason for the importance of change. Opportunity should be given to participants to ask questions to clarify the information. However, discussion of the items should be deferred until after the senior manager leaves. As indicated earlier, the presence of a high-ranking executive during discussions often inhibits free expressions of thought.

8. Report of findings

The O-MRI for Excelsior Paper identified a number of areas that were causing problems. The two most serious centered on (1) the authoritarian style of management; (not surprisingly, most of the offenders assumed that such behavior was "normal") and (2) the failure of management to effectively communicate with their staff. In addition there were a variety of lesser areas that required revised thinking before specific steps to correct them could be taken.

The O-MRI team discussed the results of these findings and, together with the consultants, wrote a detailed report to the CEO. This included recommendations for the next step: determining what changes in the culture should be made and designing the strategies to institute them.

Figure 3-1 _____

The O-MRI Review and Reminder Sheet

The following is intended to help remind you of the various important elements involved in each step of your O-MRI study. Use it as a prompt, to help plan your study, and to help assure that each step in your O-MRI process is completed properly and on time.

STEP ONE: Securing the Full, Unwavering Support of Top Management
- Who will be responsible for this step in the O-MRI process?
- Who will contact the members of top management?
- Will an appointment be set or a meeting planned to discuss the project? If so, when? Where? At what time?
- Who will prepare the agenda for the meeting?
- Who will conduct the meeting?
- Are any visual aids to be used? If so, who will prepare them?
- Who will assume responsibility for a successful outcome?
- How will we know whether or not management has committed its full, unwavering support?

STEP TWO: The Announcement
- Who will be responsible for this step in the O-MRI process?
- How will those within the organization be told about the study? Company Bulletin? Staff Meeting? Internal memorandum? Other?
- What specific benefits might employees expect to realize from the O-MRI study?
- What specific benefits might the organization at large expect to realize from the O-MRI study?
- How will these expected benefits be communicated?
- What, if any, resistance might you encounter?
- Who will actually make or release the announcement?

STEP THREE: The Confidential Employee Survey
- Who will be responsible for this step in the O-MRI process?
- Who or what organization will design the survey form?
- Are any approvals necessary before the form is printed and distributed to employees?

Figure 3-1   _____

The O-MRI Review and Reminder Sheet *(continued)*

• How will the survey forms be sent to employees? By mail to each person's home? Via the interoffice mail? By E-mail? Some other way?
• Will a return envelope and postage be provided?
• Will a cover letter to the respondent accompany the survey form?
• How will assurances of confidentiality be communicated to employees?
• How will we assure confidentiality?
• Will an independent, third-party agency be used to calculate results and prepare the reports for management? If so, which one?
• Is there a date by which all responses must be received?
• What is the budget for this step in the O-MRI process?
• How will the results of the survey be communicated to employees?
• Does the company expect to comment on the results of the study? If so, how will this be accomplished?
• How will the report to management be structured/organized?
• Will recommendations for improvement and/or follow-up action be included in the report?

STEP FOUR: The Focus Groups
• Who will be responsible for this step in the O-MRI process?
• How will those participating in Focus Groups be selected? By a random selection process? By some other way?
• Who will comprise each focus group? Employees, vendors, customers, others?
• Who will conduct/facilitate each meeting? Will an outside agency and/or facilitator be used?
• What will be the focus of each meeting?
• Will a formal agenda be prepared? If so, who will prepare it?
• How long will each meeting be?
• Are refreshments of any type to be provided?
• Who will be responsible for accumulating and organizing the data?
• Will the meeting be recorded or video-taped? If so, who will be responsible?

Figure 3-1

The O-MRI Review and Reminder Sheet *(continued)*

- Who will observe the meeting while it's in progress? (e.g. members of management, consultants, etc.)
- How many participants and observers will be invited to each meeting?
- What is the budget for this step in the O-MRI process?
- What will the facilitator do to put the participants at ease and stimulate a free flow of conversation?

STEP FIVE: The Confidential Interviews with the Leaders of the Informal Organization

- Who will be responsible for this step in the O-MRI Process?

- How will you determine who comprises the leadership of the informal organization?

- What percentage of this group will you interview? All of them? A random sample?

- How will you assure the confidentiality of whatever is learned from each person?

- How will you encourage candor?

- Who will conduct each interview?

- Where will the interviews be conducted? (Somewhere off-site is often best.)

- Who will be responsible for gathering the data generated by this step in the O-MRI?

- What is the budget for this step in the process?

- How will you notify the people invited to participate?

- How will you protect the identity of those providing sensitive or potentially troublesome insights and information?

- Will an agenda for each interview be used? If so, who will design it?

- Will the interviews be recorded? If so, how will this be explained to each participant? How will any resistance to this be overcome?

Figure 3-1

The O-MRI Review and Reminder Sheet *(continued)*

STEP SIX: The 360-Degree Assessments

- Who will be responsible for this step in the O-MRI Process?

- How will you determine who should participate in the 360-degree study? Which levels of employees? Who from outside the organization (suppliers, customers, etc.)?

- Who will design the strategy for the 360-degree assessments? The instruments and/or questionnaires? The interview formats?

- During what period of time will this step in the process be conducted and completed?

- Who or what group of people will conduct each portion of the study?

- Who will be responsible for organizing and assembling the data?

- Who will be responsible for preparing the report(s)?

- Who will interpret the results?

- What is the budget for this step in the O-MRI process?

- What follow-up action is expected once the reports are prepared and analyzed?

- Who or what group(s) will be privy to the results?

STEP SEVEN: The Multi-Level Retreat

- Who will be responsible for this step in the O-MRI process?

- Who will be invited to participate in the retreat?

- Where will the retreat be held?

- Will participants be asked to prepare anything in advance of the meeting(s)? If so, what?

- Will any social or recreational activities be included? If so, who will be responsible for organizing these events?

- Will a formal agenda be used?

- Who will actually conduct each meeting and/or facilitate each discussion during the retreat?

Figure 3-1 _____

The O-MRI Review and Reminder Sheet *(continued)*

- Will some meetings involve only distinct levels of the organization? If so, which ones?
- How many joint meetings (i.e., meetings involving those from multiple levels of the organization) will be organized?
- How will participants be notified of their invitation to the retreat?
- Are any travel arrangements required? If so, who will be responsible?
- How will the meeting conductor encourage candor and stimulate an open dialogue among the participants?
- Who will be responsible for gathering and organizing the data and other information acquired during the retreat?
- Will a summary of the meeting(s) be provided? If so, to whom?
- How are people expected to dress during each meeting? (Business casual seems best in most cases.) How will this be communicated?

STEP EIGHT: The Preparation of the Final Reports and Recommendations

- Who will be responsible for this step in your O-MRI process?
- Who will actually do the work to prepare the report?
- How will the report be structured?
- How many copies will exist?
- Who or what group will determine the recommendations to be made and included in the report?
- To whom or what group of people will the report be submitted?
- Are there any deadlines to be met?
- How will the confidentiality of certain information and the identities of those participating in all steps of the study be assured in the report?

Figure 3-1 _____

The O-MRI Review and Reminder Sheet *(continued)*

- Will a meeting be scheduled to discuss the details of the findings? If so, who or what group of people will be responsible for making the necessary arrangements? Who will be invited to attend?

- Who will conduct this meeting?

- What results are expected from this meeting?

- What follow-up or future actions do you expect after the meeting in an effort to maximize your benefits from your O-MRI study?

SUM AND SUBSTANCE

- Before an organizational culture can be changed, it must be analyzed and assessed. It's necessary to understand the current culture and determine what problems exist and how seriously they affect productivity, quality of product or service, morale of the workers and the overall efficacy of the organization.

- Perception is reality in the mind of the perceiver.

- The first step in changing an organization's culture is to identify the perception of the employees about their company's culture.

- Hard data—sales volume, market share, costs, profits, return on investment—serve an important purpose, but by themselves do not identify many of the subtle problems that plague an organization. To obtain a realistic evaluation we must delve deeper. The O-MRI provides the tool to accomplish this.

- For the O-MRI to be most effective, all levels of the organization from top managers to rank-and-file workers must become involved.

- The six best techniques of obtaining data for the O-MRI are:

  1. Meet with managers and employees away from the company environment.

2. Create focus groups.

3. Use confidential employee surveys.

4. Interview employees at all levels.

5. Conduct 360-degree assessments of key managers.

6. Hold multi-level retreats.

- The culture change program should be carefully prepared. By following the O-MRI Review and Reminder Sheet (Fig. 3-1), you will assure that all aspects of the preparation are covered.

How to Find Great People

One of the best ways to maintain a high employee-retention level is to take the time and effort in the hiring process to assure that the men and women you select have the qualities and characteristics that are congruent with the culture of your organization. It's not enough to determine if a candidate has the technical know-how to do the job. Equally important is to seek candidates who will want to remain with the company because it provides them with a climate in which they can work the way they like to work and the opportunity to meet their goals while helping the company achieve its goals.

It's not easy to locate, screen, and finally select such people—and it's not cheap. Human Resources experts estimate that hiring an employee costs a company 1.5 times his or her salary—a combination of recruiting costs, training time, and lost productivity as co-workers and supervisors pitch in during the time the job is left unfilled. And this is for an average employee. To get a top-level, "A-player", can cost considerably more.

ANALYZING THE JOB

First, let's look at the process of hiring. Why is there a job opening at this time? It may be that the incumbent employee quit, retired, was transferred, or was fired. It may be a brand new spot created in a reorganization, expansion, or diversification of the organization. No matter how the job opening developed, the first step in filling it is to study the job and learn exactly what the position entails and then determine what characteristics a candidate must bring to the job in order to be an "A-player". The process differs significantly depending on whether you are replacing a worker who has left or expanding the team or department.

First, you must analyze the job and write a job description that truly depicts what the person doing that job really does day-to-day, week-to-week, and year-to-year. You must determine what education, experience and personal traits candidates should bring to the job in order to be more than just an average worker.

It may seem that the "logical" way to start is to pull out the current job description and specifications, and start the search for somebody who qualifies. But is it really logical?

Jobs change over time. The job description may have been written several years ago. What is being done today may be somewhat different from what was done then. It's a good idea to review carefully and critically every job description before starting the search to refill it.

For example, one common reason for a job to become available is the voluntary resignation of an employee. An example of this is Lisa, a customer service representative, who notifies you that she's decided to go back to school and will leave the job in two weeks.

When Lisa was hired, customer service reps wrote out customer complaints on a form, checked them out and then telephoned or wrote to the customer with the results and suggested solutions. During her tenure all this was computerized so that many of the problems could be checked and adjusted during the first telephone call. Although Lisa was very good in her dealings with customers, her computer skills were poor and she was much slower than other reps. The job description and job specs should be rewritten with more emphasis placed on computer skills.

Sometimes the reason for hiring is to increase the staff. Your team is overworked. You succeed in persuading your manager to add one or more positions to your team. What kind of jobs will you add?

In some teams all members do the same kind of work. In a data entry team, they all enter much of the same kind of data; in a quality control team, all members may perform the same function. In these cases, you can just review the job descriptions to assure that they are current.

In other teams, one or a few members perform a specialized type of work. In a multi-functional team, part of the team may study market trends and another production capabilities. Now you have been given the added responsibility of studying financial implications. An entirely new job description is needed for the new assignment.

MAKING THE JOB ANALYSIS

Many managers fool themselves by assuming they know what a job entails and what it takes to do it successfully. Don't be so sure. Take the time and effort to make a *job analysis.* In some companies these analyses are performed by specialists. They may be industrial engineers, systems analysts, or members of your Human Resources staff. If your company employs these people, use them as a resource. The best people to make an analysis, however, are those closest to a job—you and your team members. The job analysis consists of two parts: The *job description*—what the person actually does, and the *job specification*—what characteristics a person must possess to be successful in the job.

There are several ways of developing information for the job description.

TACTICAL TIPS

When several people perform the same type of job, don't select the most or least experienced or skilled workers to observe. Studying a few mid-level performers will give you a more realistic concept of what is actually done on that job.

Observing the action

For jobs that are primarily physical in nature, watching a person perform the job will give you most of the material you need in order to write the description. If several people are engaged in the same type of work, observe more than one performer.

Even a good observer, however, may not understand what he or she is observing. Sometimes it involves much more than meets the eye. Additional steps must be taken to get the full picture. In jobs that are not primarily manual, however, there is little that you can learn from observation alone. Just watching someone sitting at a computer terminal, for example, isn't enough to learn what's being done.

Interviewing the worker

Ask the people who perform a job to describe the activities they perform. This technique fleshes out what you're observing. You must know enough about the work, of course, to be able to understand what's being said and to be able to ask appropriate questions. It's a good idea to prepare a series of questions in advance. Below are a few questions that will elicit good information. Only ask those questions which are pertinent to the job. In addition you should prepare questions that are specific to the job being analyzed.

- Tell me about how you spend a typical day.
- Tell me about some of the other work you occasionally do. How often and when do you do this work?
- What positions do you supervise (if any) and how much of your time is spent in supervising others?
- What responsibilities do you have for financial matters such as budgeting, purchasing, authorizing expenditures, and similar decisions?
- What equipment do you operate?
- What performance standards are you expected to meet on this job?
- What education and experience did you have prior to taking this job that prepared you for it?
- What training did you get on this job to help you do it effectively?

Interviewing the supervisor or team leader

If you're analyzing a job other than the ones you supervise, speak to the team leader to obtain that person's perspective of the position. Ask the supervisor or team leader questions about his or her perception of the job similar to those you asked the worker. Note variations in their answers. Probe to determine which is the more accurate description.

If you are evaluating a job that you personally supervise, try to take an objective view of the position and review it as if you were looking at it the same way a stranger might. Not easy to do, but you'll be amazed at the results. You'll see things you never noticed before and you'll interpret some of the aspects of what is being performed and how it is done in a different light.

Make it a team project

When work is performed by a team, job descriptions cover the work of the entire team. The best way to develop a complete job description is to get every team member into the act.

Have each member write a job description of the job as he or she views it. It's amazing how various people who do what ostensibly is the same job describe the work. Sure, basic aspects will be the same, but it's the differences among what each person considers to be important to the job that should be examined.

Bring the team together and discuss the differences. From this discussion will evolve a true picture of the entire job—duties, responsibilities, special activities and performance standards. Combine this with your own observations and obtain a consensus from which the final job description will be drawn.

Indicate performance expectations

Some companies prefer to call the job description a "position results description" or a "job results description." They feel that the true objective of this document is to determine what is expected of the people performing the job. Each description should include the major goal (why the job exists), the key results areas (KRAs)—aspects of the job on which the performer should focus attention, and the standards on which performance will be measured.

By indicating results expected and performance standards by which they are measured, both managers and performers are not only given a standard against which they can continually measure their performance, but a motivational instrument impelling action that will lead to desired results. This type of Job Results Description will be discussed in more detail in Chapter 9.

The job description worksheet (Figure 4-1, pages 82–83) is a helpful tool. Tailor the form you use to the type of job you're analyzing.

WHAT TO SEEK IN A CANDIDATE

After you know just what a job entails, you can determine which qualities you seek for the person who will be assigned to do the job.

The job specifications in some situations must be rigidly followed; others may allow for some flexibility. In civil-service jobs or in cases in which job specs are part of a union contract, for example, even a slight variation from job specs can have legal implications. In some technical jobs, a specific degree or certification may be mandated by company standards or to meet professional requirements. For example, an accountant making formal audits must be a certified public accountant (CPA); an engineer who approves structural plans must be licensed as a professional engineer (PE). On the other hand, if there's no compelling reason for the candidate to have a specific qualification, you may deviate from the specs and accept an equivalent type of background.

Determining Job Specs

Most job specifications include the elements in this list:

• Education: Does a job call for college? Advanced education? Schooling in a special skill?

Figure 4-1

Job Description Worksheet

Job title: _____

Reports to: _____

Duties performed: _____

_____

_____

_____

Equipment used: _____

_____

_____

_____

Skills used: _____

_____

_____

_____

Leadership responsibility: _____

_____

_____

_____

_____

Responsibility for equipment: _____

_____

_____

_____

_____

Figure 4-1 _____

Job Description Worksheet *(continued)*

Responsibility for money: _____

_____

_____

_____

_____

Other aspects of job: _____

_____

_____

_____

_____

Special working conditions: _____

_____

_____

_____

_____

Performance standards: _____

_____

_____

_____

_____

_____

Analysis made by: _____

Date: _____

- Skills: Must the candidate be skilled in computers? Machinery? Drafting? Statistics? Technical work? Are there any skills necessary to perform the job?

- Work experience: What type and duration of previous experience in related job functions are required?

- Physical strength or stamina: Does the job require heavy lifting or hard physical labor? If so, is it a significant part of the job or does it only occur occasionally?

- Intelligence: Some jobs call for a high level of intelligence. Decisions must be made that require deep thinking, solving complex problems or being able to think on one's feet. Intelligence can be measured by standard tests. For such jobs, the job specs might indicate a high score on these tests. In addition, there are jobs calling for specific types of intelligence such as working with intricate mathematical calculations, dealing with spatial relationships, or using sophisticated vocabulary. All these skills are measurable.

- Communication skills: The job spec should specify exactly which communication skills you need: for example, one-to-one communication, the ability to speak to large groups, innovative telephone sales methods, or creative writing skills.

- Accuracy of work: If a job calls for "attention to detail," specify what type of detail work. In some jobs there is no room for margins of error. Work must be done right the first time or serious problems may result. For example, working on a nuclear reactor or piloting a jet plane.

- Dealing with stress: If a job calls for "the ability to work under pressure," indicate what type of pressure (for example, daily deadlines, occasional deadlines, round-the-clock sessions, difficult working conditions, or a demanding boss).

- Extroversion or Introversion: A sales representative or an office receptionist should have an outgoing personality. Shy, introverted people will be ill at ease in such jobs. On the other hand, if the job is one in which one works alone in a confined space with little contact with others, the extroverted person is sure to be unhappy and most likely will fail.

- Special factors: Among the many other factors that may be included in the job specification are such requirements as fluency in a foreign language, willingness to travel, willingness to work on weekends, willingness to work overtime at short notice and anything else an applicant must comply with to perform the job satisfactorily.

One of the toughest jobs you have is to determine what differentiates the "A" player from the "B" and "C" players. Study the backgrounds of current employees whom you consider to be "A" players. Identify what makes them different from the average employee. Add these factors to your job specs.

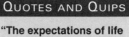

QUOTES AND QUIPS

"The expectations of life depend upon diligence; the mechanic that would perfect his work must first sharpen his tools."
Confucius

Bradford D. Smart, in his book *Topgrading* defines the "A" player as one who qualifies among the top 10% of those available for a position—the best of the class. "B" players are the next 25 percent of the talent available; "C" players are all others who meet the basic qualifications.[1]

ELIMINATING GOOD PROSPECTS FOR THE WRONG REASON

One of the most common problems in determining the specifications for a job is having the requirement of a higher level of qualifications than is really necessary, thus knocking out potentially good candidates for the wrong reason. This problem frequently occurs in these areas:

Education. Suppose that certain job specs call for a college degree. Is that degree necessary? It often is, but just as often having the degree has no bearing on a person's ability to succeed in a job. Requiring a higher level of education (or, for that matter, any qual-

---

[1]Bradford D. Smart, *Topgrading: How Leading Companies Win By Hiring, Coaching, and Keeping the Best People*, Paramus, NJ, Prentice Hall Press, 1999, pp.14 and 18.

ification) has more disadvantages than advantages. You may attract smart and creative people, but the job may not challenge them, resulting in low productivity and high turnover. More important, you may turn away the best possible candidates for a position by putting the emphasis on a less important aspect of the job.

Duration of experience. Your job specs may call for ten years' experience in accounting. Why specify ten years? An "A" player need not be one with years of experience. No direct correlation exists between the number of years a person has worked in a field and that person's competence. Lots of people have ten years on a job but only one year's experience (after they've mastered the basics of the job, they plod along, never growing or learning from their experience). Other people acquire a great deal of skill in a much shorter period.

It's not that years of experience don't count for anything. Often, the only way a person can gain the skills necessary to do a good job, make sound decisions, and make mature judgments is by having extensive experience. Just counting the years, however, isn't the way to determine that ability.

Rather than specify a number of years, set up a list of factors a new employee should bring to a job and how qualified the person should be in each area. By asking an applicant specific questions about each of these factors, you can determine what he or she knows and has accomplished in each area.

Type of experience. Job specs often mandate that an applicant should have experience in "our industry." There are some jobs where the skills and job knowledge needed can be acquired only in companies that do similar work. In many jobs, however, a background in other industries is just as valuable and may be even better because the new associate isn't tradition-bound and will bring to a job original and innovative concepts.

Preferential factors. There are job specs that are essential to perform a job, but there are other factors, which are not essential but would add to a candidate's value to your company. In listing preferential factors, use them as extra assets and don't eliminate good people simply because they don't have those qualifications.

For example, it may be an extra benefit if a candidate already knows how to use a certain type of computer software, but because that knowledge can be picked up on the job, eliminating a person who is otherwise well qualified might be a mistake.

Be Flexible

Job specs can be so rigid that you're unable to find anyone who meets all your requirements. Sometimes you have to make compromises. Reexamine the job specs and set priorities. Which of the specs are nonnegotiable? These requirements are the ones a new team member absolutely must bring to a job or else there is no way the job can be done. For example, a candidate must have a jet pilot's license to fly the company plane; the candidate must be able to do machine work to precise tolerances or the work will not pass inspection.

Suppose that your specs call for sales experience. One of the applicants has no job experience in selling, but as a volunteer, was a top fund-raiser for the local community theater. That person may be able to do the job. In seeking to fill a job, the employer should make every effort to abide by the job specs but should also have the authority to use his or her judgment to determine when deviation from the job specs is acceptable.

TWENTY-TWO MISTAKES COMPANIES MAKE IN HIRING

Let's look at some of the major errors companies make in hiring.

1. Waiting for vacancies

Sometimes you know when a team member plans to leave. He may be reaching retirement age; she may be expecting a child and has chosen to remain at home. This gives you weeks or months to find a replacement. Often, it's a complete surprise. Sarah finds a better job and gives you two weeks notice. Tom is badly injured in a car accident and will be out for months. Some jobs are more difficult to fill than others. Unless there's a plan for hiring new people, the job may go unfilled for a long time. Having an ongoing hiring program can minimize such problems.

2. Hiring a "warm body"

The job is open and the right candidate just hasn't come along. So you hire a marginally qualified person to "do the work." Big mistake. This is how companies often wind up with a glut of "C" players. You figure you can train them to become at least "B" players, but the time, energy, and money spent will rarely pay off. Better to get the work done by having other team members put in extra time to meet work schedules or to employ temps or outsource the work than to put marginal workers on the payroll. Take your time and aim for "A" players.

3. Looking for the "Dream" candidate

The "A" player may not be your dream candidate—the man or woman you imagine is ideal for the job. Don't establish unrealistic specifications that are not really needed to do the job. By including them, the best candidates may be eliminated for the wrong reason.

For example, when the Property Development Corp. expanded its Minneapolis division, one of the jobs they created was Divisional Controller. The job included managing their accounting department, dealing with banks and other financial institutions and coordinating financial matters with the home office. In determining the specifications for the job, in addition to comprehensive experience in performing similar work, the company required that candidates have a degree in Accounting, an MBA and be certified as a CPA.

Are these educational requirements truly meaningful for success in the job? Because the job calls for extensive knowledge of accounting, the degree in accounting is most likely an essential factor. But why an MBA? Graduate degrees in Business may provide a good deal of knowledge and analytical skills that may not be acquired by experience. However, depending on the program undertaken by the student, the specific skills needed for being a successful controller may have been acquired by work experience. If an MBA is a requirement, men and women who have the necessary skills, but not the degree, will be eliminated. To avoid this, the MBA may be considered as *one* of the means of acquiring the skills needed to do the job, but the lack of the degree should not eliminate an otherwise viable candidate.

Let's look at the requirement for certification (CPA). Certification is required for accountants working as *public* accountants, whose work involves dealing with clients' accounts. This certification is not needed for accounting positions in companies or organizations. Having had a background in auditing and other public accounting activities may be a valuable asset for controllers, and it certainly is not a negative factor. But to make it a job requirement may eliminate the best-qualified applicants.

4. Cloning the incumbents

In seeking to replace an effective employee who has moved on, companies often seek that person's mirror image. Or, if he or she was not effective, they search for the exact opposite.

You loved Diane. You wished you had ten like her. When she left because her husband was transferred to another city, you were devastated. Your goal: hire another Diane. So you used her background as the specs for her replacement. Diane graduated from an ivy-league college. Therefore her replacement must come from an ivy league school. Diane always dressed in bright colors—really made the place more cheerful, therefore applicants with bright clothes will be preferred. Before she worked here, Diane worked in a bank. Bank experience is important, etc., etc.

You fired Alfred. Alfred was from New York. His successor should come from a smaller community. Alfred was an avid sports fan—always talked about sports. People like that don't really concentrate on their work. No sports fans. Alfred had a background in Macintosh computers. Although he did learn your PCs, he always complained that Macs were better. No Mac users, etc., etc.

QUOTES AND QUIPS

"Never hire someone
who knows less than
you do about what he's
(or she's) hired to do."
—Malcolm Forbes,
Publisher

Do such trivial factors often enter into the unofficial job specs? Using the incumbent or a predecessor's personal characteristics as significant factors in determining the qualifications for a job can keep you from hiring the best qualified person, and may overly influence you to hire an unqualified person just because they are like (or unlike) the previous holder of that job.

5. "We only promote from within"

Promoting or transferring a current employee to a new position is commendable and should be encouraged. The internal candidates are known factors. The company has seen them in action. It knows their strengths and weaknesses, their personality quirks, their work habits, their attendance and punctuality patterns and all the little things that months or years of observation uncover. It also is good for employee morale and motivation. The problem, however, is *limiting* the candidates for a position to current employees only. In this highly competitive world, a company should attempt to find the very best candidate for open positions—and that person may not be currently on your payroll.

There was a time when companies boasted that when the Chairman retired, they hired a junior clerk. Everybody moved up a notch. It is likely that in a large organization there are many highly competent people who are available for filling the new openings and of course, they should be given serious consideration. However, a search for outside candidates may bring to the company skills and expertise that is now lacking and new ideas that often elude people in-bred within the organization.

6. Relying on personal contacts

Personal contacts are excellent sources for referrals. People you know from your business and social worlds often may be ideal candidates themselves or may recommend highly qualified people from their networks. Indeed, networking can be a prime source of potential applicants.

But using personal contacts has its downside. First, the people you contact may not know anybody at this time who is qualified. Or worse, they may palm off a friend or relative who needs a job, but has limited abilities for your opening. Turning down a friend of a friend may jeopardize your relationship with that person.

Another problem is that you may be overly impressed with the personality or sociability of a person you know and not consider their true capability for the open position. A good example of this is Harry L., the sales manager of Amalgamated Products. Harry was always looking for good salespeople. He knew Jim D. for years. They belonged to the same golf club and occasionally played together or socialized in the restaurant or bar. When Harry learned that Jim was looking for a job, he offered him a position on his sales force. It didn't take long for Harry to realize that Jim needed considerable training and supervision if he were to succeed. It was only after months of wasted effort and frustration that Harry finally let him go. Had Harry used even minimum screening, he would have learned that Jim had a pattern of failures in his previous jobs.

Many companies encourage their current employees to recommend friends and acquaintances for open jobs. This can be a valuable source and should be used. But it should be made clear that the referral by another employee is not a guarantee of a job and the applicant will be treated as any other applicant.

To get the best possible candidates for your job openings, it's smart to use as many sources as possible. Just because you found a terrific guy or gal from your old alma mater or when you had a tough job to fill, a friend recommended a great candidate is no reason to hope that this time around you can depend on them to come across again. Open your minds; open your rolodex, use your imagination. Broaden the market.

7. Writing ads that don't pull

Help-wanted advertising is expensive. Whether you are running a classified ad in the local paper to fill a clerical or blue-collar position or a display ad in a national publication for a technical expert or an executive, the results can range from just a few replies to a deluge of résumés.

No matter how many responses you receive, the key is whether the respondents actually fit the job. Too many companies place ads that either do not pull at all or bring in a plethora of responses from unqualified people.

Too many managers write help-wanted ads without giving them adequate thought. They scribble the ad on a scratch pad while waiting for a phone call to go through or on a paper napkin while eating lunch. It's worth the time to learn how to write and place effective ads

> **TACTICAL TIPS**
>
> **Studies show that when screening responses received from an ad, employment specialists spend an average of 30 seconds to read each résumé and decide whether the applicant should be given further consideration.**

8. Failure to take pro-active steps in seeking candidates

> **TACTICAL TIPS**
>
> *Top Ten Internet Referral Services*
> 1. Monster.com
> 2. Careerpath.com
> 3. CareerMosaic.com
> 4. HeadHunter.net
> 5. JobSearch.org
> 6. HotJobs.com
> 7. Dice.com
> 8. CareerBuilder.com
> 9. NationJob.com
> 10. Jobs.com

Are your recruiters surfing the Internet on a 24/7 basis? Are they visiting Web sites of competitors, identifying their top producers, and attempting to entice them away? Are they reviewing the constant flow of listings on the Internet referral services such as Monster.com, Careerpath.com, and others to look for the talents needed by your firm? (See Tactical Tips at left.) According to a poll of 400 employers taken by Recruiters Network of Milwaukee, Wisconsin in August 2000, 59 percent of the respondents reported that Internet recruiting reduced the cost per hire significantly.

9. Paper tigers: résumés that sound ideal

Whether the candidate responds to an ad or is referred by any of the other sources you use, it takes time—lots of time—to screen out the unqualified and select those whom you think are worthy of being interviewed. Once an applicant is invited for an interview, depending on the type of position involved, an initial interview can take anywhere from ten minutes to over an hour. How much time do you have to devote to interviewing? Even if you are a full-time interviewer in the Human Resources Department, there are only so many hours each day you can schedule. And if you are a team leader, department head, or senior executive, your day is probably already full and interviewing means putting in extra hours.

You must be able to pre-screen candidates so those you do interview are viable prospects for the open position. The most commonly used pre-screening device is the résumé.

Most employers ask prospective employees to provide a résumé either before they meet with them or at the interview. As résumés are written to impress prospective employers, you must learn how to separate the facts from the fluff.

Beware of the functional style résumé. In this format the writer describes the functions performed in previous jobs. This is very helpful in learning about the applicant's background, but often it is used to play up functions in which the applicant has only superficial knowledge—and it may not indicate the duration of the experience or the name or type of company in which it was attained.

For example, Gertrude S. used a functional format. She listed four functions: Administration, Data Processing, Personnel and Secretarial. Although 80 percent of her job was secretarial, her résumé gave the impression that she was equally involved in all four functions.

This doesn't mean you should not consider Gertrude for the job, but it does mean that you must be prepared to ask very pointed questions about the specific details on her experience in each of the functions listed.

When seeking an Information Technology position, Ted L. used the more traditional chronological résumé—but instead of listing the dates of his employment, he just noted the number of years in each position followed by a description of the duties performed.

Systems Specialist, ABC Co. (5 years)—(then description of duties)

Programmer, XYZ Co. (3 years)

Sales Representative, Apex Insurance Co. (8 years)

This gives the impression that the past eight years were in computer work, but in reality, the most recent job was the last one listed—selling insurance. He has been away from computer work for some time—and the field has changed significantly during those years.

10. Wasting time on unqualified applicants

Sometimes when companies are in a rush to fill a job, they may ask applicants to telephone for appointments or come right to the office. Despite all the problems of reading and evaluating résumés, they serve the purpose of helping eliminate unqualified people and saving interviewing time. When no résumé is used, it is more difficult to weed out time-wasting candidates. One way to overcome this is by a carefully structured telephone interview. Asking good questions will help determine whether or not to invite the candidate in for an interview. This will be discussed in more detail in Chapter 5.

11. The unstructured interview

The interview is more than a polite conversation. Yet, many interviewers sit down with the applicant and expect by asking a few questions and conversing about the applicant's background and the job requirements, they will get enough information to make a decision to hire or reject the candidate.

To assure that you obtain significant information about a candidate, ask very specific questions that will bring out whether that person can perform the job and what he or she offers in comparison with other applicants for the same position. This may or may not develop in a pleasant conversation. A definite structure must be designed to elicit the key points, give the candidate the opportunity to expound on his or her credentials and accomplishments, and enable the interviewer to size up the applicant's personal characteristics. More on this will be found in Chapter 6.

12. The overly structured interview

Some interviewers, in their efforts to cover all the bases, overly structure their interview plan. They make a list of questions and read them to each candidate. In this way they will get responses that enable them to determine basic qualifications and because the questions asked are the same for each applicant, answers can be easily compared and the differences among the candidates clearly defined.

Sounds good? Maybe. The problem is that quite often an answer requires a follow-up question. If you stick to the structure—with no flexibility—you may miss an important point. For example:

Interviewer: What was your greatest accomplishment on that job?

Applicant: I saved the company a lot of money.

Interviewer: What was your greatest disappointment on that job?

Note that the interviewer asked the next question on the list instead of following through and finding out what the applicant did that saved the company money. The answer to that might have opened the door to even more questions that would give considerable insight into the prospect's qualifications before moving on to the next question on the list.

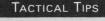

TACTICAL TIPS

Make every question count. If the answer is vague or not clear, ask an appropriate follow-up question.

13. Asking unlawful questions

It's been over 35 years since the federal equal employment opportunity law went into effect. You'd think that by now companies would no longer be asking applicants questions that are consid-

ered unlawful. Yet, every day some interviewer in some company—maybe yours—will ask a question that shouldn't be asked.

Why? Sometimes it's ignorance of the laws. Most employment
professionals know the laws and abide by them. However, as noted
before, team leaders, managers and, often, team members, participate in the interviewing process. Many of these people have only
vague concepts of the laws. And, as in many matters with legal implications, it's not always clear just what the law allows and what it
prohibits.

You may feel that in order to determine if the candidate will be
available for overtime work, you should ask if she has any young
children. Uh! uh! Illegal! The applicant has an unusual name.
You're curious, so you ask, "What kind of a name is that?" When
the applicant is rejected for whatever reason, he files a complaint
against you claiming discrimination because of national origin.
This may not have had anything at all to do with his rejection, but
because you asked, the burden is on you to prove otherwise.

Make it your business to learn what the laws require and how
you can get much of the information you need to make a hiring
decision without violating any laws.

14. Telling the applicant too much about the job

One of the major errors interviewers make is to tell the applicant
all about the job early in the interview. Often they may give the
applicant a copy of the job description before the interview begins.
Why is this bad? This enables the smart applicant to tailor his or
her background to fit the job description. For example, the open
job calls for somebody who has extensive experience in adminis-
tering employee benefits. In her last job, Shirley had some exposure to benefits. Knowing that this is an important aspect of the
open position, Shirley might play up—perhaps exaggerate—her
background in this field.

Of course, the applicant should have some concept of what job
he or she is being interviewed for. The best way to do this is to
first ask questions about the applicant's background in the area
under discussion. Then, after the response, comment about the job.

Let's see how this could be structured so the interviewer will get an unbiased response.

Interviewer: Shirley, I notice that your current job as a generalist gave you a broad background in many phases of the H.R. job. In what area did you spend most of your time?

Shirley: I guess in interviewing, but I also was involved in orientation of new employees and explaining our benefits to them.

Interviewer: Did you process claims?

Shirley: One of the other staffers was responsible for processing claims, but I sometimes helped her.

Interviewer: Processing claims is an important part of the job here. If you're hired, we'd have to give you added training in this area.

In this way the hiring decision can be made on more accurate information.

15. Inadequate reference checks

The applicant presented you with a slick résumé, and came across well in the interview. Before you make the decision, you should verify that what the applicant claims to be true is true.

The purpose of the reference check is to verify the applicant's statements and perhaps catch the "artful liar." Unfortunately, this essential part of the employment process is often disregarded or treated much too casually.

Often the background check is assigned to a junior employee who may send reference letters to previous employers or telephone them—with little training or know-how in asking probing questions and interpreting the responses.

> ## QUOTES AND QUIPS
>
> **"Don't automatically reject an applicant if you get a poor reference. Arrange for another interview. Don't mention the poor reference, but ask questions that may uncover the reason for it. Hold your judgment until you know the entire story."**
> **—Dr. Arthur R. Pell, Author from *The Complete Idiot's Guide to Recruiting the Right Stuff***

In recent years many companies have been advised by their attorneys not to give any reference information for fear of defamation suits. They limit responses to reference inquiries to the dates of employment and some generalized information about job duties.

Because of this, some organizations don't bother to check out potential employees and take them at face value. This can be a costly mistake. It's important that you make every effort to get as much information about an applicant before you make the hiring decision.

16. Being overly impressed by superficial factors

There's an old saying that the decision to hire or not to hire is often made in the first 30 seconds of the interview. There is some truth to this. One of the major factors in hiring is the first impression made by the applicant—and that is primarily physical appearance. This has been categorized as "lookism"—overemphasis on appearance.

Studies have verified that good-looking people are far more likely to be hired than equally qualified but less attractive people. In an informal exercise we administered at a series of seminars conducted a few years ago, a job description and several résumés of more or less equally qualified prospective candidates were distributed to the participants. Half the class received résumés with photos of the applicant attached; the other half had no photos. In virtually every instance, the participants who received photos selected the more attractive candidate, while the choices of the non-photo group were about equally divided among all the candidates.

Common sense tells us that just because a person is attractive is no assurance of competence, yet both men and women may decide in favor of the better looking applicant. Perhaps we just like to have nice-looking people around us.

Some first impressions create a "halo-effect." Because you are so impressed by some superficial facet, it is assumed all other aspects of his or her background are outstanding. He's so charming, he must be a good salesman. She speaks so well, she'll make a great supervisor. Halo effects are not limited to first impressions.

Sometimes because an applicant is highly competent in one aspect of a job, it is assumed he or she is equally competent in others. Charles could type on the word processor at 90 words per minute. With that speed, the supervisor figured he had hired a winner. But it wasn't until after Charles started work that they realized that speed was his only asset. He was a poor organizer, he was temperamental and didn't work well with others and had other unsatisfactory work habits.

Poor first impressions may cause you to reject an otherwise well-qualified candidate. An applicant may be downgraded in your mind because he or she does not speak well—important if the job calls for oral communication, but it should not be a factor in jobs where that is not required. One of our clients wouldn't even consider an applicant who had a straggly beard and long, unkempt hair. Only after the person who referred the applicant persuaded him that the man was a computer whiz did he hire him. This man has since solved countless problems for the company and has saved them tens of thousands of dollars.

Smart employers don't make hiring decisions based on one or two factors. No matter how impressed you may be by an applicant, learn as much as you can about him or her before choosing the new employee.

17. Subconscious biases—pro or con

We all have biases. Biases are not limited to prejudice against people because of their race, religion or sex. They may be based on long-held beliefs or stereotypes—true or false. They may be caused by our personal tastes or idiosyncrasies.

At one seminar participants were asked to share with the group some of their hiring mistakes. Most people told about people they hired who didn't make the grade. But, one of the participants told about a salesman he had rejected.

He said: "At a luncheon meeting of our trade association, the sales manager of one of our competitors was bragging about his top sales rep. He said that in his first year, he broke all records for bringing in new accounts. When he mentioned his name, it rang a bell. I recalled having interviewed him some time ago. When I returned to my office, I checked my files. Sure enough, I had interviewed and rejected him. Why? My notes on his application just said: "not suitable." Then I remembered. I turned him down because he was wearing a bow tie. My stupid bias against bow ties had kept me from hiring a potential winner."

Many people have biases in favor of people like themselves. One manager reported that his boss preferred to hire people who graduated from the University of Michigan, and would never—no matter how qualified he or she may be—hire a Michigan State grad.

> **TACTICAL TIPS**
>
> **To get the best people, you have to identify your own biases and compensate for them in making the decision.**

18. Mismatching candidates with job specs

The importance of having realistic job specs was noted earlier in this chapter. The whole purpose of developing a list of specifications is to assure that the person hired can do all (or most) of the facets of the job.

Often it is difficult, if not impossible, to find somebody with all of the requirements. In such cases, choose which of the specs are absolutely essential and in which areas a new employee can be trained after employment. There are certain aspects of most jobs in which experience or technical know-how is essential and cannot be taught on the job. The big mistake organizations make is to hire a candidate who may qualify in several of the specs but is weak in the essential areas.

19. Overlooking the intangibles

When making a hiring decision, it's just as important to evaluate the intangibles as the ability to perform the job. Too often, the employer limits the selection procedure to determining if the applicant is technically qualified and overlooks such factors as whether the person can work in a team, can communicate ideas, can work under pressure, has the capacity to be flexible, and the countless other personality factors that make up the human being.

The intangibles that make for success on a job are just as important as education, skills, and experience. In making your job analysis, be as diligent in determining the intangible factors as you are the tangible factors.

20. Making job offers that won't be accepted

You have screened hundreds of résumés, interviewed dozens of applicants, tested or sent many of them for evaluation and checked references. You finally make up your mind and make an offer, only to have it rejected by the applicant. This is the most frustrating experience one can have in the hiring process. Why should this be?

The terms of employment that are offered should be well thought out long before an offer is made. However, too many companies have a pre-conceived idea of the offer before they even interview applicants. This makes for sound business, but unless the offer is shaped to fit the needs of the applicant, there's a good chance it will not be accepted.

One major part of the job offer is the salary. We'll talk about this in the following section. Other factors that should be clearly understood prior to making a job offer are such key aspects of the job as amount of travel required, hours of work including the likelihood of extensive overtime, whether the job will call for relocation now or in the future, and any other special aspects of the position. Don't surprise the applicant at the time of the offer with "By the way, you will have to go to our plant in California for three months' training."

21. Negotiating the financial package

With lower-level employees, salary is non-negotiable. It's "take it or leave it." But when the position is hard to fill, you must be more flexible or you'll lose the best applicants.

It's not necessary or even advisable to commit to a salary too early in the interviewing process. There may be many factors that should be considered in determining the final financial package. But, it makes sense to have an approximation of the salary range clearly established early on. If you and the applicant are far apart about salary, there's no point in considering the applicant seriously.

Perhaps your benefits package is significantly poorer than other firms in the community or industry. Despite the increasing cost of health insurance, for example, unless your medical plan is in line with those of other firms, many applicants will turn you down.

Most benefits plans are standardized. However, more and more organizations are constructing individual benefit programs for each employee. The amount paid into the package may vary with the position and pay scale. The specifics of what is covered within the package can be tailored to fit the desires of the employee. This will be discussed further in Chapter 8.

22. When the current employer makes a counteroffer

Talk about frustration? Here is one of the worst examples. After all the time, energy, thought and emotional turmoil you have experienced in the hiring process, you offer the job to Tom, and he accepts it. You think your troubles are over and you can get back to work. A week later, Tom calls and tells you he gave notice to his boss, and was made a counteroffer, so he decided to stay. You have to start all over.

You must expect that counteroffers will be made to good workers. You probably have done the same when one of your best people gave notice. To beat this, you have to be proactive. You must prepare the person to whom you make a job offer to expect and reject a counteroffer. How to do this will be discussed in Chapter 7.

INTERNAL TRANSFERS AND PROMOTIONS

One way to attract and retain "A" players is to have an active program of internal transfers and promotions. When a change of job involves a promotion, most people are delighted and welcome the opportunity. However, not every transfer is a promotion, but it's often an opportunity for someone to learn, gain experience, and take a step forward in preparing for career advancement.

Seeking to fill a vacancy from within a company has many advantages. People who already work in your company know the "lay of the land." They're familiar with your company's rules and regulations, customs and culture, and practices and idiosyncrasies. Hiring these people rather than someone from outside your company saves time in orientation and minimizes the risks of dissatisfaction with your company.

You know more about these people than you can possibly learn about outsiders. You may have worked directly with a certain person or observed him or her in action. You can get detailed and honest information about a candidate from previous supervisors and company records.

Offering opportunities to current employees boosts morale and serves as an incentive for them to perform at their highest level. An important side effect is that it creates a positive image of your company in the industry and in your community. This image encourages good people to apply when jobs for outsiders do become available.

However, it has its share of problems. Although the advantages of internal promotion usually outweigh the limitations, there are disadvantages to consider:

- The job may require skills not found in your company.

- If you promote only from within, you limit the sources from which to draw candidates and you may be restricted to promoting a person significantly less qualified than someone from outside your company.

- People who have worked in other companies bring with them new and different ideas and know-how that can benefit your team.

- Outsiders look at your activities with a fresh view, not tainted by over-familiarity.

Most companies use a judicious mixture combining internal promotion and transfers with outside recruitment to get and keep the best candidates for their openings.

QUOTES AND QUIPS

I know I'm happier and healthier today because I decided long ago to do what I loved doing. I also think people sense the enjoyment I get from my work. I'm always pleased when people say they actually enjoy coming to see us. It tells me we've succeeded in creating the kind of work environment I always intended for my business.
— Carmine Fischetti, Small business owner

One of the major problems in inter-departmental transfers is the reluctance of department heads to release efficient and productive workers to other departments. One of the first actions of a company planning a policy of internal recruitment is to notify all department heads and team leaders that it will overrule any attempts to keep people who could be more valuable to the organization by transfer to another position. It should also be mentioned that people who are passed over for better positions in other departments are unlikely to remain with the company, and probably will seek another job elsewhere—so both the department and the company will lose a valuable employee.

Finding the Right Candidate from Within the Company

Many organizations have developed training programs that provide them with a steady stream of trained people for their expanding job needs. In some companies there's a plethora of talent to choose from.

However, there are times when there are no obvious candidates for a vacant job. You may have people in the company who are qualified to do the job—and you don't know it. What can you do?

Search the Personnel Files

If properly maintained, personnel records can be a major resource. Examination of these records may uncover people working in jobs below their education or skill levels. It may also reveal people who have had additional training since they were employed.

Any training given by the company, whether internal or outside seminars or programs, should be noted. If the company has a tuition reimbursement policy, any courses falling into this category should be noted. Employees should be encouraged to inform the Human Resources Department of other courses, programs or outside training they may have completed.

Personnel records can be an important means of locating people urgently needed by a company. A major aerospace firm recently spent several thousand dollars in advertising for specialized engineers needed for a new project in one division of the company. The recruiters were shocked to receive letters in reply to the ad from engineers in another division of the same company. The engineers claimed that their specialized knowledge was not being used in their current jobs and were seeking a position where it would be. Had the HR department known of them, it would have saved the company money and time.

> ### TACTICAL TIPS
>
> **Send periodic questionnaires to all employees to bring the personnel records up to date. Ask about new skills or knowledge acquired at the annual reviews. All this should be incorporated in the personnel records.**

Ask the Supervisors

Supervisors and team leaders know a good deal about their associates. Take advantage of this. Let them know what jobs are open in other departments. They may have associates who are qualified.

There are two dangers here. One is that team leaders may be reluctant to lose a good worker, even if the transfer would be advantageous to both the worker and the company. It's not easy to overcome this. The company must have a strict policy on this as noted earlier in this section.

The other is that the team leader may refer somebody he or she wants to get rid of. Give as careful screening to applicants referred by their team leaders as to every other candidate for the job.

Job Banks

To systematize internal searches, many firms have established databases listing all of the skills, talents, experience, education and other backgrounds of all of its employees. These are usually referred to as *job banks,* sometimes called *skill banks.*

For example, under "Lotus 123," are listed the names of all persons who have worked with this program at any time in their careers, whether or not they are currently using this skill. If a need for a team member with this background occurs in Unit A and the bank indicates there is a person who has had that experience in Unit B, but is employed in another capacity, he or she may be approached about transferring to Unit A.

As new skills are acquired, internal training programs completed, and outside training reported, they are added to the database.

Job Posting

Many companies make a practice of posting job openings on bulletin boards or listing them in company newsletters so that any employee who believes he or she is qualified can apply. Indeed, many union contracts require that job openings be posted.

Posting a job opening encourages current employees who may qualify for the job, but are not known to the manager or team leader seeking to fill the job, to apply. Sandra L. worked in the order-processing department, but her career goal is in sales. Everybody tells her she has a "sales personality," and she has had some part-time selling experience. When an opening for a sales trainee is posted, she applies. The sales manager interviewed her and recognized her talent. She was transferred into the sales training program and in time, became one of the company's star sales reps. Had the job not been posted, Sandra would not have known there was an opening, and the sales manager would not have known about Sandra. The company would have missed a high potential employee.

There are still companies where minority and women employees are not usually considered for certain jobs. Job posting enables members of these groups to apply and be given serious consideration for them. For this reason, many compliance agreements with the EEOC include a requirement that all jobs be posted.

However, there's a down side to posting jobs. When a current employee applies for a posted job and is rejected, you have a disgruntled employee. Some may quit, causing the loss of a good employee. Some of those who stay lose self-confidence and make little effort to build up their competence. Some go back to work and bad-mouth the company to their co-workers, leading to low morale.

When rejecting an employee for an internal transfer or promotion, take the time to explain in detail why he or she did not qualify. Point out what might be done so that next time this type of job is posted, the employee would be better equipped to qualify for it and would have a good chance of getting it. Suggest what additional training is needed, and if pertinent, what the company will do to help the employee attain that training.

Promotion Policies

Advancement within the organization is an ideal way to fill higher level jobs. Although there are many people who are not career oriented and shun moving into positions demanding responsibility, a great number of men and women look for advancement as a means of career growth. If they cannot advance in your company, they'll move to another where they can. Successful companies recognize this and provide opportunity for their best staff members. Let's look at some commonly followed policies.

The Einstein Theory of Promotion—Relativity. If you're a relative of the boss, you get the promotion. Nepotism has been a factor in promotion from ancient times. Popes and kings appointed nephews and cousins to cushy jobs. In the world of business, parents "hire" their sons or daughters as vice presidents. Even distant relatives get preference over "strangers."

If you don't quit or die, you're promoted. In many companies promotions are based on seniority. When an opening occurs, the most senior member of the department or the team moves up. Fair? After all, doesn't a person who has served long and loyally deserve a promotion? Not necessarily: A long term, loyal employment record is commendable, but it doesn't necessarily qualify the member for the higher level. Often the position requires skills not used at the lower level. Not only may specific educational or professional experience be needed, but leadership skills may be essential to the job.

When a position develops at any level, it should be analyzed to determine what the person who will perform it must bring to the job in terms of education, training, experience and personality. If the most senior person in the group falls short in any of these areas, somebody else should be considered. You may have to select a person from the group with lesser seniority, transfer somebody from another part of the company or hire an outsider.

Telling the senior member he or she is not getting the promotion must be done with sensitivity. The person by-passed has most likely been a productive worker who may have been waiting for years for this opportunity. Don't surprise him or her with the public announcement of the appointment. Explain as well as you can why the decision was made before it is announced to the other employees.

The best worker gets the promotion. When promotion by seniority is not mandated, employers can select the best worker for the job. The best mechanic is promoted to master mechanic, the best accountant to controller, the best sales rep to district manager. This is an excellent way of choosing a person for a higher-level technical position such as moving a programmer up to a systems analyst, but if the job is at the management level, it is not enough

Promotion resulting from competence is an incentive for team members to work hard and smart with the carrot of promotion dangling in front of them. But, the best worker may not necessarily be the best leader or manager. It takes additional and often different skills to be successful in the higher-level job.

This doesn't mean that good performance should be ignored. Doing good work certainly should be a factor in making the decision, but as pointed out before, it is only one of the facets of succeeding in a leadership position.

To qualify for any position, the candidate must meet a variety of qualifications as determined in the job specification. To determine whether the persons you are considering are qualified, you must undertake the same procedures as you would if you were screening outside applicants. Indeed, you can obtain much more information about the internal candidates than you can about outsiders.

> **QUOTES AND QUIPS**
>
> "Your best worker may not be your best bet for promotion to team leader or supervisor. More important than technical competence are leadership ability, communication skills and superior interpersonal relations."
> —Scott Ventrella, Management consultant

Career Pathing

When Southeast Utilities hired Kevin K., he went through a series of evaluations and was assigned to a training program. When the program was completed, he was assigned to a team in the Technical Support Department. Over the first few years he was given progressively more responsible assignments and did very well in each of them. He was identified as a potential "A" player.

At his third annual performance review, he was informed that because of his excellent record, he was chosen to participate in the company's career pathing program. In order to assure that the expanding needs of the company are met, several men and women were selected each year to be assessed and trained to move up the corporate ladder.

The first step in this process was to report to an "assessment center" where he was given a series of tests and interviews, and participated in interactive exercises with other participants. After the results were analyzed, he met with the Career Pathing Team of the Human Resources Department, to discuss their findings, his own ambitions and the opportunities available in the company. Kevin was told that there were many opportunities for a person with his talents in the organization and suggested several areas he should consider for his career path. They pointed out that to become better equipped for growth within the company, he should acquire more knowledge in the information technology areas and develop managerial skills.

To start the ball rolling, he was advised to sign up for an advanced computer training program and when completed successfully, he would be transferred to a position in the IT department where he could hone these skills. In addition, to prepare him for eventual promotion to management, he was advised to enroll in an MBA program at the local university under the company's tuition reimbursement plan.

This career pathing program was not just an altruistic action to help Kevin grow in his career. It created within the company a core of well trained, highly motivated "A" players to fill their ever-growing need for technicians and managers.

SUM AND SUBSTANCE

Before starting the search to refill a job, review the job description carefully and critically.

- Job specifications—the experience, education, skills and traits an applicant should bring to the job—should be realistic and meaningful. Don't establish specifications that are not really needed to do the job. By including them, the best candidates may be eliminated for the wrong reason.

- The intangibles that make for success on a job are just as important as education, skills, and experience. In making your job analysis, be as diligent in determining the intangible factors as you are for the tangible factors.

- Don't limit the candidates considered for a position to current employees only. In this highly competitive world, a company should attempt to find the very best candidate for open positions—and that person may not be currently on your payroll.

- Interviewing is time consuming and expensive. Pre-screen applicants by carefully studying their résumés and by telephoning candidates before inviting them in.

- Don't let superficial factors such as appearance dominate your decision. Watch out for the "halo effect."

- Prepare the selected candidate to expect and reject a counteroffer.

- Current employees should be given the opportunity to develop skills needed for transfer and promotion to better positions. Good training and career pathing programs will enable you to build a cadre of qualified people to fill hard-to-fill jobs on an ongoing basis.

Pre-Screening Applicants

Screening candidates to find that one person who is most likely to be an "A-player" is the most challenging part of the selection process. Interviewing is still the most frequently used technique in choosing a new employee. Interviewing is expensive. It's time consuming. It takes the managers who do the interviewing away from their regular, productive work.

The solution: Get rid of those unqualified applicants before taking the time to interview them. How? Well, you can't just dump their résumés. But by good pre-screening you can reserve your valuable time for people who at least are good possibilities.

USING THE RÉSUMÉ IN PREPARING FOR THE INTERVIEW

Everybody has a résumé. Put an ad in the paper and you may be deluged with résumés. Reading all these responses takes valuable time. You have to know what to look for. If the person reading the résumé recognizes it for what it is, it will be much more useful as a screening tool.

There is no such thing as a standard résumé. Many résumés are badly written by the applicant and may fail to highlight qualities that are important to success on a job. Others may be prepared for the applicant by a professional résumé service that may exaggerate the candidate's experience and give an impression of experience and competence that exceeds the reality.

Let's look at what the résumé really is and how you can weed out from all the verbiage whether an applicant is worth spending time on. You can't read every line of every résumé. You don't have the time and probably most are from people who are not qualified for your job opening. You have to skim, but there's an art to skimming.

TACTICAL TIPS

According to a survey made by the Society for Human Resources Management (SHRM), 88 percent of respondents indicated that they spend less than three minutes reading a résumé. A decision that may affect the profitability of the company and the life of the applicant is based on these few minutes.

Knock-Out Factors

Review the job specs. There are certain qualifications that the prospect must possess in order to make the first cut. For example, a job calls for a degree in Electrical Engineering. Assuming that there is no flexibility for this requirement, look first at the education section of the résumé for that degree. If there's no EE degree—dump the résumé.

The job calls for experience in design of servomechanisms. The applicant worked for a manufacturer of servos, but says not a word about designing them. Put this résumé in the second choice pile. When you complete your first scanning, if there are relatively few respondents who specify this type of experience, you may telephone people in this pile to determine if they have the requisite background.

Be careful in choosing knock-out factors. By making qualifications that are desirable, but not really essential, you may eliminate well-qualified applicants.

In this computer age, software has been designed to screen résumés. The résumés are scanned into the computer and then searched for key words. If the key words are

QUOTES AND QUIPS

"Writing one's résumé is like writing one's own obituary. You only put in what you want to be remembered for."
       Erwin S. Stanton,
       Industrial psychologist

not found, bye-bye résumé. It sure makes it easier for the re-cruiters.

But in any of these situations, computers can't use judgment. An applicant may be well qualified but has failed to use that key word in the résumé. A human being reading the résumé could eas-ily see that the respondent has a viable background, but the com-puter only searches for the words that have been programmed for the job.

Reading Between the Lines

Don't take what you read in the résumé at face value. Read be-tween the lines. Applicants may have hidden negative factors, or neglected to note assets that may be of value to your company. Let's look at some of these:

Many people have had short-duration jobs and leave them out of their résumés. Some signs to watch for are:

1. Listing dates of jobs by specifying years only rather than months and years. For example 1994-1996 for one job and 1996-2000 for the next. It may mean a short period of unem-ployment in between jobs in1996, but it could also hide a short duration job in 1996 from which the applicant was fired.

2. A variation of this is listing the number of years worked instead of dates of employment. For example, Job A: 4 years; Job B: 3 years. This may indicate the covering up of unfavorable factors in job history. It could also indicate the emphasizing of older background when more recent work experience is not relevant. For example, the job sought is a Human Resources Manager. The applicant did have that experience—ten years ago, but has worked in an entirely different area more recently.

3. More space is given to earlier jobs than to more recent ones. Often this is due to poor judgment on the part of the applicant. He or she "updated" an earlier résumé and added a few lines at the bottom to describe the most recent job. This may not be

important in many jobs, but it's a sign of poor planning or possibly laziness. It also may mean that the last job wasn't as important as previous jobs or was held for a much shorter period of time. It's not necessarily a negative factor, but it indicates the need for a more careful look at the applicant.

4. There is an overemphasis on education and non-job factors. If a person is out of school for more than five years, the résumé should predominantly indicate work experience. What he or she did in high school or college is secondary to what was accomplished on the job. The applicant who gives details on current non-work aspects of his or her life such as hobbies or volunteer work, may be subconsciously showing where his or her interests really lie.

None of the above is a knock-out factor. They simply suggest further exploration during the interview. If the résumé gives you any indication that problems may exist, note them, so that when you interview the applicant, they can be brought out and discussed.

> **QUOTES AND QUIPS**
>
> **"To think is to differ."**
> **Clarence Darrow,**
> **Noted attorney**

Résumé Styles

One of the reasons that a résumé might be misleading is the style in which it is formatted. Applicants can select the style they believe will do them the most good and sometimes this can hide negatives in their backgrounds or overemphasize those aspects that they want you to know about. Let's look at the most commonly used styles.

Chronological résumés

This is the most frequently used style. Typically it starts with education and then lists the work experience by dates starting with the most recent job.

Nancy Noname
111 Eleventh Street
Yourtown, USA

Education: B. A., New York University, 1992
Majored in Economics

Certificate in Human Resources Management, University College for Continuing Education, Hofstra University, 1998

Experience:

Sept. 1994-Current: Asst. Director of Human Resources, ABC Co.
* *Administration (description of administrative duties and accomplishments)*
* *Employment (description)*
* *Training (description)*

Sept. 1992-July 1994, XYZ Company, Employment Interviewer
* *Recruiting (description)*
* *Interviewing (description)*
* *Job Analysis (description)*

This is easiest for the employer to read. It provides a clear overview of the education and work history of the applicant. It parallels the typical company application form; however, as there are no space limitations, it gives the writer freedom to expand on job activities. A well-constructed résumé will describe each major phase of the job in enough detail to make it meaningful to the reader. Duties, responsibilities and achievements are discussed for each job held. Unfortunately, too many résumés are not well constructed and give little information other than job title.

Functional résumés

The functional résumé gives an applicant the opportunity to play up job duties, rather than duration of a job. This enables the reader to readily note what the candidate has done. It's a more effective sales tool for the applicant, but can be used to mislead the reader. Let's see how Nancy Noname's résumé would look in functional form.

Nancy Noname

111 Eleventh St.

Yourtown, USA

Experience in Human Resources Management:

Recruiting:	(description of recruiting experience and accomplishments)
Interviewing:	(description)
Administration:	(description)
Training:	(description)

The names of employers and dates of employment may be listed separately or in some cases omitted. Education and any other information may be listed at the end of the résumé.

A functional résumé is an excellent way to highlight the background of a person who has done similar work with more than one company, alleviating the need to repeat the same information for each job. But it's often used to mask frequent job changes or to give the impression that the candidate has worked much longer in the highlighted functions than he or she has.

> **TACTICAL TIPS**
>
> When reading a functional résumé, place it side by side with the candidate's completed application form to compare job history with functions indicated on the résumé.

Résumé experts recommend a combination of the chronological and functional résumé. It gives the applicant opportunity to describe each job more fully and gives the employer more information than is usually obtained from the traditional chronological résumé. Here's an example:

Nancy Noname

111 Eleventh St.

Yourtown, USA

Education: B. A., New York University, 1992

Majored in Economics.

Certificate in Human Resources Management, University College for Continuing Education, Hofstra University, 1998

Experience: *Sept. 1994 - current, Asst. Director of Human Resources, ABC Co.*

- *Administration: (description of administrative duties and accomplishments)*

- *Employment: (description)*

Training: *(description)*

Sept. 1992-July 1994, XYZ Company, Employment Interviewer

- *Recruiting: (description)*

- *Interviewing (description)*

- *Job Analysis: (description)*

Gimmicky Résumés

In order to get your attention, some applicants will send you a cute résumé. Companies have received résumés in the form of poems, fairy tales, greeting cards, fancy brochures, audio or videotapes and all kinds of gimmicks created by computers. If the job is for a person who has creative talents, this may be an asset. It shows their creativity. However, for most jobs, it should be looked at as a gimmick and be judged on its content, not its style.

Evaluating a Résumé

The résumé can provide a great wealth of information, or it can be a lot of sizzle, but no steak. By carefully evaluating the résumé, you can save yourself much time by eliminating people who really are not worth seeing and by preparing good questions for those whom you invite for interviews.

Here are some suggestions to help you seek important information about the applicant when reading a résumé:

Study the job specifications

Prepare a list of the significant qualifications the applicant must have. This is a much more detailed list than the knock-out factors noted earlier in this chapter. Does the applicant have experience in all or a good portion of these qualifications? If yes, has this experience or training been acquired in a setting comparable to your organization? (For example, systems analysis in a bank is much different from that in a manufacturing company.)

Ask about missing qualifications.

If the applicant does not indicate experience in one of your qualifications, it doesn't necessarily mean he or she does not have it. Often a person may overlook an important factor of experience in writing a résumé or omit it to keep the résumé brief. If the applicant has much of what you need, but omits a key qualification, phone him or her for more details.

Consider depth of experience.

The résumé indicates experience in a desired area, but you can't tell from the description how deep the experience is. Make a note to probe for more details when you interview this candidate.

Look at size of company

The type of experience a person has is often conditioned by the size of the companies in which it was obtained. For example, a person working in a large department of a large company may do only a specialized aspect of a job. Patti J.'s first job was a marketing analyst for a large food company. However, all she did was compile sales statistics. On the other side of this coin, Jeffrey R. worked as a marketing assistant in a small housewares company. He performed a variety of marketing functions, but as the company was very small, it didn't have the tools or techniques he might have acquired in a larger organization. In interviewing these candidates, ask good questions about what they actually have done and learned in their current or previous jobs.

Look for accomplishments

What makes the applicant stand out in competition with others who have similar experience? Many applicants describe their jobs by echoing the company's job description. This is fine up to a point, but if they added some of the specific results they achieved doing this job, you get an answer to this question.

The "Paper Person"

In reading a résumé, always keep in mind that the piece of paper in front of you cannot completely describe the applicant. The résumé is just a one-dimensional sketch of a multi-dimensional individual. Yet, the key decision is often made from this "paper person." If you choose *not* to see the applicant based on the résumé, you'll lose this prospect forever—and he or she might have been the best applicant. It's easy to discard a résumé.

Before putting it in the discard file, ask yourself these questions:

> *Is the reason for rejection based on the applicant's lack of qualifications or is it lack of information presented on the résumé?* If the latter, on the basis of the types of jobs the applicant has held, is it likely that the experience may be there, even though it's not specified? If so, it may pay you to telephone the applicant to obtain the missing information before making a decision.

> *Is the reason for rejection due to a poorly written or poorly presented résumé?* If the position calls for communication skills, this is a valid reason for rejection. On the other hand, eliminating the ré-

sumé of a master mechanic because it is poorly written may deprive the firm of a highly skilled potential employee.

In case of doubt it pays to obtain further information before making the final rejection. If there is time, you may mail the applicant an application form to complete and return. If not, the telephone is your best bet for determining whether to invite the candidate for an interview. Losing a qualified person because the résumé is unsatisfactory is not fair to the applicant or to your company.

Detecting Résumé Fraud

Everybody expects résumés to exaggerate a little. Candidates present themselves in as favorable a light as possible and if they stretch the truth a little, we can pick it up by good interviewing.

But real résumé fraud is a much deeper problem. There have been numerous cases where candidates lied about key factors such as the level of education completed, degrees or licenses received, companies where they never worked and similar misrepresentations.

Educational background

Lots of people claim degrees they don't have. They may have attended the university for a year or two and claim a degree. A few years ago one of the authors interviewed a man who claimed he had an MBA from a university where the author was an adjunct professor. After a few questions, it was obvious he never attended that school. He shamefacedly admitted that his only contact was taking a one-day seminar there.

One of our clients was about to hire a man who claimed to have a degree in Accounting from a prestigious college. Only when we called to their attention that the school was a liberal arts college that didn't give a degree in accounting, did they realize the candidate was lying.

It's relatively easy to check colleges. Most schools will verify whether a student attended and graduated if you write to them. If you want a transcript, you must have written authorization from the applicant and may be charged a small fee.

Exaggerated or misleading claims of expertise or experience

Watch out for phrases like "supervised a department," "managed a team," "increased sales," or "created a program." They may be true, but can be misleading unless they are related to and supported by specific accomplishments, such as the size of the department or team, the percentage of improvement in sales, or the scope of the program. Be sure to question all such claims at the interview.

The self-employment cover-up

Many résumé fakers claim to be self-employed to cover up periods of unemployment or a job they don't wish to reveal for a variety of reasons. It's very difficult for an employer to confirm self-employment. If it's legitimate, you can usually check the bank where the business had an account or through Dun and Bradstreet or other credit organizations. But this takes time and sometimes money, so many employers will not bother to check it out, particularly if it is for a relatively short period of time. Use your best judgment. Ask a lot of questions about the nature of the business, what customers or clients were served, financial reports, and get the names of the accountants, attorneys, and bankers the company used.

Another ploy applicants use to hide periods of unemployment or jobs they'd rather not discuss is claiming to be "a consultant." Often, this is literally true. Many executives take on consulting assignments during periods of unemployment. It's a good way to make a few bucks while looking for a job. Don't just accept this at face value. Ask for details about clients and projects to verify the claim.

The "out-of-business" excuse

It's not unusual for a résumé faker to claim employment with a company that is out of business. We've seen résumés that claim employment in well-known firms that have closed shop, and we've seen claims of employment by companies that never existed, but are listed on the résumé as being out of business. It's sometimes not possible to check these claims. One way, of course, is to ask for paycheck stubs or W-2 forms issued by the company. This will at least prove that they worked there. If they have no proof, be skeptical about that claim.

If, on the basis of the résumé, you decide to interview the applicant, make a list of questions to verify the facts and probe for details about that job. How to do this and to check the accuracy of the information will be discussed in the following chapters.

Can They Do the Job?

In reviewing the résumé and the application form, determine whether the applicant has the basic requirements to do the job. Check to see if at least the basic educational requirements are met and if the jobs held are in line with the experience needed. If so, prepare to explore this at the interview.

It's reasonable to assume that an applicant who has worked in your field may have the background you are seeking. Some recruiters or team leaders are overzealous in their screening and eliminate well-qualified prospects because of lack of information. If the background you are seeking is not clearly stated on the application and résumé, don't automatically reject the candidate. Pick up the telephone and call him or her to clarify the situation. Don't make a rash decision to eliminate the applicant solely on the basis of inadequate information. On the other hand, applicants who don't meet the basic requirements should not be given further consideration

The résumé should also give the person reading it enough detail about the candidate's previous job duties to see how much can be transferred to the needs of the company. It can specify information such as experience in using certain computer software, operating certain equipment or possessing skills needed on the job. If the application form used has been designed for specific jobs as described earlier in this chapter, the answers to the special questions asked about background in that area can be very helpful in making the decision on whether the applicant should be brought in for further processing.

Progress

The applicant's progress and growth in jobs and career should be evaluated as well as specific experience. For routine jobs this may not be significant; indeed, it can even be a negative. A person who has moved up rapidly will expect to continue to move up rapidly. If your company cannot offer opportunity for this continued progress, the employee will probably become unhappy and in a short time seek employment elsewhere. On the other hand, if a job offers opportunity, but demands ambition and drive, the applicant should have manifested this by the progress made in previous jobs.

Progress can be measured by positions held and salaries earned. A person who has worked for the same firm for many years and has only received automatic annual salary increments has actually made no real progress even though earnings have gone up. Position and salary should be compared with those of other people in that field with similar education and experience.

If an applicant for a position of marketing administrator is a Harvard graduate, age 32 and is earning well below what his classmates are earning, it may be indicative of some problem. It may indicate that the applicant has no drive and is content to work in a routine job with modest earnings and no real responsibility.

Caution: Again, never take anything of this sort at face value. There may be legitimate reasons for lack of progress. Some years ago an applicant was almost rejected because she had worked for a company for several years and made no progress. When the interviewer probed, it came out that she had joined the company when it started with promises of big opportunity once it got off the ground. Unfortunately, the firm never could raise the capital needed to move ahead. It had nothing to do with her capability. When hired, she became one of the company's most productive employees.

The earnings record should not be the only measure of progress. More important is to determine whether the applicant shows a pattern of increasing responsibility in his or her career to date. Have promotions been in line with the person's experience? Has he or she moved more rapidly than might be expected? If so, was this due to personal capability and accomplishments? Was it due to growth of the industry or the company rather than individual efforts? Was it based on nepotism?

Comparing several applicants' progress in their careers will develop a pattern for growth in any occupation. One could find, for example, that advertising people move faster in both position and earnings than persons in the banking field. Salespeople may make more money faster than in most jobs, but they don't move up to management positions as rapidly as their co-workers in administrative jobs. Comparison of progress rates must take all of these factors into consideration. One can't make arbitrary judgments and rate one occupation against another.

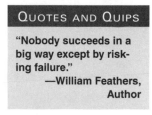

QUOTES AND QUIPS

"Nobody succeeds in a big way except by risking failure."
—William Feathers, Author

TACTICAL TIPS

In today's hot market for technical personnel, qualified people are likely to move from company to company far more frequently than their non-tech colleagues. Over the past few years the typical tenure of a "techie" on a job has fallen from five to three years.

Stability

Another factor the application form indicates is job stability. Many employers will automatically reject an applicant who has changed jobs too often. Some companies have made this a knock-out factor: If a person has had more than two jobs in five years or some similar combination of years and jobs, he or she is knocked out.

There is much to be said in favor of this policy. Frequent job changes may indicate restlessness or boredom with a job. It's unlikely that the candidate's next job will be any different. Some people are "two-yearers,"— the time it takes to master the intricacies of the job and then tire of it. Others may be marginal workers, employees who are not bad enough to discharge, but are the first to be laid off when business slows down. In other cases there may be personality problems. The employee may never have been able to get along with co-workers or their bosses.

On the other hand, it may be just bad luck. The person may be on the job a short time when the company suffers a business reversal resulting in a mass downsizing or a reorganization, which eliminates the job. Sometimes a person may start a job and rapidly realize it was a mistake. It's better to quit immediately than stay around just to keep the work record from looking bad. Young people particularly, may make several job changes over a short period of time. They are feeling their way and it may take a while to find their right careers.

Before arbitrarily rejecting an applicant as a job hopper, it's important to determine the reason for the apparent instability. There are often good reasons one changes jobs. Don't lose a potentially good employee because of some arbitrary policy on "instability."

SUM AND SUBSTANCE

- Interviewing is expensive. It's time consuming. Get rid of unqualified applicants by good pre-screening before taking the time to interview them.

- The first step in culling out unqualified applicants is to review the job specs. There are certain qualifications that the prospect must possess in order to make the first cut.

- The résumé can provide a great wealth of information, or it can be a lot of sizzle, but no steak. By carefully evaluating the résumé, you can save yourself much time by eliminating people who really are not worth seeing and by preparing good questions for those whom you invite for interviews.

- In case of doubt it pays to obtain further information before making the final rejection. Telephone the applicant to clarify and expand on the information in the résumé. Losing a qualified person because the résumé is unsatisfactory is not fair to the applicant or to your company.

- To assure the truthfulness of the résumé, verify education and employment data before making the final decision.

- The applicant's progress and growth in jobs and career should be evaluated as well as specific experience.

- Before arbitrarily rejecting an applicant as a job hopper, it's important to determine the reason for the apparent instability. There are often good reasons one changes jobs. Don't lose a potentially good employee because of some arbitrary policy on "instability."

6

Sharpening Your Interviewing Skills

Interviews are more than just pleasant conversations between you and the applicant. How the interviewing process is planned and followed can make the difference between hiring the best candidate and just selecting one by instinct.

The first step is to determine who will do the interviewing, what types of interviews will be conducted, and what other selection techniques will be used. Then questions must be framed that will bring out the information needed to judge the qualifications of the candidate.

Each applicant brings to the interview his or her own special qualifications and personal characteristics. Be prepared to tailor your interviewing plan to accommodate for this.

A basic part of any interview is proper preparation by the interviewer. The two essential sets of documents that must be reviewed are the application form and its accompanying résumé, and the job description including the job specifications.

REREAD THE PAPERWORK

Before an applicant enters the interviewing room, the application and résumé should be thoroughly studied. Any areas that require more information, or are indicators of strengths or weaknesses, should be noted so that questions may be asked about them.

Keep in mind the objectives of the interview: first, to determine whether the candidate has the technical qualifications needed for the position; second, whether the applicant has the personality traits needed to be successful in the job.

Job skills are easy to identify and are clearly indicated in the job specification. Questions geared to job skills should be prepared. They may take the form of test questions, such as "What type of equipment would be most suited for this process?" or questions about experience, such as "What software did you use to determine marketing trends?"

Personality qualifications are much more difficult to measure. Some of these intangibles may be listed in the job specs. For example, "must be able to work under pressure," or "should be able to present public speeches." It's not easy to reduce many personality factors to a simple statement. The interviewer's knowledge of the job, the people with whom the applicant will have to work, and the company culture must be taken into consideration.

> **TACTICAL TIPS**
>
> **All persons assigned to conduct interviews should be carefully trained in interviewing techniques.**

The First Interview

In most companies the first interview is with a member of the Human Resources Department. As HR staffers are usually well trained in interviewing, they generally do a credible job in determining if the candidate is worthy of further consideration.

However, many firms, particularly smaller organizations, don't have Human Resources departments. Even in larger companies, the HR department may be located at the home office and the job opening is in a distant facility. In these cases, some other manager or supervisor will conduct the first interview. Unfortunately, many of these people are not trained in interviewing.

The hiring decision is rarely made at a first interview, but it is a key phase of the process. Good applicants are lost because the interviewer didn't ask the right questions or misunderstood the answers. Good applicants may be lost because they get a bad impression of the company at that interview and decide not to pursue the position. In addition, applicants who should have been rejected may be referred for subsequent interviews, wasting the time of higher-level managers.

Know the Equal Opportunity Employment Law

Most human resources professionals are carefully trained in what questions an interviewer may and may not ask applicants under federal and state laws. Unfortunately, this important information may not be clearly understood by line managers who often interview applicants. It is essential that before anybody in the company conducts an employment interview, he or she is given thorough training in this sensitive area either by a member of the HR staff or by the legal department.

Subsequent Interviews: When and By Whom?

If as a result of the first interview, the applicant appears to be viable, arrangements should be made for additional screening without delay. Particularly when jobs are plentiful and applicants scarce, qualified applicants are lost because of procrastination.

A candidate for all but the most basic jobs should be interviewed by at least one member of the HR department and by the team leader, supervisor, or manager for whom he or she will work. The HR staffer screens to determine whether the applicant meets broad job specifications and analyzes the applicant for personality, attitude, and general background. The team leader or supervisor is better suited to evaluate specific knowledge of the job and whether the prospect will fit in with the group.

In many companies, several managers may interview the candidate before a final decision is made. When teams are used, members of the team, other than the team leader, may also interview prospects for that team.

In most companies, the head of the department in which the employee will work makes the hiring decision. He or she is usually the last interviewer. For example, a member of the HR department may first interview an applicant for a tax accountant. If warranted, the leader of the tax accounting section interviews the applicant. If passed, the chief accountant or controller will conduct an interview and make the hiring decision. In this process, the decision maker sees only the very top candidates.

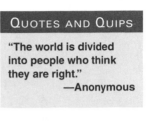

QUOTES AND QUIPS

"The world is divided into people who think they are right."
                    —Anonymous

Planning the Questions to Ask

Some interviewers sit down with the applicant with only a general idea of what questions they plan to ask. They may start with a general question such as "Tell me about yourself." From the response, they then pick aspects of the background to explore. This may be okay for an experienced interviewer who just uses that question as an opening device and has thought out what added questions to ask. However, the danger here is that the applicant may tell you only what he or she wants you to hear and you may never get around to asking about areas not mentioned.

TACTICAL TIPS

To ensure attainment of all relevant information, prepare a list of key questions that must be asked during the interview before you sit down with the applicant. But don't limit yourself to asking just those questions. Be alert to responses and ask additional questions based on answers received.

Make a List of Key Questions

In planning for the interview, develop a list of questions you plan to ask. An effective interview is well planned. The interviewer doesn't ad lib questions. Some interviewers write down the questions they plan to ask and refer to them during the interview. Others make notes on the applicant's application form to remind them about areas they wish to explore. Still other interviewers depend on their knowledge of the field to develop questions as they move along in the process.

General questions about work factors

To evaluate the applicant's qualifications, questions should be developed that give you enough information to make a hiring decision. Some of these will be broad general questions to get an overview of the candidate's education, experience, and personality. Once you are satisfied that he or she meets these requirements, you should be prepared to ask additional questions that will probe for very specific details. Here are several suggestions of areas to explore.

Education and skills

Level of education (secondary school, college, grad school)

Majors or courses related to job requirements

Scholastic achievements

Licenses, certifications

Other skills acquired (for example, foreign languages, computer know-how, mechanical skills, etc.)

Jobs held

Include in this category all full-time jobs, part-time jobs, volunteer work related to the job being filled, and military service.

Titles

Companies

Description of duties

Earnings

Progress

Achievements

Physical qualifications (where relevant)

Energy

Strength

Health

Vision

Hearing

Appearance

Dexterity

These can be observed at the interview and questions can be framed to verify how these characteristics were manifested in previous jobs.

Character

Reliability

Honesty

Integrity

Conscientiousness

Values

Loyalty

Work ethic

Environment (where pertinent)

Ability to get to the place of work

Willingness to travel

Ability and willingness to be on job during hours required

Ability and willingness to work overtime when required

Willingness to work at pay scale and/or pay system offered (for example: lower salary than previously earned; working on commissions or other incentives)

Level of Intelligence

Mental ability

Judgment

Breadth of experience

Communication skills

Aptitudes

Personality Factors

Reaction to pressure

Motivational factors

Drive

Initiative

Adaptability

Emotional stability

Self-confidence

Interpersonal relations

Questions to Ask

Framing questions to elicit the information needed is not easy. Here are some suggestions:

It's best to use open-ended questions. For example, instead of asking "Have you worked with EXCEL?" ask "Tell me about your experience with EXCEL." This allows the respondent to answer in an unstructured manner, thereby giving more information and often answers that would not have been elicited from closed-end specific questions.

Here are some examples. Note that most are open-ended questions.

Education

- I see that you majored in Economics; why did you choose that major?

- If this was not your original major, tell me what that was and why you made the change.
- In what extracurricular activities did you participate and what role did you play in them?
- What internships or summer jobs did you have? What was the most significant thing you learned from each of them? How did they affect your career choice?
- What were the high points in your college career? The low points? Why do you consider them this way?

The following questions are for applicants who attended graduate school. For those attending immediately after receiving their undergraduate degree:

- Why graduate school? Why that particular program? Why at that time? What plans do you have to continue your education?

For applicants who attended graduate school at later dates:

- When did you decide to attend graduate school? Why? Why that particular program?
- What do you feel were the significant values of obtaining an advanced degree?

Work experience (for each job held)

- Describe your responsibilities and duties. How do you spend an average day?
- How did you change the content of your job from when you assumed it until now?
- Discuss some of the challenges you encountered on the job. How did you deal with them?
- What do you consider to be your chief accomplishments on this job?
- What about some of the disappointments or set-backs on this job?
- What did you like best about this job? Least? Why?

- Tell me about the progress you made in that company.
- What was the most valuable experience you obtained in this position?
- Why did you leave (or, if employed, desire to leave) this company?

Relationship of background to open job

- How do you view the job for which you are applying?
- In what way will this job meet your career objectives?
- What in your background particularly qualifies you to do this job?
- If you were to be hired for this job, in what areas could you contribute immediately?
- Where would you need additional training?
- In what ways have your education and training prepared you to do this job?

Stability

- What were your reasons for leaving each of your jobs?
- Why are you seeking a job at this time?
- What were your original career goals?
- How have these goals changed over the years?

Resourcefulness

- How did you change the scope of your previous jobs?
- What were some of the more difficult problems you faced on the job? How did you solve them?
- To whom did you go for counsel when you couldn't handle a problem on the job?
- What was the most radical idea you introduced to your company? How did you persuade management to accept this idea? How did you implement it?

- You are under extreme pressure to complete a job by a deadline. Two days before the deadline, you discover a major error in your calculations. How would you deal with this?

- You're a sales rep. You just learn that another company has acquired your biggest customer and the acquiring company will do all the purchasing. How will you handle this?

Taking criticism

Nobody likes to be criticized. Some people are very sensitive and become upset and resentful. Here are some questions to ask about this:

- In your last performance review, what did your boss tell you that you felt was accurate; in what areas did you feel the boss was unfair in the assessment?

  In evaluating the response, consider the importance of the "unfair" areas, the applicant's attitude when he or she discussed it. Did the applicant sound upset or resentful? Did he or she dwell on it, or pass over it rapidly?

- Your boss blasts you for making a decision with which she disagrees. You feel you were right. What will you do?

- One of your employees files a complaint against you with the union, claiming you treat him unfairly by assigning him all the "dirty work." Your argument: "That's all he's capable of doing." During the period that this is being adjudicated, how will you deal with the complainant? The other employees in the department? Your boss?

Working under direction and with others

- Describe your supervisor's management style.
- How would you evaluate his or her supervision methods?
- On what task forces, committees or teams have you served?

- What did you contribute to the work of this group?
- What aspect did you enjoy most? Why?
- Give me an example of an order or instruction you received from your boss with which you disagreed. What did you do?
- You are a member of a team. When the team is assigned a project, all team members participate in planning the work. You disagree with the majority. What will you do?
- In your previous jobs, how much of your work was done as an individual? As part of a team? Which did you enjoy more? Why?
- How would you describe your relationships with your co-workers on your present (past) jobs?

Career goals

- What are you seeking in this job that you are not getting in your present job?
- What are your long-term career objectives? How do you plan to reach them?
- What goals did you set in school? At previous jobs? What did you do to accomplish them and what were the results?

Potential and self concept

How a person views his or her life to date is an indicator of that person's future. People who look upon themselves as being successful are likely to continue to be successful. People who are dissatisfied with their lives will likely become dissatisfied employees. On the other hand, people who are complacent with their progress may not have the motivation to push ahead. These questions will bring out the applicant's self concept:

- How would you evaluate the progress you have made so far in your career?
- What do you think has contributed most to the successes you have made?
- What have you done in the last five years that has given you the greatest personal satisfaction?

- What has been your biggest disappointment in your career? How has it affected your life?

- Why do you think you can be successful in this job?

- In what way can we help you become successful in this job?

- Do you have a plan for self-improvement? What have you accomplished on this plan thus far? What do you plan to accomplish this year?

Special characteristics

Some companies look for special characteristics in an applicant. For example, in addition to looking for specific knowledge and skills, Andersen Consulting looks for what they call "softer attributes:" how people go about doing their jobs; their intelligence, work ethic, and motivation; the ability to adapt to constantly changing circumstances; and, perhaps most important, a characteristic of lifelong learning. Everything changes so quickly in their business that they really need people who are able to learn new things and apply them very, very quickly.

These are more difficult to assess. Everyone at Andersen Consulting who interviews job seekers goes through fairly rigorous training that teaches them how to tease out and then recognize whether or not somebody possesses these attributes. They go through two days of training, which is instructor-led, with classes of 20 to 24 participants. It's very hands-on. They even bring in real candidates—not actual candidates for a job, but people who want interviewing practice.

An interviewer might ask: "Can you give me a recent example of a situation where you dealt with a difficult problem? What was the problem, and how did you go about solving it?" Then the interviewer would spend the next 15 to 20 minutes trying to understand the situation and specifically what the individual did and said and thought and so forth. The advantage is that it's a real-life situation. It's not a hypothetical question, where an applicant can tease out what he or she thinks the interviewer is trying to determine. They try to figure out what the person did in that situation because it's very likely that he or she will act in a similar way on the job applied for.

Preparing Specific Job Related Questions

The responses to these general questions will give you enough information to determine if the candidate is basically qualified for your job opening. However, there are in every job certain very specific areas of knowledge, experience, and expertise that the applicant must demonstrate to be capable of becoming productive rapidly. To determine this, you should also prepare a list of questions that will probe for these details.

As the questions differ from job to job (even jobs with the same or similar titles may require different specific factors), you must develop appropriate questions for each job. To do this, you must study not just the job specification, which lists the qualifications required, but also the job description, which gives details of the job functions.

For example, if your opening is for a medical technician, you should prepare questions about the types of medical equipment the applicant has learned to operate in school, about the applicant's experience in operating the equipment, and about the venues in which the person worked (at a hospital? clinic? physician's office?) If you are not fully knowledgeable about the job, have the person to whom the job reports design these questions for you—and, of course, the answers.

Some HR staffers prefer to leave the asking of specific questions to the team leader or department head. However, if there are several applicants who appear to be qualified, and the line managers are overloaded with work in their functional areas, it's advantageous for the first interviewer to use these questions as screening tools.

TACTICAL TIPS

A good source of specific questions for over 100 job categories is *Be A Better Employment Interviewer* by Dr. Arthur R. Pell (Personnel Publications, PO Box 301, Huntington, NY 11743).

THE STRUCTURED INTERVIEW

Most good interviews have structure. If not, they result in a chaotic exchange of questions and answers with little possibility of making reasonable decisions. However, some companies use specially prepared structured interview forms, which interviewers must follow virtually line by line.

One reason for this is legal; another psychological. Some labor lawyers advise that by asking each applicant exactly the same questions in exactly the same order, you provide a defense against charges of discrimination. Some psychologists have designed structured interviews with the objective of uncovering patterns of behavior by asking questions in the exact same order in the exact same way to all applicants.

Advantages of Using a Structured interview

Whether the reason is legal, psychological or just pragmatic, there are some advantages to using some form of structured interview. By asking questions that are printed on a form, you won't miss asking an important question. You have to ask it. The structured interview form provides space next to the questions to record answers. This helps the interviewer remember the responses. And, as all applicants are asked the same questions, it makes it easy to compare applicants when making the final decision.

Consider the Downside

The negative side of a formal structured interview is that it stifles creativity and flexibility. In the formal structured interview, you are not allowed to deviate from the form. Both the forms developed for legal reasons and those with psychological implication require strict adherence to the structure. As noted before, flexibility is important in an interview. The answer to one question may require follow-up to obtain more or better information.

Using a Less Formalized Structure

One way of using the structured interview effectively is to use it as a guide. This cannot be done if the format you use is psychologically based. In this format, the exact words, where questions are placed in the interview, and the interrelationship of one question with another are designed to enable the psychologist to make the evaluation. However, most structured interviews are not of this nature and variations and flexibility can be built into them.

CONDUCTING THE INTERVIEW

TACTICAL TIPS
An important objective of the interview is to create a favorable image of the company in the eyes of the applicant. The reputation of the firm may be improved or harmed by the manner in which applicants are treated. You want an applicant to accept a job offer, and even rejected applicants may be potential customers.

The interview serves several purposes in the selection process. Its obvious first purpose is to obtain enough information from the applicant to determine whether he or she is qualified for the job. But it is not just an interrogation. It also enables the interviewer to observe the candidate, interpret and evaluate the answers to the questions, and compare the candidates. In addition, an important function of the interview is to give the applicant information about the company and the job.

Getting Started

In order to obtain the best results from an interview, the interviewer must put the applicant at ease. Tense applicants are ill at ease, and don't respond fully to your questions. Establishing rapport with the applicant takes a little time, but even in a brief interview it is well worth it.

To make the applicant feel at ease, as the interviewer, you must be at ease and feel comfortable about the interviewing process. An ideal setting for an interview is a private room, comfortably furnished with a minimum of distracting papers on the desk. To avoid telephone interruptions, turn on your voicemail or have somebody else answer your phone.

Go out and greet the applicant. It's much better to personally go to the reception area than to send a secretary to fetch the applicant. So get up from your chair and get out there. Introduce yourself and escort the applicant to the interviewing room.

When greeting the applicant, use his or her full name. "David Livingstone? Hi, I'm Henry Stanley. This makes the applicant feel you identify him or her as an individual, not just another candidate. Dale Carnegie said. "Remember, a person's name is to that person the sweetest and most important sound in any language."

By using both the first and the last name in addressing the applicant and in introducing yourself, you are putting both of you on equal footing. If you call yourself Mr. or Ms., and call the applicant "Dave" it sounds condescending.

Start the interview by making minor observations and asking noncontroversial questions. It's not necessary to talk about the weather or last night's game or television special.

The opening should be related to the interview, but should not make the applicant defensive or upset. Don't start with such questions as "What makes you think that you could handle this job?" or "Why were you fired from your last job?"

A better approach would be to select an innocuous area from the application and comment on it. It may be based on something in the background that you relate to. For example, "I see you went to Lincoln High School. Did you know Mr. Salkin, the drama teacher?" or "I see you live in Chelsea. That neighborhood is growing rapidly."

> QUOTES AND QUIPS
>
> **"If you don't know where you're going, you'll end up somewhere else."**
> **—Yogi Berra,**
> **Baseball player**

Asking Questions

Now's the time to ask the questions that you prepared when you were planning for the interview. If you use a structured interview system, begin now to follow the structure. If you follow a less formal procedure, ask the questions that you prepared, and others that will help get the information needed.

To get the most out of the interview, here are some guidelines to follow when asking questions:

- DON'T ask questions that can be answered "Yes" or "No." This stifles information. Instead of asking, "Have you any experience in budgeting?" say, "Tell me about your experience in budgeting."

- DON'T put words in the applicant's mouth. Instead of asking, "You've called on discount stores, haven't you?," ask "What discount stores have you called on?"

- DON'T ask questions that are unrelated to your objectives. It might be interesting to follow up on certain tidbits of gossip the applicant volunteers, but it rarely leads to pertinent information.

- DO ask questions that develop information as to the applicant's *experience* ("What were your responsibilities regarding the purchasing of equipment?"), *knowledge* ("How did you, or would you, cope with this problem?"), *attitudes* ("How do you feel about heavy travel?" or "Why do you wish to change jobs now?").

An effective way of probing for full information is to use the "W" questions: "What," "When," "Where," "Who," and "Why." With the addition of "How," you can draw out most of the information needed. For example:

- "What computer software was used?"
- "When did you design that program?"
- "Where was the program installed?"
- "Who was responsible for supervising that project?"
- "Why did you make that decision?"
- "How did you implement the new system?"

Ask Situational Questions

Give the applicant a hypothetical situation and ask how he or she would handle it. The situations should be reasonably close to actual problems found on the job. Judge the response by knowledge of the subject, approach to the solution, value of the suggestions, and clarity in communicating the answer. A variation of the situational question is to ask the applicant to describe difficult situations faced on previous jobs and how they were resolved.

Summary Questions

When you have completed questioning the applicant about a phase of background, ask a question that will summarize what has been presented. For example, "You certainly have extensive background in quality control; briefly summarize what you can contribute to make our company more effective in that area."

This gives the applicant a chance to bring together the highlights of his or her experience in that area and enables you to review the highlights of that person's background.

At the end of the interview, a good summary question is: "Now that you've learned a bit about our job and had a chance to tell me about yourself, please tell me briefly what you bring to this job that will assure your success."

From the responses, determine if the candidate is a team player, an easy-going conformist, or an individualist. Base your judgment on the culture of your company.

Use Non-Directive Techniques

It's not always possible to obtain necessary information by direct questioning. Non-directive approaches may help in these cases. Non-directive questioning uses open-ended questions such as "Tell me about...." The applicant then tells whatever he or she feels is important. Instead of commenting about the response, you nod your head and say, "uh-huh," "yes," or "I see." This encourages the applicant to keep talking without your giving any hint as to what you are seeking.

TACTICAL TIPS

Try this: After the applicant responds to your question, count to five slowly (to yourself, of course) before asking the next question. By waiting five seconds, you'll be surprised how often an applicant adds something—positive or negative—to the response to the previous question.

In this way, the applicant may talk about problems, personality factors, attitudes or weaknesses that might not have been uncovered directly. On the other hand, it may bring out some positive factors and strengths that were missed by direct questioning. Another way of using the non-directive approach is to be silent. Most people can't tolerate silence. If you don't respond instantly, the applicant is likely to keep talking.

Giving Information to the Applicant

An important part of the interview is giving the applicant information about the company and the job. All the work and expense undertaken to get good employees is lost if the applicants you want don't accept your offer. By giving them a positive picture of the job at the interview, you're more likely to have a higher rate of acceptances. One significant reason for employee turnover is that the new employee has a misconception of what the job entails. Giving accurate information about the job and the company and assuring that the applicant fully understands and agrees is essential to getting an acceptance and to retaining people once employed.

When and what to tell about the job

Some interviewers start the interview by describing the job duties. Some give the applicant a copy of the job description in advance of the interview. *This is a serious error.* If an applicant knows too much about a job too soon, he or she is likely to tailor the answers to all of your questions to fit the job.

For example, suppose you tell a prospect that the job calls for selling to department store chains. Even if the applicant has only limited experience in this area, when you ask, "What types of markets did you call on?"—you can guess which one will be emphasized.

The best way to give information about duties and responsibilities is to feed it to the applicant throughout the interview—after you have ascertained the background of the applicant in that phase of the work. For example:

Interviewer: What types of markets did you call on?

Applicant: Drug store chains, discount stores, department stores, and mail order houses.

The interviewer then should ask specific questions about the applicant's experience in each of these markets. If the department store background is satisfactory, the interviewer might then say: "I'm glad you have such a fine background in dealing with department store chains as they represent about 40 percent of our customer list. If you should be hired, you'd be working closely with those chains."

If the background in this area was weak, the interviewer might say: "As a great deal of our business is with department store chains, if you should be hired, we would have to give you added training in this area."

At the end of the first interview, the interviewer should have a fairly complete knowledge of the applicant's background and the applicant should have a good idea of the nature of the job. At subsequent interviews, the emphasis will be on obtaining more specific details about the applicant and giving the applicant more specific data about the job.

TACTICAL TIPS
Don't give the applicants copies of the job description before an interview. Their responses to your questions will be influenced by what they read.

Answering applicants' questions

Most interviewers give the applicant an opportunity to ask questions about the job and the company at some point during the interview, usually at the end. The questions asked can give some insight into the applicant's personality and help you in your evaluation.

Are the questions primarily of a personal nature (such as vacations, time off, raises, etc.), or are they about the job? People who are only concerned about personal aspects are less likely to be as highly motivated as job-oriented applicants. Their questions can also be clues to their real interest in the job. If you feel from these questions that a prospective candidate might not be too enthusiastic about the job, it gives you another chance to sell the prospect on the advantages of joining your company.

You are always "selling" when you interview. It's important that you present your company and the job in a positive and enthusiastic manner. This doesn't mean that you should exaggerate or mislead the applicant.

Tell the applicant the negatives at the interview, but show how the positive aspects outweigh them. For example: "Our company does require its engineers to put in a great deal of overtime because we're working on very urgent matters. However, even though as an exempt employee, we are not obligated to pay for overtime, we do give extra pay for the extra time. Moreover, the work is exciting and rewarding. I'm sure you'll get as much satisfaction as all our engineers do from the challenges of the job."

Closing the interview

Once the interviewer has all the information needed, and the applicant has been told about the job and has had the opportunity to ask questions, the interview can be brought to a close.

All interviews should end on a positive note. The applicant should be told what the next step would be. In most cases, if there is an interest in the candidate, additional interviews—sometimes with the same interviewer, more often with another person—will be arranged. This should be done as soon as feasible. If possible, make the appointment for that interview before the applicant leaves the office. If testing, psychological appraisal or other steps are part of the process, tell the candidate what to expect and set dates for them.

In many cases, the first interviewer will see several applicants before deciding which ones will be sent on for subsequent interviews. Unless you have already decided that this applicant is not to be considered further, tell him or her that once you have interviewed the other candidates, you will select those who will be invited for further discussions. Tell the applicants that as soon as this decision is made, you will contact them.

Giving the decision to the applicant

If, on the basis of the first interview, you have decided that the applicant is not to be considered, it's only fair to tell them. In most cases, the reason may be obvious. During the interview, if it becomes clear to both of you that the applicant is not qualified, just say: "Joe, as you don't have experience in area X and Y, which are essential to being able to do this job, we cannot consider you for it."

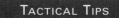

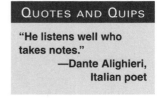

TACTICAL TIPS

Don't keep applicants on a string waiting to hear from you. If you are not interested in a candidate, write or phone him or her no later than a week after the interview. If the applicant is still being considered, but the decision is delayed, keep the applicant advised of the status.

If the reason is not directly job related, such as a lack of certain personal characteristics or your reaction to the applicant, rather than reject him or her outright, say, "We have several more applicants to interview. Once we've seen them all, we'll make a decision."

Remembering the Applicant

You've seen a dozen applicants for the open position. Unless you take notes, it's unlikely that you will remember what each one has told you and your reaction to them. It's essential that some method be devised to record the highlights of the interview, and in due course, the decisions made. It's not possible or even desirable to take stenographic transcriptions or tapes of every interview. Enough information should be noted so that you're able to remember who each applicant is, what makes one different from another, and how each applicant measures up to the job specifications.

QUOTES AND QUIPS

"He listens well who takes notes."
—Dante Alighieri,
Italian poet

Good notes keep you out of trouble. When you evaluate several candidates for the same job, if you've kept good records of the interviews, it's easier to compare them. By rereading your notes rather than depending on your memory, you are more likely to make sounder judgments. When several people interview the same candidate, a consistent system of recording information will facilitate an in-depth analysis of the applicant's qualifications.

Good records help if you face legal problems. In case of an investigation by government agencies such as the EEOC or state civil rights divisions, good records of the interview can be your most important defense. Where no records or inadequate records have been kept, the opinion of the hearing officer is dependent on the company's word against the applicant's. Good, consistent records provide solid evidence.

Taking notes

TACTICAL TIPS

Taking notes is important, but it may stifle applicants and it may keep you from fully listening. Write brief notes during the interview. Immediately after the interview review them and write a summary while the interview is still fresh in your mind.

Taking notes often has a negative effect on applicants. Some get very nervous when they see you write down everything they say. They may be inhibited from talking freely and hold back on important matters.

Taking notes may have a negative effect on you, the interviewer. You're so busy writing what the applicant just said, that you don't listen to what is now being said.

Some companies have special forms designed for interview recordkeeping. Others suggest you make notes on the application form or on a paper to attach to the form after the interview. In any case, a summary form should be completed *immediately* after the close of the interview.

Figure 6-1, *Interview Summary Sheet,* is a good example of a form useful in summarizing interview results. Note that it provides space to list the job factors as indicated in the job specification with space in the next column to record highlights of the applicant's background in that factor. On the reverse side of the form is a place to record personal factors and the interviewer's overall comments.

Figure 6-1 _____

Interview Summary Sheet

Applicant _____   Date _____

Position applied for _____   Interviewer _____

	Applicant's
JOB FACTORS[1]	**Background**[2]

Duties: _____ | _____

_____ | _____

_____ | _____

_____ | _____

Responsibilities: _____ | _____

_____ | _____

_____ | _____

Skills Required: _____ | _____

_____ | _____

_____ | _____

Education Required:[3] (level) _____ | _____

   Specific types: _____ | _____

_____ | _____

   Educ. achievement _____ | _____

_____ | _____

Other Job Factors: _____ | _____

_____ | _____

_____ | _____

_____ | _____

[1]Job factors should be listed from job specifications for position applicant applies for.

[2]Interviewer should note aspects of applicant's background that apply to each factor in this column.

[3]Level of education = how much schooling completed; type represents subjects related to job taken; achievement represents grades or standing.

Figure 6-1 _____

Interview Summary Sheet *(continued)*

PERSONAL FACTORS	Comments
Growth in Career	
Accomplishments	
Intangibles	
Appearance	
Motivation	
Resourcefulness	
Stability	
Leadership	
Creativity	
Mental alertness	
Energy level	
Communication skill	
Self Confidence	

COMMENTS

    Applicant's strengths: _____

_____

_____

    Applicant's limitations: _____

_____

_____

❏ Applicant should be hired. _____

    Recommendations for additional training: _____

_____

❏ Applicant should not be hired._____

    Reasons: _____

_____

    Additional Comments: _____

_____

Recommendations of Interviewers

Each person who has interviewed the applicant should make comments on the same type of form. After going over the comments, a recommendation should be made:

Recommend hiring ____

Recommend consider as a possible hire ____

Don't hire ____

Reasons for recommendations should be given. Compelling the interviewer to succinctly state a reason helps overcome the intuitive decision based on some vague like or dislike. Interviewers must remember that the reason may be challenged by EEOC or other agencies.

In Chapter 7 we'll discuss in detail the factors to consider in making the hiring decision.

MAKING INTERVIEWS MORE MEANINGFUL

Interviewing can be tricky. You think you're asking the right questions, but the answers don't give you the information you expected. Maybe you're doing it wrong. Maybe the applicant is maneuvering around the questions. Maybe you lost control of the interview.

Ten Common Mistakes Interviewers Make

By being aware of some of the traps interviewers fall into, you can catch yourself and keep the interview moving along productively.

1. The haphazard interview

Earlier in this chapter, we discussed how by establishing a systematic approach to the interview, you'll get the information you need. Although using a formal structured interview has advantages, many people are not comfortable working within its limitations. It was suggested that an informal structured format be used. Unfortunately, in their attempts to be flexible, some interviewers go to the other extreme, ask questions in a haphazard manner, and as a result get little information.

Bill W., who had been interviewed for a job in the accounting department of the Goody Gumdrop Candy Co., left the interview with the feeling that the Chief Accountant, who conducted the interview, had obtained little information about his qualifications. Bill reported that the interviewer had jumped from one subject to

> **TACTICAL TIPS**
>
> By planning the questions to ask in a systematic manner, you'll cover all the bases. Be flexible within the structure so you don't fail to probe areas of interest that may develop as you go along.

another—talking for a moment about education, shifting to some phases of work experience, back to schooling, over to attitudes, to job objectives and then back to work background. Not only did the interviewer fail to get a comprehensive view of Bill's fitness for the job, but also he turned Bill off about wanting to work for a person who was so disorganized.

2. Interviewing for the wrong job

Some interviewers don't pay adequate attention to the job specifications. This is likely to happen when you are interviewing for a variety of jobs in the same department. Barbara P. applied for a job analyst's position. The interviewer asked all kinds of questions on every aspect of human resources administration, but only a very few were about job analysis. Barbara commented that the questions asked were very good for somebody applying for a more general job in the department, but didn't bring out information about her background for the open job.

Always reread the specs before the interview. It will help you set your mind on what you really seek in the applicant's background and enable you to frame appropriate questions.

3. Letting the applicant dominate the interview

A savvy applicant can so dominate the situation that he or she only tells you what is most favorable and manages to de-emphasize negative facets. The good interviewer must maintain control. When you have an applicant who doesn't let you get one word in, who twists your questions to fit his or her desires, who keeps adding information that isn't relevant, but that is designed to boost the applicant's assets, *cut it off.*

One polite way of doing this is to say: "That's most interesting, however would you mind giving me specific details on..." The best way to counteract an applicant's attempt at domination is to insist that he or she answer your questions to your satisfaction.

> ## TACTICAL TIPS
>
> **Don't let the applicant dominate the interview. If he or she spins answers that are not responsive to the questions asked, repeat the question and demand specific information, not just broad generalities. Keep probing until you get a satisfactory response.**

4. Playing God

One of the major complaints applicants have about interviewers is that they condescend to them. They act so superior, that the applicant feels uncomfortable. Because the interviewer has the power to hire or at least to refer the applicant on for further consideration, there is a tendency to "play God" and smugly savor the power.

Cool it. Keep your objectives in mind. You don't want to turn off the candidate. A little humility will pay off in better rapport, obtaining more and more meaningful information, and, if an offer is extended, a better chance of the candidate accepting it. It will also win friends for you and your company.

5. Telegraphing the right response

Some interviewers are so anxious to fill a job, they help the applicant respond correctly to their questions. They "feed" the applicant the expected answer. "This job calls for experience in handling customer complaints. You've done this, haven't you? Nobody ever says "No."

6. Talking too much

Some interviewers talk too much. They start the interview telling the applicant all about the company. Then they spend more time telling about the job. Sometimes they'll tell you about their job. Finally they get around to asking a few questions. But often, before the applicant has a chance to complete the answer, they interrupt to make a comment or worse, tell you about something in their history that your answer reminded them of. There's an old saying that you can't learn anything when your mouth is open. The interview is a two-way process. If you do all the talking, you'll stifle the applicant and get little information. Let the applicant do most of the talking, but keep her on track by asking good questions.

> **QUOTES AND QUIPS**
>
> **"We have two ears and only one tongue in order that we hear more and speak less."**
>
> **Diogenes,
> Ancient Greek
> philosopher and orator**

7. Playing the district attorney

Some interviewers get a kick out of catching the applicant in inconsistencies. They repeat questions in several forms to ascertain that the answers are the same. If they find an "error," they pounce on the victim. Such people should not be interviewing applicants. They belong in the Police department or the C.I.A. Most of the so-called inconsistencies found by this type of interrogation are insignificant and have little or no bearing on ability to do the job. It is not only a waste of time, but it may cause the company to lose highly qualified prospects who are rejected by these "D.A.s" for the wrong reasons.

8. Playing psychologist

Just because you took Psych 101 in college doesn't qualify you to be a psychologist. Some interviewers assume far more psychological knowledge than they have. They look for hidden meanings in everything the applicant says. They ascribe Freudian motives to work experience, family relations, attitudes, and even casual comments made by the applicant. The fact that they are not really qualified to make these judgments doesn't bother them one bit. They are so absorbed in their "psychological" evaluations, they fail to determine if the applicant can or cannot do the job for which they are being interviewed.

9. Falling in love (or hate) with the applicant

Sometimes an interviewer is so impressed with one aspect of an applicant's background that it dominates the evaluation. This is called the "halo effect." It may be a person's appearance or charisma. It might be the possession of a specific skill that is needed by the company. Although that trait may be impressive, there may be other important facts in the applicant's background that negate it.

A good example: The interviewer was so impressed by Lara's high score in the word processing test that he hired her. Only after she was employed did he discover that she didn't have sufficient background in some of the other functions the job called for.

The opposite of the halo effect is the "pitchfork effect." The applicant displays one characteristic that turns you off. You ignore his or her other excellent qualifications.

The good interviewer will recognize that this charm or skill is an asset, and that one negative factor is only one aspect of the total person. They should be put in proper perspective.

10. Failure to probe for details

You can't accept every answer at face value. Some applicants may lie outright; more often applicants will play up their strengths by exaggerating their qualifications. When you ask about experience in a certain area, even if the experience is very light, the applicant is likely to make it sound more impressive than it really is. To overcome this, probe for details. Study the job specs. If you are not fully familiar with the job for which you are interviewing, ask the person to whom the job will report to suggest questions to ask.

The applicant says that he has designed a training program for computer operators. Don't stop there. Ask specific questions about the content of the program, the problems faced in implementing it, the results of the training and other pertinent questions.

Get examples of what was actually done. The applicant, a customer service representative, states that she dealt with irate customers. Ask for some examples of how she handled a customer.

Probe for details. Don't move on to another question until you feel you have adequate information.

Poor Communication

Good interviewing is not interrogating—asking questions and getting responses. To be effective it must be a two-way communication with feedback flowing from one party to the other on a continuous basis. The response to your question may not provide the information you desired. Why should this be?

You may not be speaking the same language

You may not be speaking the same language. I don't mean that you were speaking Latin and the applicant was speaking Greek. You may be using jargon—words or terms that are unique to your company and not likely to be understood by an outsider. You may use technical terminology that would be appropriate to use when interviewing a person experienced in that field, but meaningless to an applicant for a trainee position. If you see a puzzled look on the applicant's face when you ask a question, rephrase it immediately. The exception: if knowing the terminology is essential to job performance, this may indicate the applicant lacks the qualifications for the job.

Psychological barriers to clear communication

The following list details some of your attitudes that influence the way you interpret what you say and what you hear:

> *Assumptions.* You're a person whose highest priority in life is work. You've always worked 12-hour days and assume that all ambitious people are willing to put in the hours you do. You're likely to be wrong. Probe to learn how an applicant really feels about this and the other conditions incumbent to this job.

Preconceptions. People tend to hear what they expect to hear. The responses to your questions are distorted by any information you already know about the subject. If what the applicant says is different from what you expected, you might reject it as being incorrect.

What does this mean to you? Keep your mind open. When an applicant tells you something, make an extra effort to listen and to evaluate the new information objectively instead of blocking it out because it differs from your preconceptions.

Prejudices. Your biases for or against a person influence the way you receive what he or she says. If you have a good first impression of the applicant, more than likely you'll be inclined to accept whatever he or she says. If you took a dislike to the applicant, you'll most likely discount anything that's said.

> **TACTICAL TIPS**
>
> **Unless your perceptions of what the job requires and that of the applicant are congruent, the interview will deteriorate into meaninglessness.**

Are You Really Listening?

The applicant starts answering a detailed question. You begin listening attentively. Soon, but before you know it, your mind begins to wander. Instead of listening to the problem, your thoughts are moving on to other things: the pile of work on your desk, the meeting you have scheduled with the company vice president, the problems one of your children is having at school. You hear the applicant's words, but you're not really listening.

Does this happen to you? Of course, it does. It happens to all of us. Why? Our minds can process ideas 10 times faster than we can talk. While the applicant is talking, your mind may race ahead. You complete the applicant's sentence in your mind—often incorrectly—long before the applicant does. You "hear" what your mind dictates, not what's actually said.

This is human nature. You must anticipate that it will happen, and you must be alert and take steps to overcome it. Read on to learn how to become a better listener.

"Sorry, I wasn't listening"

Now suppose that your mind was wandering and that you didn't hear what the applicant said. It's embarrassing to admit that you weren't listening, so you fake it. You pick up on the last few words you heard and comment on them. That's good. If it makes sense, you're lucky, but you may have missed the real gist of the response.

When you're not sure what really was said you don't have to admit, "I'm sorry, I was daydreaming." One way to get back on track is to ask a question or make a comment about the last item you did hear: "Can we go back a minute to such-and-such?"

Another method is to comment: "To make sure that I can better understand your view on this, please elaborate."

When you realize that you haven't been fully listening to the applicant—when you start hearing a droning sound instead of words, when you hear only words but not ideas, or when you're anticipating what you *think* will be said—stop! Reorient your mind and start listening!

Proactive Steps to Better Listening

You *can* become a better listener. You can stop some of the main causes of ineffective listening before they begin. All you have to do is make a few changes in your work environment and in your approach to listening—a small effort with a big return.

Eliminate distractions. The greatest distraction is probably the telephone. You want to give the applicant your full attention—*and the phone rings.* Answering the call not only interrupts your discussion but also disrupts the flow of your thoughts. Even after you've hung up, your mind may still be thinking about the call.

Before the applicant comes in, arrange for someone else to handle your calls or set your voice mail to pick up all calls right away. If this isn't possible, get away from the telephone. Go to a conference room. Of course, there's probably a phone in the conference room, but no one knows that you're there, so it probably won't ring.

Get rid of excess paper to reduce distractions. If your desk is strewn with paper, you'll probably sit there skimming them until you realize too late that you're reading a letter or memo instead of listening. Put those papers away in a drawer. If you go to a conference room, take only the papers that are related to the interview.

Don't get too comfortable. One of our clients, Blake B., now vice president of Human Resources for a major company, told us this story: "Some years ago I was interviewing an applicant for a management position. As was my custom, I sat in my comfortable executive chair with my hands behind my head. Maybe I rocked a little. Was I embarrassed when the applicant suddenly blurted out, 'Mr. B., you're not listening to me!'"

"Ever since then, rather than take a relaxing position when interviewing, I've made a point of sitting on the edge of my chair and leaning forward rather than backward. This position not only brings me physically closer to the applicant, but also enables me to be more attentive, and helps me to maintain eye contact. It also shows the applicant that I'm truly interested in getting the full story he or she is relating and that I take seriously what is being said. And because I'm not quite so comfortable, I have less of a tendency to daydream."

Be an active listener. An active listener doesn't just sit with open ears. An active listener asks questions about what's being said. You can paraphrase ("So the way I understand it is that...") or ask specific questions about specific points. This technique not only enables you to clarify points that may be unclear but also keeps you alert and paying full attention.

Be an empathetic listener. Listen with your heart as well as with your head. Empathetic listeners not only listen to what other people say but also try to feel what other people are feeling when they speak. In other words, you put yourself in the applicant's shoes.

Take notes. It's impossible to remember everything that's said in a lengthy interview. Take notes, but as pointed out previously, don't take stenographic transcriptions. If you're concentrating on what you're writing, you can't pay full attention to what the applicant is saying.

More listening tips

Become an active listener. There's more to listening than just hearing what the applicant is saying. Here are some pointers:

Look at the applicant. Eye contact is one way of showing interest, but don't overdo it. Look at the whole person not just stare into his or her eyes.

Show interest by your facial expression. Smile or show concern when appropriate.

Indicate that you are following what is being said by nods or gestures.

Ask questions about what the applicant says. You can paraphrase "So the way I understand it is ...," or ask specific questions to clarify points that may be unclear.

Don't interrupt. A pause should not be a signal for you to start talking. Wait.

Don't argue. The interview is not a forum to discuss your opinions. If you disagree with the applicant's response, note it, but this is not the time or place to rebut it.

Watch the body language. Body language is a lot more important than people think. Interviewers should take a hint from top salespeople. They make a practice of carefully studying the body language of a prospect from the first few minutes of the interview. They note how the prospect's expressions often emphasize what is really important to him or her. They especially note the prospect's body language in reaction to their sales presentation, and adapt their pitches accordingly. All of us can benefit by following this practice. It will enable us to become better interviewers.

SUM AND SUBSTANCE

- A basic part of any interview is proper preparation by the interviewer. Review the application form and its accompanying résumé and the job description including the job specification.

- To ensure attainment of all relevant information, prepare a list of key questions that must be asked during the interview before you sit down with the applicant.

- Most good interviews have structure. If not, they result in a chaotic exchange of questions and answers with little possibility of making reasonable decisions.

- Basing the interview on the job specs is only part of the picture. As each applicant brings to the interview his or her own special qualifications and personal characteristics, tailor your interviewing plan to accommodate for this.

- Use non-directive interviewing. Instead of making a substantive remark after an applicant's response, make a non-committal comment, such as "uh-huh." Or just nod or remain silent. This encourages the applicant to continue talking and bring out information not directly asked about.

- Frame questions that will not only tell you about the applicant's work experience, but also enable you to determine his or her resourcefulness, ability to follow instructions, to work with others and other intangible factors.

- Taking notes is important, but it may stifle applicants and it may keep you from fully listening. Write brief notes during the interview. Immediately after the interview review them and write a summary while the interview is still fresh in your mind.

- You *can* become a better listener. All you have to do is make a few changes in your work environment and in your approach to listening.

Making the Hiring Decision

TACTICAL TIPS

Finding the perfect employee is virtually impossible. In today's market you'll be lucky if you can find a person who is 80 percent ready for the job. In making the choice, keep in mind that whoever you hire will require training, coaching and support.

The interviews are over. You now have to decide which candidate to hire. This can be one of the most important decisions you are required to make as a manager. This has become even more significant today because the old hierarchical structure in which top management made all the decisions has been replaced with a more collaborative, more team-based, more cross-functional organization, in which important decisions are made at all levels. This means that no matter what level the job is at, choosing the right person is key to the success of your organization.

JUDGING PEOPLE

Some people boast about their ability to judge people. Yet, when asked upon what basis they make this judgment, the reason is often superficial:

"He had a firm handshake."

"She looked me straight in the eye."

"He went to the same college I did."

"She comes from a fine family."

Some additional mistakes often made in judging people are:

Overemphasis on appearance

In most contacts with people our immediate reaction is to appearance. A person whose physical characteristics, dress, and presence are pleasant, neat, and attractive starts off on the right foot in most interpersonal relationships. This does not mean that you should judge the book solely by its cover, or that you should give preference to handsome men and beautiful women. Neatness, a pleasant countenance and good taste in dress and grooming are important. Caution: Overemphasis on appearance, making it the key factor, can result in a halo effect. For example, good looks alone will not make one a successful salesperson.

This doesn't mean that certain aspects of appearance shouldn't be considered. For example, if the applicant's mode of dress or other aspects of his or her appearance are unconventional, it may turn you off. "How can I hire a man with a handlebar mustache?" "Why does she wear such an odd outfit?" For jobs calling for dealing with customers, these may be negative factors. But for other jobs, they shouldn't influence your decision. Some psychologists point out that such idiosyncrasies provide insight into the applicant's personality. Probing questions and perhaps, interviews by psychologists might bring out what the applicant is consciously or subconsciously projecting.

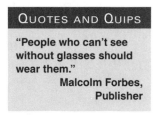

QUOTES AND QUIPS

"People who can't see without glasses should wear them."
Malcolm Forbes,
Publisher

We Favor People Like Ourselves

All of Tom's people were alumni of his university. Even though Beth worked in Chicago, her assistant and secretary were both from Iowa, her home state. When Tom and Beth were questioned on why they selected these people, their responses included comments on job qualifications, personality traits, and intelligence. Neither manager considered the similarity of their backgrounds as being a factor.

One tends to subconsciously favor people whose backgrounds are close to one's own. There is a comfortable feeling when dealing with people who have shared a similar environment or experience. This could be an asset in that working relationships can be developed more rapidly and more easily. However, it may lead to choosing a less qualified candidate. When all the people in a work group have analogous backgrounds, there's an inclination for them to think alike and to be less open to new ideas.

EMPLOYMENT TESTING

In the effort to minimize subjectivity in making the hiring decision, many companies use a variety of tests to help assess applicants. These tests vary from gimmicky quizzes that are purported to predict success or failure on a job to well designed, carefully validated instruments.

Do these tests really help? Some companies swear by tests; others swear at them. In companies in which tests are used extensively as part of the screening process, the HR department or an independent testing organization does the testing. In other firms, applicants are sent to a testing organization or an industrial psychologist.

Let's look at the most frequently used preemployment tests:

Intelligence tests

Like the IQ tests used in schools, these tests measure the ability to learn. They vary from simple exercises (such as the Wunderlic tests) that can be administered by people with a minimum of training, to highly sophisticated tests that must be administered by specialists with a Ph.D. in psychology.

The major flaw in using general intelligence tests is that two individuals who receive the same score can earn it in very different ways. One may be high in reasoning, low in numerical skills, and average in verbal skills. The other may be high in numerical skills, low in reasoning and high in verbal skills. They display entirely different intelligence profiles. Judging them by the total score can be misleading. To get the true picture, the test has to be evaluated by the scores of its components.

Another problem is that some tests violate the Equal Opportunity laws. To assure that a test is in compliance, it must be validated to be free from *cultural bias,* and that the score on the test must be directly related to the ability to do the job. Most test publishers have taken steps to eliminate cultural bias, but it is up to the company itself to prove that the test does have relevance to job success. For example, a test may contain questions about Greek mythology—a subject biased against minorities who come from cultures where this subject is less likely to be studied, and which are not relevant to the ability to learn the job. The Equal Employment Opportunity Commission has issued guidelines on validation of tests, which can be obtained directly from its office in your area.

Aptitude tests

These tests are designed to determine the potential of candidates in specific areas such as mechanical ability, clerical skills, and sales potential. Such tests are helpful in screening inexperienced people to determine whether they have the aptitude in the type of work for which you plan to train them.

Performance tests

These tests measure how well applicants can do the job for which they apply. Examples include operating a piece of machinery, entering data into a computer, writing advertising copy, or proofreading manuscripts. This hands-on type of testing is usually not controversial, and in most instances gives the employer a realistic way of determining the ability to do a job. Caution: If performance tests are used, the exact same test, under the same circumstances must be used for all applicants. For example, in a recent case, in which a company testing applicants for a clerical job gave each candidate a spelling test, black applicants were given words that were much more difficult than those in the test given white applicants.

Designing performance tests for more complex jobs is not easy. There are no performance tests for managerial ability or for most advanced jobs. Some companies, as part of the screening process, have asked applicants for such jobs to develop programs or projects for them. This makes sense. Asking an applicant for a marketing position to develop a marketing program for a new product can provide insight into his or her methods of operation, creativity and practicality. However, such tests can be carried too far. One company asked an applicant for a training director's position to create a leadership-training program for team leaders. He worked on it for several days, submitted it, but didn't get the job. Some months later, he learned that the company was using his plan to train team leaders. He billed the company for providing consulting services. When the company ignored his bill, he sued and won the case.

Personality tests

Personality tests are designed to identify personality characteristics. They vary from quickie questionnaires to highly sophisticated psychological evaluations. A great deal of controversy exists over the value of these types of tests. Supervisors and team leaders are cautioned not to make decisions based on the results of personality tests unless experts make the full implications clear to them.

A large number of organizations offer personality tests. You can obtain information about approved tests from the American Psychological Association, 750 First St., Washington, DC, 20002. Phone 202-336-5500 or at www.APA.org.

Selecting tests or similar assessment tools must be done very carefully. In buying a published test, ascertain the legitimacy of the publisher and the test by checking with the American Psychological Association and by contacting current and, if possible, past users of the test for their opinions.

Eric Samuelson, president of Management Development Institute of Alexandria, Virginia, poses five questions to ask when choosing an assessment tool:

1. What traits does it measure, and are they related to the job?
2. Is it validated? What studies have been done to prove it works?

3. Does it detect faking? How does it let you know about the accuracy and objectivity of the results?

4. Does it compare applicants against a standard for the job?

5. What can I do with the information after hire? For instance, can I use the results to coach and supervise the applicant?

Human resources managers should always remember that the administration of one or more personality tests is not the same thing as a comprehensive personality assessment provided by an organizational psychologist. A comprehensive pre-employment assessment by an industrial psychologist should include ability and personality measures, plus an extensive interview. These assessments typically cost in the neighborhood of $500 to $1,000 per candidate, and are usually based on an hourly rate charged by the psychologist.

Are these tests worth the cost? It depends on whom you speak to. Most of the companies that use some form of testing report mixed results. However, as many factors—not just the test results—were considered before making the hiring decision, it's difficult to determine just how valuable the tests were. In some cases, they could show that persons who did not do well in the tests, but

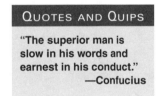

QUOTES AND QUIPS

"The superior man is slow in his words and earnest in his conduct."
—Confucius

were hired anyway, failed in the job; but there were also people who didn't test well who became very successful. And there is no way of knowing how many people who might have become A-players, were rejected as a result of a poor test showing.

CAN THE APPLICANT DO THE JOB?

Before even starting the screening process, it is essential to know exactly what an applicant must bring to the job in order to become successful in doing it. The basic tools to determine job qualifications are the job description and the job specifications. As pointed out earlier in this book, some job specs are absolutely essential. Applicants who don't meet these specs should have been elimi-

nated in the early stage of the process. All those under consideration at this stage of the process should be qualified to do the job.
Your responsibility is to select the best one.

Although all the surviving applicants meet the basic specs, they
all offer different degrees of expertise in the key areas as well as
additional qualifications. For example, Betty and Sue both have
been operating room nurses. Betty's experience has been in a hospital in a small community, and she hasn't worked with the sophisticated equipment that Sue, who worked in a large hospital, has.
Your hospital doesn't have this equipment at this time, but is planning to install it. Your decision between Betty and Sue would depend on their total backgrounds. Sue's experience is an asset, but
perhaps Betty is a better overall candidate with the potential to
learn to use the new equipment when it is installed.

Do They Have Those Critical Intangibles?

Meeting the job specs is just part of the decision-making process. Equally important is having those intangible factors that make
the difference between just doing a job and doing it well. Let's
look at some of these factors and how to evaluate them when interviewing the candidates:

Self-confidence

When Jeremy was interviewed he exuded self-confidence. He was
not afraid to talk about his failures and was not like other people
who tried to impress interviewers by bragging about their accomplishments. Jeremy was matter-of-fact about his successes. He projected an image of being totally secure in his feelings about his
capabilities. It is likely that Jeremy will manifest this self-confidence on the job, enabling him to adapt readily to the new situation.

Fluency of expression

Laura was able to discuss her background easily and fluently. She
did not hesitate or grasp for words. When the interviewer probed

for details, she was ready with statistics, examples and specific applications. Not only does this indicate her expertise, but her ability to communicate—an essential ingredient in many jobs. However, beware of some glib people who can talk a great job, but have only cursory experience or knowledge of it. They learn and use the jargon of the field. To determine if an applicant is a talker but not a doer, ask in-depth questions and probe for specific examples of their work. Glib phonies cannot come up with meaningful answers.

Alertness

Diane sparkled at the interview. She reacted to your questions and comments with her facial expressions and gestures. You could see that she was on her toes. Alert, sparkling applicants are usually dynamic and exciting people who give all to their jobs.

Maturity

Maturity cannot be measured by the chronological age of a person. Young people can be very mature and older people may still manifest child-like emotions. Mature applicants are not hostile or defensive. They do not interpret questions as barbs by a "prosecutor out to catch them." They do not show self-pity, have excuses for all of their past failures or inadequacies. They can discuss their weaknesses as readily as their strengths.

Sense of humor

Evan was a sourpuss. At no time during the interview did he smile or relax. Even when you tried to lighten up the interview with a humorous comment, he barely reacted. This may be due to nervousness, but more likely Evan is one of those very serious people who never look at the lighter side of things. They are difficult to supervise and impossible to work with in a team. It is easier and much more fun to work with a person who has a sense of humor. On the other hand applicants who are too frivolous, who tell inappropriate jokes, laugh raucously or act inconsistently with the situation may be immature.

Intelligence

Although some aspects of intelligence may be measured by tests, we can pick up a great deal about the type of intelligence a person has at an interview. If the job calls for rapid reaction to situations as they develop (e.g., sales), a person who responds to questions rapidly and sensibly has the kind of intelligence needed for the job. However, if the person is applying for a job where it is important to ponder over a question before coming up with an answer (e.g., research engineer), a slow, but well thought out response may be indicative of the type of intelligence required.

Warmth

This very important intangible asset is difficult to describe but you know when it is there. The warm person reacts to you, is empathetic and shows real concern about the matters discussed. This person will talk freely about interpersonal relations. He or she is comfortable at the interview and makes you feel comfortable. An individual with this type of personality is at ease in any environment and will fit into the department rapidly and naturally. They are likeable people and easy to live and work with.

Sensitivity to feedback

The applicant who understands what you are projecting not only in your questions and in your comments, but also with your body language will probably do the same on the job. This is an asset that is invaluable in the workplace. Such people are easy to train. They readily accept and implement instruction and criticism and work well with their peers.

Naturalness

A person who is natural and relaxed probably is a well-integrated person. However, do not automatically negate a nervous applicant. To reach such a person and determine what latent characteristics may exist beneath his or her uneasiness calls for skill, patience and determination. Their nervousness may be masking their real selves.

Growth Potential

The job for which you are hiring can lead to rapid advancement into more responsible positions. In making your decision, keep in mind the potential of the candidate. Does he or she have what it takes to move up the ladder? Potential for growth is an important factor in choosing the best candidate for this opening.

Be careful, though. You cannot reject an applicant on the grounds that they don't have specific experience for a possible future job, if they meet the specs for the current job. Leonora L., an African-American woman, couldn't understand why she was rejected for a position as a data entry clerk. She had three years of excellent experience and had been told she did very well in the performance tests. She noted that the job had been filled with a white woman, and she felt her race had been a factor. In response to the complaint, the company stated that Leonora was rejected because she didn't have any background in working with spreadsheets. When the EEOC investigator noted that the job description didn't mention working with spreadsheets, she was told that to be promoted from the data-entry job, it was necessary to know that area. The EEOC ruled in favor of Leonora. They pointed out an applicant cannot be rejected for an open job on the grounds that he or she is not qualified for a possible future job. If knowledge of spreadsheets were needed in the future, she could be trained in that work while employed in the lower level position.

DOES THE APPLICANT FIT IN WITH THE TEAM?

It used to be that top management made all the decisions and filtered them down through a series of layers to the rank-and-file workers. We have seen and continue to see this being replaced by a more collaborative organization in which people at all levels are expected to contribute to every aspect of their organization's activities. Getting things done is now assumed by groups of people usually headed by a team leader who together as a team plan, implement, and control the work. The essence of a team is common commitment. Without it, the members of the group perform as individuals; with it they become a powerful unit of collective performance. In the ideal team, each associate performs his or her function in such a way that it dovetails with that of other team members to enable the team to achieve its goals. By this collaboration, the whole becomes greater than the sum of its parts. An excellent example of this is a surgical team. Every member of the team: the surgeons, the anesthesiologist, the nurses, and the other technicians—carries out his or her individual functions expertly. But when they work as a team, interactions flow seamlessly among them. All are committed to one goal—the well-being of the patient. There are examples of successful teams in every endeavor: championship sports teams, disease-curing research teams, fire-fighting rescue teams, and in every aspect of business.

In selecting members for a team, it is extremely important that you pick people who will fit in with the team. This does not mean that all members come from the same race, ethnic group, sex, or social backgrounds. But they should have certain personal characteristics, attitudes, and philosophy of work in common. If a team consists of men and women who are dynamic and fast thinking, an applicant who is a plodder, who ponders ideas before expressing them, won't fit in, no matter how competent or intelligent he or she may be.

It's a good idea to have all team members interview applicants who are being seriously considered. The team leader should elicit the opinions of all team members before the hiring decision is made. In teams where decisions are made by consensus, all members must agree on the candidate. The danger here, of course, is the biases of individuals may influence their judgment. Careful training must be given to all members to alert them to these biases so they can work to overcome them.

CHOOSING AMONG SEVERAL TOP LEVEL APPLICANTS

In a tight job market, you may have only one viable candidate. Your choice is easy: Hire or don't hire. However, in most cases, you do have several good people from which to make your final selection.

Decision-making Blunders

Comparing candidates must be done systematically. Watch out for these common blunders:

The rule of recency

You've interviewed a dozen applicants over several weeks. By the time it comes to make a decision, you have forgotten much about the first few candidates, but the ones you interviewed most recently are fresh in your mind. You're more likely to hire one of them. To overcome this, keep good records of each interview. Discuss all candidates who have been passed on for subsequent interviews with all of the people who have interviewed them. If your notes indicate that an early applicant appeared to be a good prospect, but after seeing several others, you have only a vague memory of his personality, it's worthwhile arranging for a refresher interview before making the final decision.

Overemphasis on one factor

You were very impressed with Jonathon because he has an excellent background in designing Web pages. This is one of the first tasks the new employee will be assigned. However, the job will involve other areas in which Jonathon is not as well qualified as other candidates. Put all the applicants' backgrounds in perspective. Keep in mind the entire job—not just one part of it.

Applicant's interest In the job

When an applicant shows interest in the job, follows up with phone calls, e-mail, or letters, it's an indicator of interest in the job. This is good, but it also can influence you more than it should. Yes, you want the person you hire to be excited about the job and really want to be accepted. This is a factor that should be taken into consideration, but this does not mean that he or she is the best candidate for the job.

Pressure from another source

Stacey L. has gone through the process and is one of four candidates to reach the final stage. You get a call from a customer, a good friend, or maybe your boss, pressing you to hire Stacey. She's obviously qualified or she wouldn't have reached this stage, but it's your decision to make. Is she the best of the four? If you select another candidate, you'll have to explain why you didn't hire Stacey to that customer or friend, or most difficult, to your boss. The easy way out is to hire Stacey, but if, in your judgment, one of the others is better suited, don't let others influence you.

The Final Selection Spreadsheet

To systematize making the decision, compare applicants by placing their backgrounds side by side. One way of doing this is to use a worksheet such as the one shown in Figure 7-1.

Intuition or gut feelings

Often candidates are very close in their qualifications for the job. You have to make a choice among relatively equally competent people. Now it is a matter of your judgment. Choosing a candidate purely on gut feeling without systematically analyzing each prospect's background in relation to the job specs is a mistake. But, when the decision is choosing the best among equals, you have to trust your gut-feelings on which one to pick. As we said, hiring is both a science and an art. When you've exhausted the "science"—the systematic comparison of candidates—then the "art," your gut feelings, takes over.

MAKING THE OFFER

Once you've made your decision as to the person you want to hire, you are now ready to make a job offer. All through the interviewing process, you have been getting feedback from the applicants as to their interest in the job. Any applicant who has not expressed serious interest in the job should not have reached this point, but this does not necessarily mean that he or she will automatically accept your offer. Before making the formal offer, there should be a clear understanding by the applicant and the company on what the job entails, what the company expects from the applicant and what the applicant expects from the company.

Figure 7-1 _____

Final Selection Spreadsheet

Job Specs:	Applicant #1 NAME:	Applicant #2 NAME:	Applicant #3 NAME:	Applicant #4 NAME:
Education:				
Experience:				
Intangibles:				
Other:				

Before Making the Offer

Don't take anything for granted. During the entire process, the candidate has been enthusiastic about the job, has expressed sincere interest and seems anxious to start work. Before making the offer, it's important to review the job and make sure that both you and the applicant are on the same track.

QUOTES AND QUIPS

Restlessness and discontent are the first necessities of progress.
—Thomas Edison

Clarifying the job duties

Go over the job description point by point. Although the candidate may have read it already, most job descriptions are not comprehensive and there are many facets not specified. Discuss each aspect of the job to ensure that it is what the applicant has understood.

During the interviewing process, Ken L. was so excited about the job that the team leader was sure that he would accept the offer. But, when the team leader went over the details, Ken was not so sure it was the job he wanted. He had misunderstood some of the major duties and had assumed the job was at a higher level. He said, "I've done all of these things for years. What I'm looking for is more advanced work not just a repeat of what I have now."

What the company expects

In addition to the job duties expected of a staff member, most companies have policies and practices that should be made clear to an applicant before making a job offer. If the job requires travel, overtime work, work on weekends, or unusual working conditions, this should be made clear to the applicant before making a formal offer. Indeed, this should have been brought up early in the process, so if there is a problem in complying, the applicant could withdraw before reaching this point.

Often what appear to the company to be minor matters may be important to an applicant. Raul's résumé mentioned that he taught two nights a week at a local university. Nothing was said about this during his interviews. After he accepted the job and started work, he was told it was company policy not to permit employees to hold any other job, and he would have to give up his teaching position. Had Raul known this, he wouldn't have accepted the job. The result: a discontented employee who will probably be looking for another job.

What the employee can expect from the company

In today's competitive market, the applicant often has to be sold on accepting your job offer. Salary and the entire compensation package are important and this will be discussed in the next section. But often, it isn't money that will make the difference between acceptance and rejection of a job offer by the person you really want.

For years companies have provided "fringe benefits" such as company cars, memberships in country clubs, and the usual insurance packages. Recent innovations include such things as childcare facilities, fitness programs, flexible hours, and casual-dress days. In Chapter 8, some of these special "perks" will be discussed.

The Compensation Package

In most companies, except for senior executives, the HR department handles the final offer, including salary. Usually the HR representative discusses directly with the applicant the starting salary, benefits, and other facets of employment. If you're responsible for making the offer in your company, however, it's a good idea to check all the arrangements with your boss and the HR department to avoid misunderstandings.

Most companies set starting salaries for a job category. You may have a narrow range of flexibility, depending on an applicant's background. But when jobs are difficult to fill and in many higher-level positions, starting salaries are negotiable. In these types of jobs, several people usually interview an applicant, and you may have several interviews with finalists before making a decision. You should obtain a general idea of each person's salary demands early in this process so that you don't waste time considering people whose salary requirements are way out of line.

TACTICAL TIPS
Don't let your anxiety over losing a desirable candidate tempt you to make an informal offer—promising a higher salary or other condition of employment that hasn't been approved—with the hope that you can persuade management to agree to it. Failure to get this agreement will not only cause the applicant to reject the offer but can also lead to legal action against your company.

Salary alone isn't a total compensation package. It includes vacations, benefits, frequency of salary reviews, and incentive programs. All these items should be clearly explained.

Hiring bonuses

When applicants are scarce, companies resort to whatever they have to fill them. One rapidly growing approach is the hiring bonus. According to the American Management Association's survey of 334 HR managers, 44 percent of them said that their companies offer bonuses, up from 30 percent the previous year. Bonuses are no longer reserved for senior executives. Companies are using signing bonuses to secure all kinds of employees including technicians, IT staff, skilled factory workers, and specialists in most areas. One advantage of the hiring bonus is that it saves money down the road because base salary and benefits are not affected. It also is less likely to cause tension between old and new employees because it doesn't upset the compensation program.

The amount of the bonus often ranges from $50 for rank-and-file positions all the way to $25,000 or more for executives. The average runs about $5,000. Most companies pay the bonus in one lump sum with the new employee's first paycheck. Some companies stretch it out over the first six months or year. Some companies require the new employee to sign an agreement to remain on the job for a specified period of time, but such agreements are difficult to enforce.

> **QUOTES AND QUIPS**
>
> **Service without reward is punishment.**
> —George Herbert,
> English clergyman
> and author

OVERCOMING OBSTACLES

What do you do if at the time you make the offer, the applicant brings up new objections? Just as a salesperson must be prepared to overcome last minute reservations to buy a product, you must be ready to face and overcome these objections. Let's look at some common problems.

"The salary is too low."

Your first choice is Hillary. Early in the interview process, you explored her salary requirements, and your offer is in line. At least that's what you thought. Now Hillary demurs. "If I stay where I am, I'll get a raise in a few months that will bring me above that salary. You'll have to do better."

Having received approval of the hire at the salary offered, you have to either reject it, persuade her to take the job by selling her on other advantages, or go back to your boss for approval of the higher rate. What you do depends on many factors. Do you have other viable candidates for the job? If, not, how urgent is it to fill the job? Determine whether you can legitimately offer other benefits, such as a salary review in six months, opportunity for special training in an area in which she is particularly interested, or other perks. Think over the situation carefully, and discuss it with your manager. Caution: Don't make commitments you don't have the authority to honor.

If you and your boss agree that Hillary should still be considered for the position, determine how much above your original offer you're willing to pay and what else you can offer. The meeting with Hillary should take place as soon as possible after you and your manager have determined the maximum deal you can offer. With this in mind, you can negotiate with her and try to reach an acceptable arrangement. Usually, if this new negotiation doesn't lead to agreement, discontinue the discussion and seek another candidate. Continuing to haggle over terms of employment is not advisable

"I need flexible hours."

This should have come up early in the process. However, some people may feel that if they mention a special need, they may be rejected. Once they get the offer, then they bring it up. Some companies have an established policy on flextime. If the job for which the candidate is being considered falls into this policy, there's no problem. All that has to be worked out are the hours. However, if there is no policy, whether to grant this request depends on a variety of circumstances. If you give a new employee flexible hours, will the current staff also want their hours changed? There are some jobs in which flexible hours are more appropriate than in others. Is filling this job so difficult that it pays to bend the rules?

Doubts and skepticism

Some applicants are skeptics. Perhaps they've been misled by other employers and doubt that all the great benefits you offer are for real. Some may actually challenge you; others may just look or act doubtful. Be alert for these doubts and be prepared to rebut them

Dorothy is frank with you. She says that one of the reasons she left her last job was that they promised her she would be trained in advanced computer techniques. After she started work, she received no advanced training. When she asked when to expect the promised training, the company kept putting it off. "What guarantee do I have that you won't do the same?" One way is to show her your schedule of training in the areas discussed. Point out that all employees at her level are sent through a structured program to upgrade their skills. Tell her the main reason for hiring her is not only her current expertise, but also her potential for advanced work. You may refer her to current employees who have gone through the training so she can get first hand reports on what it did for them. If a training class is in session at this time, you may invite her to sit in for a short period of time to see it for herself.

"What are my opportunities for advancement?"

Of course, you can't promise automatic advancement in most jobs. Employees have to earn promotions. You should point out that the company conducts periodic performance reviews and that advancement is based on these reviews. To show the applicant the possibilities within the organization, display an organizational chart indicating the starting position and showing the various higher-level positions to which it can lead. If the company has a career pathing program, take this opportunity to describe how it works.

"I'm considering other offers."

It's not unusual for a good applicant to be looking at several possibilities. All through the interviewing process, you should be feeling the applicant out to determine what he or she is really seeking in the new job. Keep a record of this. Does he seek rapid advancement? Does she want special training? Has he commented on a particular type of job interest? Has she expressed concern about health benefits? Here is where you can use that information to persuade the candidate you want to accept your offer.

One way to counteract this is to ask the prospect to write down all the advantages of joining the other company or staying on the present job. Then, you list all the advantages of joining your team. Be prepared to show how your job—which may even pay less or have fewer benefits than other offers—is still the best bet. Use all the information gleaned at the interviews about what the candidate desires, and show how your job will help the prospect meet the goals he or she has set for the future. If this prospect is the one you really feel will be the best for your team, it's well worthwhile to make this effort.

Countering the Counteroffer

You've knocked yourself out reading résumés, interviewing applicants, and comparing candidates. You make the decision that you'll hire Valerie, and she accepts your offer. A week later she calls to tell you that she has changed her mind: When she told her boss that she was leaving, her boss made a counteroffer.

Frustrating? You bet. To minimize the possibility of a counteroffer, assume that any currently employed candidate will get one. At the time you make your offer, bring it up and make these points:

* You know that she has done a great job in her present company. You also realize that when she notifies her company that she's planning to leave, it will undoubtedly make a counteroffer. Why? Because they need her now.

* If the company truly appreciated her work, it wouldn't have waited until she got another job offer to give her a raise. It would have given it to her long ago.

* Many people who have accepted counter offers from a current employer find out that, after the pressure is off the company, it will train or hire someone else and let her go.

* From now on, she will always be looked on as a disloyal person who threatened to leave just to get more money.

* When the time for a raise comes around again, guess whose salary has already been "adjusted"?

When these arguments are used, the number of people who accept counteroffers decreases significantly.

SUM AND SUBSTANCE

• Don't hire or reject an applicant because of superficial aspects of his or her background. Look at the whole person in relation to the job for which he or she is being considered.

• Be aware of your own biases—pro and con. If you know that you are influenced positively or negatively by certain aspects of an applicant's background, neutralize it when you make the hiring decision.

• Meeting the job specs is just part of the decision-making process. Equally important is having those intangible factors that make the difference between just doing a job and doing it well.

• In selecting members for a team, it is extremely important that you pick people who will fit in with the team. This does not mean that all members come from the same race, ethnic group, sex, or social background. But they should have certain personal characteristics, attitudes, and philosophy of work in common.

• To systematize making the decision, compare applicants by placing their backgrounds side by side. Use a candidate comparison spreadsheet to make this comparison easier.

- When candidates are very close in their qualifications for the job, you may have to make a choice among relatively equally competent people. When the decision is choosing the best among equals, you have to trust your gut feelings on which one to pick.

You Don't Have to Pay the Most to Get and Keep the Best

Sure, money is important. There's no doubt that people will be attracted to companies that pay well and will remain in jobs where the compensation is satisfactory. But if that were the only reason for joining and remaining with a company, the job market would be a constant bidding war—and it isn't.

Surveys over the years have shown that although money plays a significant role in what employees want from a job, it rarely leads the list. According to a recent survey of 3,000 employees quoted in Bottom Line Business's May 2000 issue, salary and competitive benefits rank 11th out of 18 reasons given by employees for staying in their current jobs.

The employees gave higher ranks to intangible factors such as these:

1. career growth and learning;
2. exciting and challenging work;
3. meaningful work and the opportunity to make a difference;
4. great co-workers;
5. being part of a team;
6. a good boss;
7. being recognized for a job well done;

8. having fun on the job;

9. autonomy or a sense of control over their own work; and

10. flexibility in work hours and dress code.

In our research for this book, we found that most employees felt that if the basis for their salary was equitable, the other factors indicated in the surveys became more significant. However, if they believed they were not fairly compensated, salary and other financial rewards did become a major concern. The great percentage of respondents to our queries agreed that money alone was not the main reason they remained with their current employers.

Everybody wants to get paid. Money buys us the necessities of life and more money enables us to buy added comfort and enjoyment. But is money the best motivator to keep people from leaving?

> QUOTES AND QUIPS
>
> "The reward of a thing well done is to have done it."
> —Ralph Waldo Emerson, American essayist

SATISFIERS VS. MOTIVATORS

One of the earliest studies of employee motivation was conducted by a team of behavioral scientists led by Frederick Herzberg, which researched what people want from their jobs and classified the results into two categories:

- *Satisfiers* (also called *maintenance or hygiene factors*): These are the factors people require from a job in order to expend even minimum effort in that job. These factors include working conditions, money, and benefits. After employees are satisfied, however, just giving them more of the same factors doesn't motivate them to work harder. What most people consider motivators are really just satisfiers.

- *Motivators:* These are the factors that stimulate people to put out more energy, effort, and enthusiasm in their work and more commitment to the company.

To see how this concept works on the job, suppose that you work in a facility in which lighting is poor, ventilation is inadequate, and space is tight. The result: Low productivity. A few months later the company moves to a new site with excellent lighting, air-conditioning and lots of space—productivity shoots up; turnover goes way down. The company interprets this as a solution to its productivity problems. Managers assumed that by improving working conditions, workers would produce more. They decided to make the working conditions even better. They painted the walls a cheerful color, placed potted plants around the facility, and installed Muzak. The employees were delighted. It was a pleasure to work in these surroundings —but productivity didn't increase at all.

Why not? People seek a level of satisfaction in their job—in this case, reasonably good working conditions. When the working environment was made acceptable, employees were satisfied, and it showed up in their productivity. After the conditions met their level of satisfaction, however, adding enhancements didn't motivate them.

Money Is a Satisfier

Money, like working conditions, is a satisfier. It's generally been assumed that offering more money generates higher productivity. And it works—for many people, but not for everyone. Incentive programs, in which people are given an opportunity to earn more money by producing more, are part of many company compensation plans. Why should this work for some people, but not for others?

Let's look at one company's sales department. Salespeople usually work on a commission, or incentive basis. If salespeople want to earn more money, all they have to do is work harder or smarter and make as much money as they want. Therefore, all salespeople are very rich. Right? Wrong!

How come? Sales managers wonder about this. They say, "We have an excellent incentive program, and the money is there for our sales staff. All they have to do is reach out—but many of them don't. Why not?"

Psychologists note that most people set a personal salary level, consciously or subconsciously, at which they are satisfied. Until that point is reached, money does motivate them, but once reached, money no longer is as strong a motivator. What this level is varies significantly from person to person. Some people set this point very high, and money is a major motivator to them. They "knock themselves out" to keep making more money. Others are content at lower levels. It doesn't mean that they don't want an annual raise or bonus, but if obtaining the extra money requires any inconvenience or special effort, they just won't stretch themselves. Other things are more important to them than money.

By learning as much as you can about your associates, you can learn about their interests, goals, and lifestyles and the level of income at which they're satisfied. To offer the opportunity to make more money as an incentive to people who don't care about it is futile. You have to find some other ways to motivate them

> ### TACTICAL TIPS
>
> **By learning as much as you can about your associates, about their interests, goals, and lifestyles and the level of income at which they're satisfied will enable you to determine what part money plays in really motivating them.**

People Vary in What Motivates Each of Them

What motivates an individual may change from time to time. For example, for 20 years, Glenn, a production worker in a plastics plant, did his job satisfactorily and met his quotas. Despite an excellent incentive plan for higher productivity, Glenn never made an effort to earn those production bonuses. He was satisfied with his base pay and annual raises. Two years ago, Glenn's productivity suddenly began to jump. He earned production bonuses every quarter and even asked for added training to enable him to earn even more. What happened? Glenn was planning to retire in a few years. In his firm's pension plan, the amount of the pension is based on the amount earned in the last five years. By earning this extra money, not only could he save money for the travel he and his wife planned after he retired, but it would assure a higher retirement income.

The opposite also occurs. Estelle looked for every opportunity to earn extra income. For years, she'd ask for overtime work; she'd fight to win every production bonus. Her goal was to send her son through college. After he graduated and was off on his own, Estelle no longer felt the incentive to earn more and it was reflected in her work.

THE BASICS OF COMPENSATION

Even though compensation may not be the most important factor in attracting and retaining personnel, it's essential that the employees consider the salary, incentives and benefits equitable. Unless the pay scale is in line with what companies competing for the same type of employee are paying, money will play a more important role in an applicant's decision to accept or reject a job and in a current employee's determination to stay or leave.

Let's look at how companies pay their people. Most compensation programs determine how much an employee should be paid by considering the skill level of the job as determined by a job analysis and comparing it with similar jobs in the industry and community. From these salary surveys a range is established. The amount paid to individuals performing the same job varies depending on experience, length of service in the company, and raises based on the performance review. When a person is promoted to a higher-level position, pay is raised accordingly. Supervisors and managers will get higher salaries than their staff members. Their bosses will be in a higher salary category and the CEO will get the highest salary.

In most companies, employees are reviewed annually and, unless their performance is unsatisfactory, they will usually receive an increase. In many organizations every employee gets at least a cost-of-living increase or an annual raise just for still being on the payroll.

This is changing. According to a recent survey, new trends in compensation programs are developing. Here are some of these developments:

- Rank will not be the major determinant of pay. In many companies, contribution and performance are becoming the primary bases for compensation. The sales rep who brings in the most business may be paid more than his boss, the sales manager; the engineer who develops a viable patent may receive a higher bonus than the chief engineer.

- Increases in base salary will be reduced. With inflation more or less stabilized, cost-of-living increases have become minimal. Pay-for-performance plans are replacing fixed salary increments. Workers who contribute to the company's productivity and bottom line will be rewarded. Marginal and average employees will be given minimal increases or none at all.

- Lump-sum merit bonuses are gaining in popularity. Instead of raising salary, companies are paying production bonuses. This has an advantage for companies because bonuses are not part of salary, and do not become the basis on which benefits and future salary adjustments are determined.

Incentive Pay Plans

Since the earliest part of the Industrial Revolution, companies have used financial incentives as part of their compensation programs. In many companies all compensation was based on "piecework." It was assumed that people would work harder and faster if they received a direct reward for production. This system was carried forward into the period of "scientific management." Frederic Taylor, the founder of this new movement, and his followers believed that people could be motivated by wages based on productivity, and developed variations of the "piecework" pay system to achieve their goals.

In an economy that is moving rapidly away from mass production and manufacturing-based businesses to custom-engineered production and service-type industries, pay per piece has little value. New types of incentive programs have had to be developed.

Profit Sharing

Many companies have instituted profit-sharing plans as an incentive to their employees. These are plans in which a portion of the profits the company earns is distributed to its employees. Many of these plans are informal. The executive committee or board of directors sets aside at the end of the fiscal year a certain portion of profits to be distributed among employees. Other, more formal, plans follow a formula established for that purpose.

In many organizations, only managerial employees are included in a profit-sharing plan; in others, all employees who have been with the company for at least a certain number of years are also included; in still others, the entire work force gets a piece of the profits.

A number of profit-sharing programs are based on employee stock ownership. In addition to the stock options discussed in the next section, various types of stock-ownership plans are used. Some companies give shares of stock as bonuses or encourage employees to purchase shares.

A growing variation is the employee stock ownership plan or ESOP, whereby employees own so much of the stock that they virtually own the company. Having an ownership stake in the company should be a great incentive. As stockholders, they share in profits by receiving dividends—the higher the profits, the higher their dividends. Alas, it doesn't always work that way. Factors outside of the control of employees often affect stock prices and dividends. And as the share of the company owned by each employee is very small, they have no real input in running the organization. ESOPs work well when things are going well, but may even be a disincentive when stocks are down.

> **TACTICAL TIPS**
>
> **Stock options work great when the market is rising, but can be a demotivator when the share price doesn't move up.**

Stock Options

In an economy where more and more of the teams work in jobs in which performance cannot be measured by production figures, other types of incentive plans must be developed.

Stock option programs provide opportunity for employees to benefit from an increase in the value of the company's stock. Employees are given "rights" to purchase the stock at a price that is lower than the market price. Let's say the stock is currently selling for $25 per share. Options are issued enabling employees to buy the stock at $22 per share. If they exercise the options immediately, they make a $3 per share profit. However, the incentive is to keep the options until the stock rises in value. A year later, the stock is selling at $40 per share. They can still purchase it at $22 and sell it immediately for a profit of $18. In the exploding Internet business, exercising stock options has made millionaires of many employees of those firms.

The incentive is to help the company grow through its efforts, which will result in higher stock prices. The downside is that stock price doesn't necessarily reflect the company's profitability. As noted before, other market factors may influence it. If the stock falls below the option price, the rights are worthless.

Until recently, stock options were not offered to lower-level employees. They were chiefly a major part of executives' compensation packages. Over the past few years, particularly in start-up firms, stock options have been a force in attracting and retaining much needed technical personnel.

> **TACTICAL TIPS**
>
> **Tailor your incentive plan to what the company wants to accomplish. Create innovative programs that will motivate workers to help the company meet its goals.**

NEGOTIATING STARTING SALARY

It all starts when you hire the new employee. The deal you make with the applicant not only determines the salary at which he or she will start, but becomes the basis for all future salary adjustments.

TACTICAL TIPS

Information on going rates by type of job, industry and location can be obtained from the U.S. Bureau of Labor Statistics National Compensation Survey at *www.bls.gov/comhome.htm.* Other sources are: Salary.com at www.salary.com, Wage Web at *www.wageweb.com* and American Career Information Network at *www.acinet.org.*

As pointed out in Chapter 7, salary levels are usually set by the H.R. Department. Although occasionally it is delegated to the department manager.

Most companies set starting salaries for a job category. Salaries are usually determined by what the "going rate" is for the job—what other companies in the community are paying. This varies considerably depending on location.

When jobs are difficult to fill and in many higher-level positions, starting salaries are negotiable. In these types of jobs, several people usually interview an applicant, and there may be several interviews with finalists before a decision is made. To avoid wasting time in considering people whose salary requirements are way out of line, obtain a general idea of each person's salary demands early in this process.

Companies traditionally have used an applicant's salary history as the basis for their offer. Ten or 15 percent higher than a person's current salary has traditionally been considered a reasonable offer. However, as the job market gets tighter and tighter, many companies have offered much higher increments to attract the persons they want.

The danger here is that you may be paying newcomers considerably more than you are paying currently employed people for doing similar work. This can cause serious morale problems.

There are exceptions to this rule, of course. Some applicants have capabilities that you believe would be of great value to your company, and to attract these people, you may have to pay considerably more than your current top rate. Some companies create special job categories to accommodate this situation. Others pay only what they must and hope that it won't lead to lower morale.

Some companies believe that they can avoid these types of problems by prohibiting their employees from discussing salary. This "code of silence" is virtually impossible to enforce. People talk—and discussion of who makes how much is fodder for great gossip. One of our clients gave an employee a significant raise to keep him from leaving. He and the others in the company who were aware of the raise were sworn to secrecy. That very afternoon the manager in Los Angeles called the home office to ask whether the rumor about this raise was true. Asked where he picked up this information, he said that it was on his e-mail when he got back from lunch. The grapevine in action again!

Effect of Paying More to Recruits than Current Employees

What happens when current employees learn that newcomers are being paid more—and often, much more—than they are? This causes resentment and low morale; and in extreme cases, veteran workers may get angry enough to quit, perpetuating the labor shortage that led the employer to offer higher salaries to applicants in the first place. Disgruntled workers may not leave in a huff, but they often rethink their commitment to the company. This may be manifested in lower productivity, reluctance to work overtime, and unwillingness to cooperate with the higher-paid recruits. Frustrated employees may not do anything unethical or dishonest, but they also won't do anything to help the new employee to adjust.

It's not only the established staff that may suffer. Many companies rationalize their paying higher salaries to new employees on the grounds that because of their expertise, they can become productive rapidly. The companies demand exceptional performance from them. Often this involves expectations far above that which reasonably could be attained. Two years ago one of our clients, in a desperate effort to staff a new facility, recruited 18 high-tech specialists at salaries well above what they were paying to their established workers. When the current workers complained, our client explained that the

> **TACTICAL TIPS**
>
> Even when the salary you offer is less than an applicant wants, you may persuade that person to take your offer by pointing out how the job will enable him or her to use creativity, engage in work of special interest, and help reach career goals.

higher salaries were justified because these experts would produce high revenues in a short time. Expectations of the new techies were set so high that they were impossible to meet. The pressure on the newcomers overwhelmed them, resulting in a flood of resignations. As of this writing, only three are still with the company.

Competing with "Dot.com's" Stock Option Bait

Over the past few years the high-tech companies, particularly the start-up dot.coms have lured employees away from their current employers with stock options that may well make them millionaires. Sure, it's a risk. A good portion of these ventures will not become new Microsofts or Oracles. But promising techies and bright marketers and managers are leaving the "old economy" firms to take their chances with these start-ups.

To overcome this problem and make it worthwhile for their people to resist this temptation, some companies have taken proactive steps. One excellent example is the Andersen Consulting Co., which created a program called "e-Units".

Andersen is investing $200 million in e-commerce-related companies in its employees' behalf through Andersen Consulting Ventures, which is the firm's venture-capital unit. The wealth that is created by these investments will be distributed to the employees as employee units, or e-Units, which is a unique and proprietary form of compensation that takes advantage of the value that's generated through the electronic economy.

There are two aspects to e-Units. One is what is called loyalty awards, which are granted every year to people who have stayed three years or more with Andersen Consulting. All employees are entitled to loyalty awards. The second type of e-Unit award is called the performance award, which is tied specifically to one's performance and contribution to the success of the firm and its clients. These e-Units are above and beyond regular compensation, and this is one of the ways to share the wealth with the employees who work effectively.

In addition, Andersen is greatly expanding the partnership—the ownership—of the firm. This year alone, they plan to double the size of the partnership by making more than 1,000 new partners. This will enable top performers to become owners in the business.

PERKS

In many companies, employees have been given perks—those little extras that may not seem like much, but they often are significant additions to the traditional compensation package—and have been a great help in keeping people from leaving.

Why do perks motivate people to stay on a job? Why not give the employees cash bonuses and let them purchase or lease their own car, pay their own dues to the country club, or buy what they wish? Companies have found that most employees like receiving perks. If they did get cash equivalent, they would probably use it to pay bills or fritter it away. Perks keep reminding them that the company is giving them something. Every time they step into the company car, it reinforces their loyalty to the company. Every time they pass the day-care bill to the accounting department, they thank the company for taking that burden off them.

Perks should not be confused with benefits. Benefits such as pensions, health care, and life insurance are part of the compensation package. Today almost all large companies provide these standard benefits. Perks usually are add-ons to make life more pleasant for employees.

> QUOTES AND QUIPS
>
> "What I aspired to be, and was not, comforts me."
>
> —Robert Browning, English poet

The Perk Buffet

Company perks vary. Here are some of the more commonly provided perks:

- Company cars. Cars are leased for executives, sales people, and sometimes other staff members.

- Memberships in professional associations. To encourage technical and specialized personnel to keep up with the state of the art in their fields, the company will pay their dues in appropriate associations.

- Subscriptions to professional and technical journals. Offered for the same reason as memberships in associations.

- Membership in social clubs. Because much business is conducted on the golf course or over a meal, for years many companies have paid the enrollment fees and annual dues for country clubs and dining clubs for executives and sales representatives. In recent years such memberships have been extended to other employees as an added incentive.

- Subsidized lunchrooms. We recently had lunch in the cafeteria of a large insurance company. The bill for a salad, entree, coffee, and dessert was less than half of what is normally charged at a restaurant. This is a great savings for employees.

TACTICAL TIPS
Reward longevity. Give loyalty bonuses to employees who have completed long-term projects or years of service. Let employees know you appreciate their tenure. Arcnet, a wireless telecommunications company in Holmdel, N.J., figures to slash its turnover costs by more than half with its recent offer of a "free" BMW sedan to every employee who remains with the company for at least one year.

- Coffee and —. Many companies provide a never-empty coffee pot for employees. Often the company offers free doughnuts, bagels, or sweet rolls at break-time.

- Child-care. With the great number of families in which both parents are working, child-care is a major problem. Some companies have child-care facilities right on premises or arrange for child-care at nearby facilities and subsidize the cost.

- Transportation. Vans or buses are made available to employees to bring them to and from work. It's cheaper for the employees to use the company's transportation than to take public transportation or drive one's own car. Some companies will take employees to and from the nearest railroad station or bus depot at no cost to them.

- Tuition. Companies often pick up the entire bill for courses taken by employees—even if not specific to their job training. If the company doesn't pay in full, it may pay a portion of the cost of education.

- Scholarships. Some companies provide funds for college scholarships for children of employees.

- Flextime. A very effective perk is giving team members control over their own time. Some companies have company-wide flexible hours, but others allow supervisors or team leaders to set the hours for their staffs. For example, if there is a lot of pressure to complete a project, don't insist that everybody be on the job from 9 to 5. Some people may be more productive if they can work at home for a few hours before reporting to the office. Others may want to complete work away from the office during the day. Others may do their best work in the evening. Letting each person set time schedules for the project gives that person control over his or her hours and usually pays off in higher productivity.

Now let's look at some of the less common perks that companies give.

- *Birthday celebrations.* There are a few companies that give employees a day off on their birthday. That's a nice gesture, but it can disrupt team production. Many more companies celebrate the birthday on the job—at a break, lunch, or after work— with a mini-party: cake (no candles, age is confidential), soft drinks, and a little fun. When the group is relatively small, they may go out together after work for a little party.

TACTICAL TIPS

Rather than just copying what other companies do to add perks to your buffet, talk with your employees to determine their real interests. What may work for one group may not be effective for another.

- *Pets at work.* Bringing pets to the office can be very distracting, especially if they get restless. However, some companies permit employees to bring the dog or cat to work if they are kept under control. One company sets aside one day each week as "pet day" for employees who wish to take advantage of it.

- *Casual dress days.* Offices have always been formal places. Men wore suits and ties; women wore conservative outfits. Today many companies—particularly in the high-tech fields—have no dress code. Employees can wear whatever they feel comfortable in—except perhaps beachwear or "indelicate" attire. However, most offices still have traditional dress codes, modified somewhat. Sports jackets and slacks are okay for men and blouse-skirt outfits or slacks for women. To appease and attract the younger generation, companies have instituted casual dress days, usually Fridays, in which men can replace business suits with open-necked sports shirts and slacks and women can wear sporty outfits.

- *Exercise rooms.* With so many people engaging in regular exercise routines, many large firms have built complete gymnasiums for use by employees. Smaller organizations, of course, have neither the space nor funds for a gym, but an exercise room with a stationary bike, a treadmill, or other equipment for use by employees is feasible.

- *Recreation rooms.* To give employees a chance to relax after work, during breaks, or at lunch, some organizations have recreation rooms. In an article in the *Wall Street Journal,* one firm reported that it provided a billiard table and a Ping-Pong table; another, beanbag chairs; another a Velcro wall at which employees can throw sticky toys.

- *Financial counseling.* Companies provide seminars on managing money, investment basics, credit management, and means to achieve financial security. Some companies arrange for private counseling of employees by experts in the field.

- *Banking.* Many companies now have Automatic Teller Machines on premises, while others have arranged with a local bank to set up a branch at the company's facilities.

- *Charter schools.* To help retain parents who are concerned about the quality of education in the community, Ryder Systems, Inc. in Florida established a charter school at its Miami facility. Ryder made the initial investment to build the school, which will be re- covered over time as the school is funded by state education taxes. The school now teaches 300 students from kindergarten to third grade. It has resulted in retaining many employees who might have left but for this perk.

- *Laundry facilities.* The Wilton Connor Packaging Company of Charlotte, North Carolina, offers an unusual perk. They learned that a large number of employees didn't own washers and dryers and spent an inordinate amount of time going to and from pub- lic laundromats. The company arranged with a local laundry to let employees drop off their wash in the morning and pick it up at the end of the workday at a minimum charge, subsidized by the company. The company reported that the laundry perk is one of the most popular among their employees.

- *Concierge Services.* A growing trend, particularly in companies in larger cities, is the concierge service. Just as most top grade hotels have staff members who can care for the needs of their patrons, these firms provide equivalent facilities for their em- ployees. What exactly do some of these services provide? Concierge staff can be called on to purchase tickets to theater or sports events, arrange for personal travel, make reservations at restaurants, provide messenger service and do many of the time- consuming chores that complicate the lives of employees. In *For- tune* magazines list of 100 best companies to work for, 26 offered concierge services, up from 15 just a year earlier.

Some of the more unusual chores reported by some companies include bringing employees' cars to be serviced, arranging pet care, waiting at an employee's home for a repairman to come, making arrangements for weddings and parties, and locating hard-to-find collectibles.

Rather than have company staff act as concierges, most concierge services are outsourced. Concierge services are available in most cities. Costs vary. Some services charge a per-employee rate, some charge hourly fees for actual time spent, others charge the company nothing, but take a percentage of the receipts on anything employees order from approved vendors. Some companies pay the entire cost, but may require the employee to pay a "co-payment" similar to those charged on health insurance.

Just as benefits add to the compensation package, perks provide both financial advantages and convenience factors that display the company's concern for its employees.

WORK-LIFE PROGRAMS

To attract and retain top-level employees, more and more employers are turning to work/life programs that assist employees with balancing the demands of their personal and professional lives. Companies have come to recognize that increasingly employees are complaining about not having enough time for family, personal needs, community involvement and household tasks—while work demands continue to increase.

Successful companies are reaping more than financial rewards from work/life programs. Work/life balance solutions can foster the three key characteristics common to Fortune's 100 Best Companies. Those characteristics are: engaging employees in business; creating a supportive and inclusive company culture and environment; and giving greater consideration to their employees' quality of life. Companies on the list such as Microsoft, Hewlett-Packard and Charles Schwab are among the many who have implemented work/life programs to assist their workforces.

Work/life solutions have become a major new benefit, supplementing health care and 401(k)s. These employer-sponsored programs help employees balance their work and home responsibilities, and enhance employees' overall quality of life. These programs can boost employee loyalty, morale and productivity, which in turn can improve the company's bottom line. During the last five years, the number of employers offering work/life programs has grown significantly.

A survey by *Working Mother* magazine and the Work & Family Connection Inc. reported that 70 percent of surveyed employees at a manufacturing company said they remained with their company because of its work/life benefits. And 60 percent of workers surveyed at another large employer reported that the ability to balance work with personal and family responsibilities was "of great importance" in their decision to stay with the company.

In addition, work/life benefits can pay off in other ways. Several studies have noted the link between work/life programs and employee productivity. One study, for example, reported that work/life initiatives enable employees to better manage their life responsibilities, and as a result, they can be more focused and productive at work.

Work/life programs build loyalty with employees who are strongly committed to their company and make them more productive. For example, Scott Paper Co., started work/life programs, and other efforts to support employees increased productivity by 35 percent.

Other studies have shown that often employees value work/life balance assistance more than salary. According to JobTrak.com's Career Values Poll, a great number of students and alumni consider balancing work and personal lives more important to them than money, location, and advancement potential.

All three of the factors above—employee retention, productivity and reward—can enhance a corporation's bottom line. For example, a study focusing on Sears Roebuck and Co., published in the *Harvard Business Review,* found that every 5 percent improvement in employee attitudes created a 1.3 percent improvement in customer satisfaction and a 0.5 percent increase in store sales.

Employers aren't the only ones becoming more aware of the advantages of tools that enhance their employees' quality of life. A survey by *Fast Company* magazine and Roper Starch Worldwide reported that 89 percent of college-educated, employed adults placed the responsibility of enabling people to balance their work and personal lives on their employer. With expectations like that, employees will reward the companies that reward them, through their loyalty and productivity.

According to a recent survey by Hewitt Associates, 74 percent of the respondents now offer flexible schedules. In addition, 90 percent of the respondents offer some type of childcare benefits. Other work/life benefits noted in the survey were adoption assistance, and various provisions for elder care.

> QUOTES AND QUIPS
>
> **"The way to gain a good reputation is to endeavor to be what you desire to appear."**
>
> —Socrates

SUM AND SUBSTANCE

- Even though compensation may not be the most important factor in attracting and retaining personnel, it's essential that the employees consider the salary, incentives and benefits equitable. Unless the pay scale is in line with what companies competing for the same type of employee are paying, money will play a more important role in an applicant's decision to accept or reject a job and in a current employee's determination to stay or leave.

- Most people set a personal salary level, consciously or subconsciously, at which they are satisfied. Until that point is reached, money does motivate them, but once reached, no more. This level varies significantly from person to person.

- Companies have found that perks pay off. Perks keep reminding employees that the company is giving them something. Every time they step into the company car, it reinforces their loyalty to the company. Every time they pass the day-care bill to the accounting department, they thank the company for taking that burden off them.

- Be creative in selecting perks for your company. Rather than just copying what other companies do to add perks to your buffet, talk with your employees to determine their real interests. What may work for one group may not be effective in another.

- To attract and retain top-level employees, more and more employers are turning to work/life programs that assist employees with balancing the demands of their personal and professional lives. Companies have come to recognize that increasingly employees are complaining about not having enough time for family, personal needs, community involvement and household tasks—while work demands continue to increase.

9

On-Boarding: Getting the New Employee Off on the Right Foot

You've done everything right in attracting, screening and finally hiring the person for the open job. A starting date has been set, and at last, the new employee reports to work. What you do those first few days may determine whether that person becomes a loyal, dedicated, enthusiastic staff member or a half-hearted worker already on the way to disillusionment and potential problems.

Let's look at this from the viewpoint of the new employee. Starting a new job is both exciting and scary. The new person doesn't know just what to expect. During the period of interviews and pre-employment discussions, impressions and expectations were developed, and now comes the reality check. Does the job live up to what was expected?

When the company hired Ken, he was told the job would involve creative approaches to the work, but from day one, he was told not to deviate from what the manual specified. When Dorothy was interviewed, she was given the impression that the company believed strongly in employee participation. When she was hired, she found that her boss usually ignored suggestions from employees.

Our research brought up countless similar examples. In many cases this was due to poor leadership by the immediate supervisors. (See Chapter 12 for ways of dealing with this.). However, often the problems could have been alleviated if the new workers were properly oriented so that they fully understood the company's policies, the true nature of their jobs and what they might expect over time.

Recent studies have shown that one of the key reasons a whopping 55% of newly hired employees fail or voluntarily leave their new organizations within the first two years is due to a failure to properly introduce and assimilate them into the new culture.

THE ORIENTATION PROGRAMS

Most companies have some type of orientation program for new employees. These are usually conducted by the Human Resources department on the day they report, before they are sent to the department in which they will work. They may be shown videos, be given a tour of the facilities, receive literature, or attend a lecture. They learn the history of the organization, the benefits are explained and the rules and regulations are outlined. This is a good start, but not enough.

The team leader or supervisor must augment this with an orientation to the team or department. This should include a detailed discussion of the nature of the specific job the new worker will be performing and an understanding of what the supervisor plans to do to train the employee and help him or her to become productive.

ON-BOARDING

A relatively new approach companies are using is known as *on-boarding*. This process supplements and makes more effective the traditional orientation program. Originally designed to bring newly hired executives into the mainstream rapidly and thoroughly, it is now being extended to technical, professional, and administrative personnel, and in some companies, to all new hires.

During our research for this book, we identified and analyzed a number of the most successful on-boarding strategies. Not surprisingly, we found that although the timetables and techniques varied from organization to organization, the fundamentals (as measured in retention rates) are remarkably similar.

Let's look at how a successful on-boarding process works.

The Development of a Plan

The single most important aspect of successful on-boarding is the development of a comprehensive plan to shepherd the new employee through the first several months. Unfortunately, most organizations studied during the research for this book do a very poor job at this, and even those who *said* they had a plan rarely took the time to describe it in writing.

The companies with the best record of converting new employees to happy, productive, well-integrated members of the culture have taken the time to think through the key goals and objectives for the first year, and have prepared a written set of guidelines that provide a way to avoid any misunderstanding, and to gauge progress. The best plans we've seen contain the following elements:

1. A statement of purpose
2. A clear assessment of the current environment
3. Identification of the "Critical Few Objectives"
4. The identifying and assigning of a mentor

A very clear sense of what they're trying to accomplish

All of the best plans and on-boarding strategies observed by us over the years have contained a *statement of purpose*. Obviously, this is very important in helping bring focus to the on-boarding effort, and as assurance against some future misunderstanding. In many cases, the purpose statement is no more than a sentence or two, but the effect is always the same: *To make clear the reason a successful on-boarding effort is important to both the company and to the new employee.* Rather than using a boilerplate plan for all new employees, the most effective on-boarding plans are tailored to the special needs of the new employee and the organization.

Here are some real-life samples of purpose statements incorporated into on-boarding plans:

- To introduce Ethan and his ideas into our company, make him feel welcome, and provide the tools and the support necessary to achieve our objectives for the remainder of the year.

- To work with Angela and help her earn the loyalty and friendship of the entire team and establish their willing, enthusiastic cooperation in the effort to achieve our new sales goals.

- Inasmuch as Charles previously worked in a highly centralized organization, and our firm allows much more autonomy to its managers, special emphasis should be given to explaining and practicing our decision-making policies.

- As two of the key employees in the marketing department had hoped for promotion to the job Marcia has been hired for, we must work to overcome the resentment felt by these people and prepare them to accept Marcia as a credible and very capable person who can bring needed expertise and leadership to the department.

An honest, objective assessment of the current environment

Nearly all of the managers and executives we talked to felt that a careful assessment of the current environment was a particularly important element of a good on-boarding plan. The fact is, every company culture has positive and negative qualities, and every new employee is likely to experience both. The best, most successful on-boarding plans carefully evaluate both the forces that tend to work in favor of a new employee, to increase the likelihood of a successful introduction, and those that work against it. Being sure which is which, and to what extent, can have as much to do with success and failure as anything else.

When a company hires a new employee, they are most likely to emphasize all of the positive points about the job and the company and to either hide or minimize the negatives. All jobs and all companies have facets that are not as desirable as one may wish. New employees will find them out—often during the first days or weeks on the job—and this may affect their attitude toward the company. To avoid this, any negatives should have been brought up before the final offer was made, pointing out that the positives of the job far outweigh the negatives. This will prevent potential disillusionment and unhappiness.

During the on-boarding process, the new employee should be given a full and honest assessment of the situation that he or she will face. For example, Jason expected to take over an ongoing collections program that "needed a little sharpening up." When he started the job, he found that the system was in shambles and collections were well behind schedule. Had he been given the true picture, he would have been far better prepared for the work he had to do.

Identification of the "Critical Few Objectives" (CFOs)

One of the biggest contributors to failed on-boarding attempts is taking on too-much-too-soon. It's not at all unusual for new employees to feel as though they're "in the spotlight" for some period of time. People are watching. They're forming impressions—and making judgments. As we've said, it's important that the first few months of a new employee's tenure be orchestrated, at least to some appropriate extent. One aspect of this is the establishing of expectations.

One of the best strategies in this regard is identifying and clarifying the three or four (seldom more) objectives that are *critical* to the success of the new colleague in the first 90 days. By definition, these are the handful of things that *must* be achieved if the person is to be accepted. Dr. Raymond Harrison, formerly of the University of Pennsylvania Medical School, and currently president of *Executive Transformetrics* in Princeton, New Jersey, a management consulting and executive coaching firm, is often described as the originator of the concept. In our conversations with Dr. Harrison, he emphasized that, "every new job has at least two or three *critical few objectives*. They mean so much that even if a new person does a hundred other things superbly and these few things poorly, the result will be a failure."

According to Dr. Harrison, too often companies fail to understand that most executive failure can be traced to the inadequate accomplishment of just this handful of critically important objectives. If, however, these objectives are identified and a plan is prepared to assure that they're accomplished, the probability of success increases dramatically.

Among the most common CFOs identified by Dr. Harrison in his work with new executives are:

- Developing a cooperative, trusting relationship with one or two key colleagues. If Albert T., the newly hired human resources director of the Eagle Transformer Company wanted to make any progress in the company, he had to win the respect of the manufacturing manager and the chief engineer—both of whom looked down on people who were not from the technical areas. Failure to win their trust was a sure sign of potential failure in the job. Fortunately, as part of his on-boarding program, his mentor advised him about this and helped him plan an approach to deal with it.

- Demonstrating an ability to be decisive. In many jobs decisions must be made early on. One is judged on the ability to make these decisions. If the company culture calls for this trait, a new manager must demonstrate it right away.

- Making a good first impression at an important company gathering. Rachel L. was hired as product manager just three weeks before a major sales conference was scheduled. She was asked to make a presentation at that conference about a new product for which she was responsible. This would be the first time most sales representatives would meet her. As presentations of this type were key to her job, this "test" would either make or break her.

• Delivering on short-term promises. Often, a new employee faces a critical situation when hired. Let's say that when Jason M., the collections manager mentioned earlier, found that collections were well behind schedule, he promised to straighten out the situation in three months. His success or failure in meeting this promise will affect his future with the company.

Another example of how this works is Daniel Matthew, the homeowner policy claims manager of a large insurance company. Dan is an executive who understands the nature and importance of tending to one's CFOs. When he hired Doris M. as a team leader of the fire damage team, he set three immediate key objectives for her. First, she had to win the confidence of the team members to whom she was a stranger; second, to tackle a backlog of claims that had accrued since the departure of her predecessor; and third, to study and recommend an improved system for dealing with new claims.

To do this, he agreed to be her mentor and to help "sell" her credentials and abilities to the team members. He provided the support she needed to gain their initial acceptance, and set the stage for her to take full control rapidly. He reiterated the importance of reaching each of these objectives rapidly and gave unstintingly of his time to work with her to develop and implement a plan and timetable to accomplish these goals. By focusing on accomplishing them over the first few months, Doris was able to assimilate rapidly into the company and begin a successful career with the firm.

Some other examples of typical CFOs include: building a trusting, strong working relationship with a boss or other superior, making an important deadline, keeping an important project on budget, winning the support of key stakeholders for an important initiative, and similar situations.

Identifying short-term, intermediate and long-term goals with timetables

In addition to the identifying of the critical few objectives, all of the good on-boarding plans we've seen also specify a series of key goals, and the dates by which they'll be achieved. The value and benefits of careful goal-setting isn't new to business people, but it is worth mentioning that *all* of the successful on-boarding plans studied during the research for this book contained very specific, very quantifiable goals, and specific time-tables. Interestingly, and by contrast, the overwhelming majority of candidates experiencing unsuccessful on-boarding either had plans without specific goals or seemed unclear about the overall objectives of their new jobs.

> **QUOTES AND QUIPS**
>
> "He that succeeds makes an important thing of the immediate task."
>
> —William Feather, Author

Identifying and Assigning a Mentor

The second major step in successfully on-boarding a new employee is the selecting and recruiting of a mentor. Obviously, it's important that this person be intimately familiar with the internal workings on the firm, including the key political players and the leaders of the informal organization.

> **TACTICAL TIPS**
>
> The most successful on-boardings we've seen have always included a mentor with some level of prestige within the organization, and this is particularly important when assimilating someone in the more senior ranks of the organization.

Mentors provide important advice for new employees on a range of topics. Their overall mission is to "pave the way" for the new person, make sure they're introduced to the right people, and run interference should the going get tough. Although some disagree, it is our opinion that mentors and their protégés should be within easy access of each other, allowing plenty of time for private, face-to-face conversation and the building of trust and a personal bond.

According to Dr. Paul J. Mackey, the former vice president of instruction for Dale Carnegie & Associates, Inc., the most valuable qualities and characteristics of a good (management-level) mentor include:

- A reputation for honesty and effectiveness within the firm.

- The respect of senior-most management *and* the rank-and-file.
- Strong communications skills.
- Good listening skills.
- Counseling skills or background.
- A willingness to invest the time necessary.
- A personal stake in the success of the new employee.
- A results-oriented, "can-do" attitude.
- A likable personality and a good sense of humor.

Later in this chapter we'll discuss more on the mentoring process.

Getting Focused On the First 10 Days

Once a good plan, the *critical few objectives* and a series of short-term, intermediate-term and long-term goals are identified, the focus then needs to shift to the first ten days. The reason for this is simple, but it's amazing how often even the smartest, most experienced mentors and managers miss the point entirely.

Whether justified or not, the fact is *first impressions* are lasting, and few things are more important to a new employee than making a good one. Research has shown that most people care very little about who you are or what you have to say until they decide whether or not they like you. Knowing this, mentors and new employees are wise to concentrate more on *"winning friends"* than *"influencing people"* in the first week or so of a new employment relationship.

Many of those most effective at creating and managing a public image, such as political leaders, have learned as a result of their training and experience how to bring smiles to the faces of others, and how to stimulate positive, endearing reactions. In short, they understand the value of being able to create an emotional bond in a very short period of time, and they do it well. Those *best* at creating good first impressions and strong, lasting relationships are those who do so in a very natural, genuine, and sincere way. In short, they rely much less on the acquired skill or art of making friends and much more on a deep, very genuine concern for others, and a desire to serve.

Let's always remember Abraham Lincoln's admonition that you can fool all of the people some of the time and some of the people all of the time, but you can't fool all of the people all of the time. Put another way, the best way to make a good friend (or a good first impression) is to *be* a good friend.

Here's a list of the most commonly observed attributes of those recognized as both genuine and truly good at making good first impressions.

- They smile.
- They make eye contact.
- They make an effort to remember the names of others.
- They give thought in advance to what they want to say.
- They listen well.
- They encourage others to talk about themselves.
- They pay attention to their appearance.
- They are genuinely interested in others and in the opinions of others.
- They leave people feeling good about themselves.

True, most of these traits have been developed in people over all of their lives and it's not likely that even a good mentor can change the personality of an individual over a few weeks or months. However, many people are unaware of some of the items on the list and here is where a mentor can be of great help.

For example, in Malcolm's previous job, casual dress was the rule; in his present company, they're much more formal. Unless Malcolm is counseled on the way he dresses, he will make a poor impression on others in the firm.

Sheila's bad habit is jumping into a conversation before the other person has finished speaking. Her desire to express her ideas must be controlled or she will not gain the respect of her new colleagues.

Ted has a bad habit of constantly telling his colleagues, "that's not the way we did it in my old company." This is not the way to gain their friendship and cooperation. Somebody (preferably a mentor) has to alert the Malcolms, Sheilas, Teds, and others to the type of impression they are making so it can be corrected immediately.

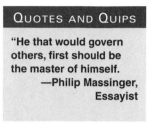

QUOTES AND QUIPS

"He that would govern others, first should be the master of himself.
—Philip Massinger, Essayist

Staying Focused, Supportive, and In-Touch

The fourth step is really more a series of mini-steps and commitments that when done well, assure the success of the others.

One of the great mistakes made by a surprising number of managers otherwise dedicated to good on-boarding is what we jokingly refer to as *mentoring fatigue syndrome.* MFS is a disease that seems to hit many mentors (and, indeed, some *protégés*) about a month or so into the on-boarding process. Symptoms vary, but often include impatience, difficulty finding time to meet, claims of success with the process and of having completed the process, and talk about workloads.

The great problem with MFS is that those who get it after a month or so almost always get worse; and those who get worse almost always end up causing headaches—and more—for others.

The best way to avoid MFS is to guard against it by accepting at the start of a mentoring assignment the fact that the process will continue at different levels of intensity for a year or more. Our experience has shown that once mentors and their protégés come to grips with the longer-term nature of their work together, they learn to pace their actions and interventions better, and in ways that are more comfortable and sustainable.

Another of the important cautions that seems to occur more often than we might have imagined is a tendency on the part of mentors to unintentionally undermine or sabotage the on-boarding effort by engaging in too much speculation and discussion about the new hire with colleagues and their own confidants. It's normal for there to be a good deal of interest and curiosity about a new hire, especially one brought into the organization at a senior level. It's also normal for people to seek out information about the new person, his or her intentions, management style and plans for the future. Not surprisingly, one of the best initial sources of current information about the new person is that person's mentor; and this is why it's particularly important that mentors show not only a great deal of discretion when discussing the progress of their protégé, but also a great deal of restraint when tempted to discuss any frustrations about the person.

Mentors (and, indeed, business people in general) are wise to assume that even the nicest, most well-intentioned people will find it hard to honor something "juicy" told to them in confidence about a new hire. We're all naturally curious and naturally drawn to gossipy tidbits about those who have captured our interest. Knowing this, mentors need to resist at every turn the temptation to win the affection of others by proving themselves a reliable source of gossipy information, and accept the need for discretion and complete trustworthiness as a condition of their role as mentors. In short, they need to fully understand and appreciate the great damage they can do to the perception and evolving reputation of a new hire when they break trust. They must place the interests of the new person ahead of both their own and those of other colleagues with whom they've had a much longer relationship.

Let's remember that mentoring is serious business and, according to recent research, can often be the most important difference between the successful retention of a new employee and a decision to leave. When done well it provides not only a platform for the ready and enthusiastic acceptance of a new hire, but also a much needed reference guide to the dangers and subtleties of the organizational culture.

QUOTES AND QUIPS

"The road to success is usually off the beaten path."
—Frank Tyger, Author

Seven Successful On-Boarding Practices

When we studied the approaches organizations were using to on-board, we found that organizations with consistently good records of on-boarding new employees used most or all of the following seven techniques.

1. Assign a coach or mentor to the new person right from the start

As noted earlier in this chapter, the mentor's job is to shepherd the new executive or employee through the first few days or weeks. This includes introducing them to the men and women with whom they will interrelate on the job, give them the opportunity to discuss benefit-related issues, get a clear focus on what the job will entail, and basically, just learn the ropes.

The mentor also serves as an unofficial advisor to the new employee, offering counsel about the culture, how best to handle any conflicts, manage any politics, and related issues.

When the new employee is relocating from another area, the mentor will arrange for the new person and spouse to become acquainted with the community, locate a realtor, learn about schools and religious facilities, and other areas of family concern.

Because the on-boarding process is so important and so tied to the longer-range success and assimilation of the new employee, the mentor should always be someone with both a thorough knowledge of the organization and a good measure of clout. In addition to the obvious, partnering with this type of person also sends a signal to the rest of the organization that the new hire is important, worthy of the personal attention of one of the company's heavy-hitters, and not to be taken lightly.

2. Arrange for some early successes

One of the biggest problems new employees face in assimilating to the culture of a new company is a lack of initial focus. One way organizations have found that helps a new hire get off on the right foot is to enable them to achieve some significant successes during the first couple of weeks on the job.

Let's see how this worked with one company. As part of the on-boarding process for Ben G., an assistant marketing manager, he was given an assignment to study the possibility of using e-marketing outlets for the company's products. As Ben had worked with e-markets in his previous job, he had a good deal of knowledge in this area. By enabling him to use his expertise immediately, the company gave him the opportunity to demonstrate his value to the organization early on. This not only was a benefit to the company, but also made Ben feel a part of a winning team from the beginning. It also enabled his colleagues and teammates to observe their new team member at his very best—assuring his acceptance by the group.

> **TACTICAL TIPS**
>
> **Give the new employee a chance to show early successes by assigning projects in which the expertise of the employee can be utilized immediately.**

3. Identify and concentrate on a handful of key, strategic objectives

Another on-boarding technique, as noted earlier in this chapter, is establishing for the new hire what executive coach and clinical psychologist, Dr. Raymond Harrison, calls the *Critical Few Objectives* or *CFOs*. These are the limited number of essential objectives that *absolutely, positively* must be accomplished by a new hire if he or she is to assimilate successfully into the new culture. You may wish to review the examples given in that section.

4. Develop a job description, with performance standards

Few things are more helpful to a new employee, and contribute more to a successful assimilation, than the development of a well-conceived job description. The majority of organizations identified in our best practices study make a practice of using what we call a *Job Results Description (JRD)*, which focuses on the results expected and how they will be measured.

Let's look at an example. When the Controller of Allied Merchants left the company, the CEO retained an executive search firm to fill the job. He handed them a copy of the job description, which had been written a few years earlier, as a guide for what to seek. This description emphasized the accounting aspects of the job and may have been accurate at the time it was written. Fortunately, the account executive assigned to this search did not accept it at face value. He investigated, studied what the controller actually did, learned from the CEO some of the functions he would like the new controller to be able to implement, and rewrote the description to represent what was really needed. The revised Job Results Description (JRD) is shown in Figure 9-1 (pages 222-223).

Note that the JRD is divided into several Chief Result Areas (CRAs). These are the major aspects of the job that must be accomplished by the person(s) holding it. Each is then supplemented by a list of standards on which performance will be measured— the results that the person performing the job is expected to accomplish.

Allow new employees at all levels ample time to learn, study, and plan before assuming any major responsibilities

We were delighted, and even a bit surprised, by the number of surveyed organizations who reported they are giving new employees, particularly in the management and technical areas, up to three months (and even more in some instances) to settle into their jobs and "learn the ropes" before assuming major responsibilities. The research on this is still developing, but it seems likely that the results of this practice will prove significant to the successful assimilation and retention of new hires.

We recognize that this is not always possible. There are times when the pressures of the job require the immediate assumption of duties and responsibilities. To avoid this, wherever it is possible companies should have "succession plans" in place so that replacements for retiring staff can be chosen, trained, oriented and actually functioning in the job before the incumbent leaves. This is particularly important when the successor comes from outside the company. It facilitates the transition for both the new person and the people with whom he or she will work.

Figure 9-1 _____

Job Results Description

CONTROLLER

OVERALL GOAL: To establish and implement policies and procedures that will maintain the financial health and continuing growth of the organization.

Chief Result Area 1: Financial Planning

The functions of this area will have been satisfactorily performed when:

a) the executive committee has been provided with long term financial goals that are realistic and attainable.

b) relations with investment banks, security houses and other outside financial sources are effective and profitable.

c) annual budgets are submitted on time and approved by the executive committee.

Chief Result Area 2: Accounting

The functions of this area will have been satisfactorily performed when:

a) the general accounting, cost accounting, credit and collections, and payroll departments are operating at optimum capacity.

b) systems and procedures for accounting operations are developed and implemented to meet the changing needs of the department.

c) audits by our CPA firm confirm the accuracy and effectiveness of our accounting procedures, reports, and other activities.

Chief Result Area 3: Money Management

The functions of this area will have been satisfactorily performed when:

a) short-term cash surpluses are invested for optimum returns.

b) loans for short-term cash requirements are obtained when needed at favorable rates.

c) favorable credit lines are available when needed.

Chief Results Area 4: Taxes

The functions of this area will have been satisfactorily performed when:

a) all federal, state and local taxes are paid as scheduled.

b) consultation with tax accountants and attorneys are maintained to assure best tax advantages.

Figure 9-1 _____

Job Results Description *(continued)*

Chief Results Area 5: General Administration
The functions of this area will have been satisfactorily performed when:
a)   all positions in the office are satisfactorily filled
b)   employees are fully trained to perform their jobs
c)   performance of all employees in the office are regularly evaluated
d)   the central filing system is functioning effectively
e)   office equipment and supplies are purchased when needed and properly maintained.

6. Overcome resentment of "by-passed" employees

When outsiders are hired for higher-level jobs, it's not uncommon for it to lead to jealousy or resentment of the new hire by a current employee or group of employees. They may feel they were unfairly "overlooked" for the job. In some cases, it may lead to flagrant attempts to undermine the new person through whispering campaigns, unjustified criticisms, rumor-mongering, and subtle refusals to cooperate, and a generally lowering of morale in the department and perhaps the company itself.

All of the very best organizations we visited openly acknowledged their struggles with these, and other, major internal obstacles to success, but also moved swiftly to minimize their impact. Many reported a history of great difficulty converting those harboring resentments into supportive colleagues, and sometimes found that the only way to resolve the situation was to remove or reassign the most egregious.

When the purchasing manager of one of our clients suddenly died, his three assistants all assumed that one of them would be selected to replace him. However, management felt that as each of them had specialized knowledge in only one phase of the purchasing job, it would be better to hire an outsider who had a more comprehensive background and could bring new ideas and expertise to the job. A highly qualified purchasing executive was hired to take over the position. The three assistants were never told about the decision until the new manager reported to work. The result was not surprising. They complained to the CEO. "You have always told the employees of this company that there was opportunity for advancement, that you firmly believed in promoting people when openings developed. One of us should have gotten that job." Nothing the CEO could say appeased them

You can guess what happened. No. They didn't quit; they didn't sabotage their new boss; they did their jobs—but with little enthusiasm, no extra effort and a minimum of cooperation.

Could this situation have been handled more effectively? Here are some ways that other organizations have used under similar circumstances:

- Eliminate emphasis on promotion from within. All employees should know what is required for the jobs above theirs and what they must do to qualify for them. Longevity, seniority, and good performance are important factors, but these alone will not assure promotion. Help the employees gain the skills they need for that promotion. If the purchasing assistants had worked to acquire the needed skills and knowledge, one of them would likely have qualified for the promotion.

- Once the decision is made not to promote, let the employees know in advance that an outsider will be hired. Explain the reasons for the decision.

- Don't secretly seek the new manager. Post the job. Announce that it will be advertised or an executive recruiter has been retained. Be frank about your search.

7. Provide unwavering support

There seems little question that the single most valuable contribution company executives can make to the assimilation of a new hire is the offering of unwavering support. Too many organizations badly underestimate the importance of this, and as a result, begin encouraging, however unintentionally, subtle challenges to their decision. In all of our research on this and related issues, we've found no better way to assure the failure of a new hire than to make a decision on the person's value or effectiveness in the first few months; or worse, allow the person to be put "on trial" by those around him. The results of practices like this are almost always negative and destructive, and remain a leading cause of failed assimilations, and the early exit of those who might otherwise have made important contributions. Obviously, it's the job of those with authority to be sure things like this simply don't happen.

A good example of this is giving the new employee a "baptism of fire." This happened to Carlos D. on the first day on his new job as a systems engineer. He was given a tough, major assignment that required him to work day and night for a week to identify the problems and come up with solutions. When he complained to his boss, the response was. "If you can't stand the heat, get out of the kitchen." Carlos quit. When the human resources manager asked his boss why Carlos left so soon, he was told, "I give the new guys tough problems to solve, so I can test their mettle. He didn't make it." This doesn't really make sense. Had Carlos been properly broken in, given a thorough orientation, given an original assignment he could readily accomplish, he most likely would have developed into a highly productive employee.

> **TACTICAL TIPS**
>
> Providing the new employee with full support, training, and encouragement over the first few months will maximize the chances of developing a productive and loyal staff member.

The Five Worst Practices

Having discussed the *best practices* in on-boarding strategy, now let's look at some of the *worst practices* we've seen. Usually they'll be found in organizations with the least impressive records of retaining new hires.

1. Delegating the orientation of new hires to clerical and administrative employees

This is particularly true when the new employee is at the management or higher technical or specialized levels. Allowing persons well below the level of the new employee to be responsible for the orientation sends a signal that senior management doesn't value the assimilating of new employees enough. But please don't misunderstand, it's not at all uncommon for members of the clerical or administrative team to play a very important role in the success or failure of a new hire, and to know more—even much more—about the real inner workings and culture of the company than the heavy-hitters. That said, it's also important to remember that the perception of unconditional support from senior-most management is the single most important determiner of a successful assimilation. Without it, the job is much more difficult.

Andrea F. was hired to head up the installation and operation of a new on-line reservation program for a hotel chain. Her work involved making major decisions and she reported directly to the executive vice president. However, when she started, the EVP was "too busy" and delegated "breaking her in" to an administrative assistant. Although this assistant was an intelligent and knowledgeable individual, she had neither the clout nor the stature within the organization to provide Andrea with the tools she needed to succeed and to project to other employees the true status of Andrea's position. This resulted in a long delay before Andrea was fully accepted by the staff and before she felt comfortable enough in the job to really become productive. This process would have been greatly accelerated, had the executive vice president taken the time to be personally responsible for helping Andrea assimilate into the organization.

2. Having a hands-off, "Survival of the Fittest" mentality

Our studies showed that very trusting managers with a largely "hands-off" management style were found in a surprisingly large percentage of organizations with poor records of retaining new employees. These managers tended to believe that remaining detached from the day-to-day details is the best way to encourage leadership and a "take charge" attitude among workers. While that may be true in some cases, it does appear that managers of this type, on average, have more difficulty retaining outstanding workers than those with a more involved management style. One of the reasons for this evidently is the increased likelihood that new hires will come to feel "abandoned" or "tossed to the wolves" by their perhaps well-intentioned but still ill-advised managers.

This doesn't mean that the boss should micromanage the new employee, but neither should that person be told, "Here's what I expect of you, go do it" with no other guidelines. Even highly experienced and self-confident new employees need guidance when starting in a new position. They don't know the culture, the history, the mores, the working style, the inner soul of the company, the varying personality quirks of the people with whom they will interact and the management philosophy of their new boss. It's worth the time and effort it takes to provide new hires with a set of guidelines on all of these facets and to work closely with them over the first weeks and months to monitor their progress.

3. Expecting significant results too soon

In the last decades of the twentieth century, in their desire to cut costs, many managers have overly downsized their organizations. This has often resulted in those workers who survived the lay-offs having to work longer and harder. When business picked up in the late 1990s, these same companies began to rebuild their workforces. However, due to the emphasis placed on maintaining a favorable bottom line, they often had lofty expectations of their new hires. To get them to be productive as soon as possible, on-boardings were minimized, often lasting less than a day before they expected the new hire to start "pitching in" and demonstrating his or her value. The results of this practice—asking too much too soon from a new hire—are almost always negative, and almost always lead to an increased likelihood of an early exit.

4. Evidence of overly aggressive or deceptive recruiting practices

Few things contribute more to the loss of good people and, sometimes, lead to expensive lawsuits, than evidence of dishonesty or deceptive business practices among the upper reaches of an organization. With increasing regularity (no doubt driven largely by extremely low unemployment rates in the United States and elsewhere) this includes deceptive hiring practices.

According to our own informal survey of new hires at over a dozen organizations researched for this book, a surprising 50% said they felt misled or intentionally deceived by some aspect of their interviewing process. In many cases this involved claims of alleged promises made by company personnel that eventually proved untrue or went unfulfilled. Among new hires opting to leave their new companies within sixty days, claims of deceptive and/or misleading hiring practices were reported by nearly 80%, with most indicating the deception or broken promise involved something the departing employee viewed as "extremely important"

Among the most common were misrepresentations about the nature of the job. At one company, applicants were told that there would be "occasional overtime." After they were on the job, they found they were expected to work many hours overtime each week and, as exempt employees, they were not compensated for this. Another company boasted about its "generous" health insurance plan, only to offer an HMO that had a reputation for denying benefits for trivial reasons. Other frequent complaints were that special training that was promised was never given, salary readjustments that had been promised were not made, and "moderate travel" turned into long assignments away from home.

5. Failing to anticipate jealousies and resentments, resulting in efforts to undermine the new hire

One of the surprising factors uncovered in our research was that so many companies almost completely failed to grasp the extent to which politics, jealousy, and at times, the wholesale sabotaging of people and projects, had infiltrated the organization and become a part of the day-to-day experience of a very large percentage of the workforce.

Very few things are more lethal to a new hire, especially those in new management-level jobs, than to be thrust, unsuspecting and unprotected, into this kind of environment. According to one battered former executive we interviewed, "it was like being blindfolded and thrust into a pool of hungry sharks. No matter what you did, you just knew you'd been targeted and that once the feeding frenzy started you'd be torn to shreds." Can this be prevented? Jealousy is incumbent to human nature. It's natural for a person to resent and even fear people whom they perceive to be a threat to them. And they do perceive new employees, especially those hired at equal or higher levels than themselves, to be rivals and threats. There is no way that this can be eliminated, but here are two approaches that have worked in minimizing this problem.

- *Prepare the new hire.* In the very early stages of the on-boarding program, have a frank discussion with the new person about the backgrounds, functions, and personalities of each of the people with whom he or she will interrelate. This must be handled with tact and consideration for the dignity of these people. For example. "Sam, our division controller, is a highly efficient accountant. However, he needs help in people skills. He tends to be a perfectionist and can be irritating when things are not going as well as he demands. He had hoped to be promoted to the job you have, and he expressed his disappointment. You'll be able to win him over when he sees how your expertise will make his work more successful. Be patient with him as this may take some time."

- *Prepare the current staff.* As pointed out earlier in this chapter, it's not a good idea to surprise employees when a new manager is brought aboard. When the new hire is to be a team leader, supervisor or manager, the senior executive should sit down with the group and tell them about the new manager and what this person can contribute to the organization.

When one or more of the current staff had expected to be promoted to that job, the executive should have a private meeting with that person and explain why the company went outside. He or she should explain what assets the new person brings to the job and ask for cooperation. "Sam, you have done a fine job as divisional controller and we seriously considered you for the corporate controller's job. However, our great need at this time was for somebody who could bring expertise in the development of financial control systems, and Bob has many years in this field. We do appreciate the work you are doing and I want to assure you that as our expansion plans develop, there will be opportunities for you. I'm sure we can count on your cooperating with Bob."

Dr. Edward G. Verlander, president of E.G. Verlander & Associates, an international management consulting firm, has developed a 10-step approach to on-boarding which synthesizes much of what we have found to be the essential ingredients of getting a new person effectively assimilated into the new job.

THE TEN COMPONENTS OF AN EFFECTIVE INDUCTION PROCESS

1. The Company

Most new employees will already know something about the company from going through the recruitment process. It makes no sense to repeat all of that. Management must now describe and explain how the company is structured, its value-chain and hence how the company makes money. Emphasis must be given to the company's views on and treatment of its customers. Also, the connection between the company's vision and values must be made clear and that all employees are expected to live up to the values, every day. Facts, stories and anecdotes will make the importance of these connections real and clear.

2. Function and department

All employees work in a function and in a department within that function, such as applications engineering in the Information Technology department. A clear understanding must be established in the new employee's mind about how the department fits into the function and what the department is expected to contribute in the value chain, especially goals, projects, timetables, deliverables, demographics, and human resources capabilities. Policies and procedures must be made clear to show how work gets done and contributes to the overall function, and hence the company's ability to meet the customer's needs (internal as well as external customers). Also, both functional standards and professional standards must be emphasized so the new employee knows that professional standards are not only expected, but that this is a place where one's profession can be applied to high degree.

3. Colleagues

Meeting and getting to know one's colleagues is extremely important and must be done at the outset, both in a formal way by announcing/publishing the new employee's arrival, and informally by walking the employee around and making personal introductions, extending invitations to lunch, and making sure the employee attends meetings. The key here is to make the employee feel a part of the organization and to build the perception that relationships count. Teamwork is critical and "pulling for the team" every day, even when faced with adversity, is a daily responsibility. Colleagues create the culture; pointing out the nature and dynamics of the culture (i.e. the company/function values, beliefs and behaviors) serves to reinforce how the new employee must act to assimilate and eventually contribute to the desired culture.

4. Role and responsibilities

This will probably already be known by the new employee, but at a very high conceptual level. Job descriptions and the interview discussion will have pointed out the major components of the job. Now is the time to be specific. Don't assume the employee knows what to do and how to do it. Employees in technical roles will bring training and experience, but these often must be adapted to the new organization's policies and practices. Explain that a variety of roles will be required of the employee including project work, project leadership, coaching colleagues, communicating the status of work, communicating across the department, and producing timely work. Responsibilities will include meeting accelerated deadlines, exceeding performance expectations, working late, expanding work loads, reducing costs, improving quality and certainly working effectively with other people in ways that fulfill the requirements of company culture. Remember that roles and responsibilities always involve what is done and how the employee must go about doing it. This will inevitably require being clear about building collaborative work relationships, handling conflict, disagreeing maturely, and getting along well with others, or what we now call emotional intelligence.

5. Job standards and contribution

All work must be done according to established procedures and up to the standards of quality set by the department management. We often assume that new employees will "learn the ropes" on their own. Management must talk to employees about what is expected in job contribution, the timelines, accuracy and comprehensiveness of work. Do not assume that this is understood, or that they will "pick it up." Coaching and task training employees is very important at this stage and fosters the attitude of continuous learning and improvement by the employee. It is a good idea to find the employee's limits and make the job requirements exceed them both in quantity and quality. Provide help, but send the message very early on, that this job will require new skills and knowledge over time. In short, that change is inevitable and to expect the job to change. Also, make sure the employee has a clear understanding of the authority level that comes with the job for expenditures and commitments of the department resources.

6. "White Space" management

This refers to the informal relationships that occur around the formal organizational structure. The task here is to help the new employee to balance and navigate the roads and boundaries of the

informal political relationships. Managers need to encourage cama-
raderie and to make the employee feel it is a good idea to develop
collegial relationships, to feel a part of the department and not to
just stick to the desk and work with the head down. At the same
time, the new employee needs to know about company policies regarding such things as personal use of the telephone and e-mail,
personal relationship behavior on the job, appropriate and inappropriate language and behavior, special company rules and regulations, and any limits to the job.

7. Performance management

All new employees want to know how they will be measured and
rewarded. The closer an employee can see the link is between effort and reward, the higher the probability (not certainty) of satisfaction. The keys here are: clear performance goals, good
delegation, clear work standards, regular feedback, just-in-time
coaching, sensitive and balanced dialogue on performance, performance reviews and the message that both results and company values are important for success.

8. Career development

During the on-boarding process, all employees are interested in
what lies ahead for them. This interest may be in terms of job expansion, more money, promotions, interesting job assignments, and
special projects, as well as interesting people to work with from
whom they can learn a great deal. The employee must be able to
see the career potential while getting the message that advancement only occurs with success in this first job. Everything rides on
doing what is right and proper in the first assignment; not to expect
too much too soon; to work hard and become assimilated into the
culture—to develop a personal identity with the company. This is
especially important for professional employees who always have a
"loyalty tension" between their profession and the company. A
good induction sets the stage for building strong loyalty to the
company, which will be successful if all of the induction steps are
taken and management invests quality time in their execution.

9. Professional development

In general, all employees want to learn and grow in their work. The "quality movement" has proven this many times in the last fifteen years, even in routine manufacturing jobs suitable for high school graduates. It is absolutely critical to attract and retain professional employees, especially those in the rapidly accelerating information technology jobs. The best way to retain professionals is to carefully and systematically induct them into the new organization with challenging and important work that pays market rates. Then, as they reach the limits of their contribution, to give them access to new skills, new organizational challenges, stretching experiences that make them conclude in their minds that only by staying here in this job, can they get the professional challenge and learning they desire. Therefore, the induction process must demonstrate this by its thoroughness. This will show that the company values its employees, provides training and development, invests in people and teams, expects a lot, and hires a person because management agrees the person was up to the challenge. The fear and shame of not living up to this initial positive judgment will mitigate against new employee turnover.

10. Climate contribution

The final thing that the induction process must do for a new employee is to embed the idea that the new employee has a stake in creating the tone, feel, atmosphere and climate of the organization. That is, each employee contributes to "what it's like to work around here." Quite often the climate is positive and collaborative. But, it may still have employees who point fingers at others, especially management, when they are unhappy with the work climate. New employees have to be insulated from infection and bad features in the climate. The insulation protects new employees from becoming demoralized and worrying about whether they have made a bad decision to join the company. The manager's job at induction time is to explain the reality of the climate as it is today and what the game plan is to change it and where necessary, to improve it. All organizations have problems. A perfect one does not exist. There are always problems with certain employees, or deliverables, or workloads. Managers must explain the truth and be realistic about the political nature of the organization. This will give the new employee a "heads up" and alertness to negative and mixed messages from existing employees who may try to recruit them to their cause.

Taken together, these ten components will go a long way to improving the on-boarding process. This in turn will help new employees to assimilate into the organization. If the process is one of careful explanation of the company's conditions and expectations, combined with an eagerness on the part of management to support new employees' needs, it will definitely help to create and solidify the all-important psychological contract. Both employees and employer alike have a vested interested in successfully forging it. As the psychological contract is formed, the employee will develop an understanding about what it can expect from the company in exchange for the employee's labors and knowledge. At the same time, the company will have done a good job in understanding what it can reasonably expect from the employee in exchange for the money, benefits and challenging work it offers. Once this is in balance, the employee will have a sense of psychological well-being, motivation and fairness, and this in turn will increase the probability of long-term satisfaction and retention. And that is the goal of an effective induction and orientation process: to convert today's short job tenures into long-term employment satisfaction.

SUM AND SUBSTANCE

- A relatively new approach companies are using is known as *on-boarding*. This process supplements and makes more effective the traditional orientation program.
- Successful on-boarding plans should include:
  1. A statement of purpose
  2. A clear assessment of the current environment

3. Identification of the "Critical Few Objectives"—objectives that are critical to the success of the new colleague in the first 90 days.

4. The identifying and assigning of a mentor with some level of prestige within the organization. This is particularly important when assimilating someone in the more senior ranks of the organization.

- Few things are more helpful to a new employee, and contribute more to a successful assimilation, than the developing of a well-conceived job-results description.

- Give new employees, particularly in the management and technical areas, up to three months (and even more in some instances) to settle into their jobs and "learn the ropes" before assuming major responsibilities.

- The single most valuable contribution company executives can make to the assimilation of a new hire is the offering of unwavering support.

- Even highly experienced and self-confident new employees need guidance when starting in a new position. In the very early stages of the on-boarding program, have a frank discussion with the new person about the backgrounds, functions, and personalities of each of the people with whom he or she will interrelate. Work closely with the new employee over the first weeks and months to monitor progress.

- Few things contribute more to the loss of good people and, sometimes, lead to expensive lawsuits, than evidence of dishonesty or deceptive business practices among the upper reaches of an organization.

- A well thought out on-boarding program will help new employees to assimilate into the new organization. Both employees and employer alike have a vested interest in successfully forging it. It solidifies the employee's understanding about what he or she can expect from the company in exchange for labors and knowledge. At the same time, the company will have a better understanding of what it can reasonably expect from the employee in exchange for the money, benefits and challenging work it offers. Once this is in balance, the employee will have a sense of psychological well-being, motivation and fairness, and this in turn will increase the probability of long-term satisfaction and retention.

10

Why Good People Leave

There are few things more draining to an organization—and more telling about the state of its culture—than the steady, systematic loss of highly effective and productive people. Years ago when the labor pool was larger and outstanding people were more plentiful this was less of a problem. Today, with unemployment rates and worker loyalty statistics at record lows it's one of the hottest, most compelling business issues of our time.

There's nothing new about good people trying to improve their lot. In truth, many outstanding people still use periodic job changes as a key part of their career management strategy. The problems arise, however, when evidence of dissatisfaction among top workers seems to be the major recurrent reason for high turnover rates. When that happens the results are almost always disrupting, if not severely damaging to the organization.

Can you save these people before they take that drastic step that will separate them from the organization? Not always. It may be too late to make the changes that precipitated that individual's decision to leave. There are situations in which you can reach a dissatisfied employee and make changes that will encourage a change of mind. However, even if that fails, you may learn what to do that will change the circumstances and prevent other good people from quitting.

Some companies have taken pro-active steps to identify specific problems that an employee may have that might lead to voluntary separation. For example, when the HR manager of a multi-unit, multi-state financial institution accidentally found one of his key employees' résumés on an online job service, he met with her, learned why she was seeking a change, and was able to retain the employee. As a result, he assigned one of his staff to surf the major job-posting services seeking the bank's employees. This program, which he dubbed "salvaging" has resulted in four "saves" in the first six months and has provided critical information about the bank's human resources practices.

Another example is a retail chain in Illinois. At the annual performance review, the supervisor or team leader records on each employee's report what they say they want from the company over the next year that will help them meet their goals. Every month, the supervisor reviews these reports and determines what has been done or not done to meet these needs. This follow-through has led to greater productivity, higher morale, and a significant reduction in turnover.

THE REASONS PEOPLE LEAVE THEIR JOBS

Let's look at some of the top reasons good people give for leaving their organizations. The list was compiled from data collected during over 40 interviews we conducted with former employees from a host of industries and organizations, and the surveying of over 300 others.

Loss of Faith in Management

There seems little doubt that one of the big reasons good people leave their jobs is a gradual (and, alas, sometimes sudden) loss of faith in management. In fact, of all of the answers received during our conversations with recently departed employees, this remained the one most frequently cited.

The loss of faith in a boss or colleague is nothing new in business, or in life, for that matter. People disappoint. They exaggerate. They make mistakes. What surprised us about our findings, however, is not so much the fact that highly marketable people said they left their jobs because they had lost faith in management, but rather how quickly they came to the decision and how little patience they seemed to show for any transgressions.

"Good people are much less forgiving today," says Pam Bradley, a leading human resources consultant in Manhattan. "They know they have options and that they don't have to take as much nonsense or tolerate as much incompetence as they did before."

There's also evidence that good people have a good deal less patience today for behaviors they consider shady or dishonest. "In times past," says Bradley, "many people were basically forced to turn a blind eye and a deaf ear to management practices that seemed to test ethical borders. They were afraid that they'd get in trouble or even lose their jobs if they said something. Today, many of these same people say they're more concerned with their reputations than they are their paychecks. They say they're worried about the stigma that could come from an association with a manager—or a firm— with a questionable history or reputation. They're just refusing to participate in things they find uncomfortable. They're confident that they can find another job quickly, and they're expressing their disgust not only with their mouths, but also with their feet."

According to a report on Work Practices and Employee Loyalty made by Walker Information, Indianapolis, Indiana, companies viewed as highly ethical by their employees are six times more likely to keep their staff. Nearly 80 percent of 2000 employees who questioned their bosses' integrity said they felt trapped at work or uncommitted and were likely to leave their jobs soon.[1]

---

[1]Reported in *Success in Recruiting and Retaining,* National Institute of Business Management, September 2000, p.4.

Feeling Unappreciated

Not surprising, another major reason good people give for leaving their jobs is a sense that their efforts and contributions are not appreciated enough. According to recent surveys, over 80 percent of those who had made a decision to change jobs during the past year reported they did so, in part, out of a feeling that their contributions had gone largely unnoticed or were simply taken for granted by their superiors. "It's a remarkably simple concept, and one that's been talked about and written about for thousands of years," says Bob McCarty, president of RJM Associates in Rutherford, New Jersey. "Having said that, the simple fact is that people *really do* need to feel they're appreciated and that what they're doing for their company is valuable and noteworthy." According to McCarty, "We often find managers who *say* they agree with our findings and the findings of others on this topic, but in truth do very little to send the kinds of signals that provide for people that sense of value. These folks are often notorious for their high turnover rates and poor performance on 360-degree assessments and other performance evaluations. They may say they care and that they appreciate the efforts of others, but the evidence seems to contradict it. They just don't seem to understand how important something so simple and so easy to do is to people."

William James, the great American psychologist, stated that the deepest urge in human nature is the craving to be appreciated. Yet, in our daily lives, we take so much for granted that we often forget to express our appreciation to others in our lives who make our successes possible and our daily lives more enjoyable. This is particularly true in the workplace. Managers and supervisors often assume that if employees are not criticized or reprimanded, they "know they're doing okay." Wrong! People need to be told that their work is good and is appreciated.

> ### QUOTES AND QUIPS
>
> **There is no reward for finding fault.**
> —Arnold Glasow, Author

Appreciation must be sincere. Phoniness is easily perceived. Insincerity cannot be disguised by fancy words. Your voice, your eyes, your body language reflects your true feelings. There is no reason to fake expressions of appreciation. Look for something specific that the employee has done that is worthy of praise and let it be known that it's appreciated. Supplementing your verbal comments with an occasional note of gratitude reinforces your appreciation and helps build a sense of loyalty.

Feeling Bored or Unchallenged

It came as no surprise to us that boredom and a sense of having "stagnated" at work is another major reason good people give for resigning. In fact, 67 percent of those surveyed by us listed it among the four leading reasons for their exit.

"Organizations make a big mistake when they assume highly competent and well compensated people are also happy with the routine of their jobs," says Dr. Paul J. Mackey, president of Mackey Communications in Bradenton, Florida. "The fact is, terrifically capable people get that way as a result of having searched for and accepted new challenges over the years. They're the type of people who relish change and thrive on new experiences."

Some jobs are basically boring, but any job can become boring when you do it over and over again, day after day, year after year. In many companies, jobs are enriched to minimize boredom. By adding new functions and combining several simple tasks into a more challenging total activity, jobs can be made less boring.

Some ways to prevent jobs performed by your team members from becoming boring

- Reexamine all routine work that your team performs. Encourage all people who perform the work to suggest ways of making it more interesting.

- People performing routine work often get into a rut. They start out every day performing phase one, and then go to phase two and three, and so on. Unless it's essential that work be done in a predetermined order, suggest that they change the pattern. Start one day with phase six, and then go to phase three or seven or one. Breaking the routine alleviates boredom.

- Cross-train staff members to do a variety of jobs so that they can move from one type of work to another and be less likely to become bored.

- Encourage members to help associates—particularly new team members—by becoming mentors to them.

A Highly Politicized Workplace

Another reason good people give for leaving their jobs is excessive politics. A full 75 percent of the people surveyed during the research for this book said they believed the level of trust in their management had deteriorated over the past two years; and that office politics and employee tensions had increased. The result, many claimed, is an environment less conducive to good work and good working relationships. In our opinion, this is a startling statistic and one that suggests any number of troubling trends.

Company politics has always been a factor, particularly in larger organizations where there is an ongoing rivalry among departments for higher budgets, better assignments, and favored positions. This is aggravated by competition for promotion, advancement, and control within the employee ranks.

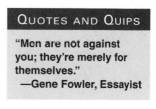

QUOTES AND QUIPS

"Men are not against you; they're merely for themselves."
—Gene Fowler, Essayist

Some executives encourage this type of competition on the mistaken notion that it will motivate each of the competitors for higher positions to be more creative and productive. Sometimes this does happen, but often the creativity is channeled into seeking ways to discredit rivals rather than promoting what is best for the company.

A few years ago the CEO of a major manufacturing company was nearing retirement and two of his senior vice presidents were under consideration to succeed him. The rivalry between them degenerated into a bitter conflict. Each man had his set of backers who knew that if their man were selected, they would personally benefit by more power, status, and financial reward. The two years preceding the decision were fraught with rancor, "dirty tricks," and even sabotage. When one of the competitors was finally chosen, the unsuccessful candidate and several of his key supporters resigned. It took years for the company to recover.

Most company politics may not be as traumatic as this, but petty politics destroys morale, reduces productivity and is a significant contributor to the loss of highly competent people, who may not be politically astute.

A More Lucrative Compensation Package

People have suspected for eons that the number one reason good people leave good firms is to accept a better compensation-related package. Not surprisingly, our interviews found this to be the case in a significant percentage of instances. "The simple fact is money still motivates," says Travis Jones, co-owner of *Personnel Consultants,* a temporary help services firm in Tulsa, Oklahoma, "especially when the package contains a large signing bonus and plenty of stock options. It's often just too much to resist."

> QUOTES AND QUIPS
>
> "What's money? A man is a success if he gets up in the morning and gets to bed at night and in between does what he wants to do."
> —Bob Dylan,
> Song writer

According to Jones, "Outstanding people today are clearly at a premium. It seems at times that there just aren't enough to go around, especially in hot areas like IT and healthcare. It's all supply and demand, with the worker winning most of the battles."

As pointed out in Chapter 8, the compensation package must be, at the least, in line with those of other companies in your industry and community if you want to attract and retain good people. However, just paying more than others will not necessarily result in lower turnover. Money is important, but unless the corporate culture meets the needs of employees, money alone is unlikely to keep them from leaving.

Feeling Used or "Exploited"

More serious than simply feeling unappreciated or unchallenged, we were surprised by the number of departing employees who said that one of their key motivations for leaving was that they felt "used" or exploited by their companies recently. In many cases, this feeling had developed after a downsizing, or other effort to reduce costs or reassign work. Nearly 85 percent of those surveyed said they felt too much was being asked of them, and that work was not being distributed in a fair and equitable way. According to one outstanding supervisor with over twenty-five years of service at the same company, "extra work just always seemed to gravitate toward those with a reputation for efficiency and an ability to get things done. It started to seem as though the more you did the more the company expected. I just got tired of making twice the effort as the other guy."

Sally's experience exemplifies another form of exploitation. She had been an auditor for a retail chain for six years and had built up a reputation for her ability to pinpoint errors in sales reports. She told us "I just have one of those minds that focus on figures and when I scan a report, mistakes seem to just pop up. Twice during the last two years I worked there, I was by-passed for a promotion. When I asked why, I was told I was too valuable as an auditor. I told them that superiority in my present job should warrant a promotion, but the company ignored it. When it happened a third time, I quit."

Concern About the Future of the Firm

In addition to losing faith in one or more bosses, another frequent reason good people give for leaving their jobs is a declining faith in the performance and viability of the firm itself. This has become particularly prevalent in a high percentage of "dot-coms" and other high-risk, new economy ventures. Many departing employees responding to our surveys said that although they often liked the people they were working with and the nature of the work they were doing, these considerations were tempered by the doubts they had about the "survivability" of the firm. Interestingly, a majority of those involved in the riskiest situations (often a dot-com in dire need of capitalization) said a kind of transient mental-ity seemed to actually impart itself on the corporate culture. "Nobody wants to be teth-ered to a sinking ship," says Dr. Edward Verlander, president of E.G. Verlander & As-sociates, "and in many cases terrifically good people develop an instinct that seems to in-dicate to them when it's time to go."

> **QUOTES AND QUIPS**
>
> **It's so much easier to suggest solutions when you don't know too much about the problem.**
> **—Malcolm Forbes, Publisher**

A similar situation occurs when a company announces that it is closing a plant or even going out of business. Quite often, it's es-sential that they maintain a workforce to cover work in progress and fill customers' orders during the final stages. How can they re-tain workers who feel they should be out looking for new jobs and preparing for the future?

Many companies faced with this situation offer bonuses to workers who remain with the company until they are no longer needed. This works if the employee feels that getting the extra money makes up for the extra time it may take to find a new job. However, when jobs are scarce in the community or in the indus-try, many people choose to take what's available immediately rather than risk not getting a job later on.

When a major aircraft manufacturer in California acquired a former competitor in New York, they planned to close a good por-tion of the New York facility. It would take from six to nine months to accomplish this and they needed many key workers to remain for that period. Those workers who were asked to stay were given bonuses, plus promises of jobs in the California plant, if they wished to relocate. For those who chose not to relocate, they re-tained an out-placement organization to try to place them with local firms who were willing to wait until they were released and to work with those who hadn't been placed until they found new positions. This resulted in a smooth transition.

Departure or Retirement of a Close Colleague

Although it's seldom mentioned as a leading factor in a decision to change jobs, organizational psychologists have known for a long time that the departure or retirement of a trusted colleague can result in significant reductions in morale and enthusiasm among those remaining. According to Dr. Raymond Harrison, a clinical psychologist and the president of Executive Transformetrics in Princeton, New Jersey, "the retirement or departure of a close colleague can stimulate a kind of grieving process in some people, and even lead to symptoms of depression. In some ways, it's akin to the feelings many people get when a close friend moves to another neighborhood, or, in more extreme cases, when a child goes off to college."

According to our research there actually seems to be a very direct relationship between the exiting of a trusted colleague and increasing levels of discontent among those remaining. In fact, we found that in about fifty percent of the cases, the person most affected by the departure also chose to leave within two years.

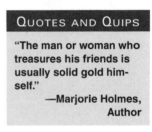

QUOTES AND QUIPS

"The man or woman who treasures his friends is usually solid gold himself."

—Marjorie Holmes, Author

A More Flexible Benefits Package

Another top reason good people leave their jobs has to do with their company-sponsored benefits. As recently as just a few years ago it was very unusual to see a company venturing out too far beyond the standard fare in health and retirement packages. Today, it's not at all unusual to see people being offered all sorts of perks and conveniences specially customized to their individual lifestyles and preferences. As pointed out in Chapter 8, items like flextime, flex benefits, childcare allowances, telecommuting, dress down days, first-class airline travel and generous stock options are far more common today than ever before.

"Companies have recognized the need to get more creative in their packaging of benefits," says HR consultant Pam Bradley, "they've been forced to react to a shift in the wishes of workers in much the same way as they'd react to a shift in the wishes of customers."

ADDITIONAL REASONS

In addition to the reasons expressed in our survey, we picked up some of the following complaints in the post-exit interviews we conducted for several clients, six months after separation. (See Chapter 11.)

Career Stagnation

Studies over the past few years have verified that most employees today don't expect to stay with the same company all of their lives. They'll change jobs if they feel it will help them meet their career goals. We frequently heard such comments as:

Figure 10-1 _____

Percentages of Surveyed "Outstanding" Employees Who Listed Each Item Among the Top Four Reasons for Their Resignations

LOSS OF FAITH IN MANAGEMENT	74%
FEELING UNAPPRECIATED	67%
FEELING BORED OR UNCHALLENGED	54%
A HIGHLY POLITICIZED WORKPLACE	50%
A MORE LUCRATIVE COMPENSATION PACKAGE	50%
FEELING USED OR "EXPLOITED"	41%
CONCERN ABOUT THE FUTURE OF THE FIRM	38%
DEPARTURE OR RETIREMENT OF A CLOSE COLLEAGUE	30%
A MORE FLEXIBLE BENEFITS PACKAGE	25%

- "The job was not leading to where I want to go."
- "There was no opportunity to advance at that company."
- "I have more talent than was being used on that job."
- "I was not given the type of training I needed to prepare for advancement."
- "The company's promotion policy was based on seniority not capability."

It's not always possible for an employee's career goals and a company's needs to be congruent. However, in many cases accommodation can be made to bring these closer together.

A good example is how the Comprehensive Insurance Co. kept one of its "A-players," Richard B. Richard was hired as a trainee when he graduated from N.Y.U. in 1993 with a degree in accounting. Over the first few years of his tenure, he acquired experience in several departments and five years later headed an underwriting team. He took advantage of the company's tuition reimbursement program and in 1998, achieved his MBA with a concentration on Information Technology. At his annual review that year, he expressed interest in moving into a division of the company in which his newly acquired training could be used. His boss pointed out that he was scheduled for a promotion in the underwriting department that could lead to a senior management position and persuaded Richard to accept the new job. Although he was successful in this advanced position, he was not happy. He planned to begin a search for a job in IT, but first he went to see the human resources manager, with whom he had established a personal friendship.

"Tom," he said, "I really like this company, but my real interest is in information technology. What should I do?" Tom pointed out that the company was planning to establish an e-marketing department. Although they were seeking people already experienced in that field, Tom persuaded the new department's manager to see Richard. The result: a transfer to the new department, where Richard has already contributed to its early successes.

> **TACTICAL TIPS**
>
> Learn the career goals of your "A players" and find ways to help them meet them in your company.

Unsatisfactory Company Practices

Another common cause of employee discontent is a poor work-ing environment. This may take a variety of forms.

Unreasonable working hours

Employees are often required to work longer hours than they really want to work. Sure, there are many workers who seek the oppor-tunity to earn overtime pay, but others would prefer to put in fewer hours. And, when the employee is in the exempt category, there is usually no added compensation for the extra hours.

Adding additional staff so overtime isn't needed, or making all overtime voluntary are ideal solutions, but unfortunately, not al-ways practical. Some companies pay their exempt workers over-time bonuses. This often alleviates the objections to working the added hours, but it is expensive. Often, better planning and more efficient techniques can help overcome this problem.

Unpleasant working environment

There's no question that a pleasant working environment is con-ducive to high morale and better productivity. But let's be realistic. There are many workplaces that by their very nature are dirty, noisy, or reek with unpleasant odors. Some of this may be allevi-ated. Dirty spaces can be spruced up by better waste control, a new paint job or other forms of "beautification." Noise can some-times be reduced by soundproofing or providing ear protectors such as those worn by workers in airports. Some chemical com-panies have found ways to minimize the bad odors that emanate from their processes.

One of our clients, a large financial institution, raised the morale of its staff (and reduced turnover) by replacing the tradi-tional cubicles, which many employees considered like jail cells, with work stations in which several people were grouped as teams and the spaces separated by planters.

Lack of "state of the art" equipment

Another complaint frequently received in our exit interviews was the failure of the company to use the most effective equipment. These included the accountant whose company was still using IBM punch-card type computers, the chemist who worked in a lab that was still using the equipment that they purchased when they were founded 20 years ago, and the HR Manager who had to maintain a personnel card-index for 3500 employees.

True, some workers are so accustomed to working "the old way," that they rebel at installing new equipment; but your "A-players" insist that they be provided with the best equipment available so they can keep at the cutting edge of their professions.

Bureaucratic bog down

"It took weeks to get a decision. I had to go to three committees before I could even present my programs to management." Organizational red tape plagues many companies. Many successful organizations have reduced red tape by evaluating and redesigning their policies and procedures. "A-players" want results and you won't keep them if bureaucratic stalling frustrates them.

Personal Work Preferences

If an employee can work in the manner with which he or she is most comfortable, that person will be more productive. Some people prefer to work in collaborative teams; others prefer to be given specific directions; still others want the autonomy that goes with working alone. It's not possible to please everyone, but it pays to learn about the work-style preferences of employees and, where possible, to place them accordingly.

Working Schedules

Another often-reported reason for leaving is not the number of hours worked, but the work schedule. Many companies work on shifts. In some, the employees always work the same shift: day, evening, or sometimes in companies that work 24-hour days, the midnight-to-dawn shift. In other companies, shifts are rotated so each worker takes a turn at each shift. In still other organizations, they work split shifts. For example, school bus drivers may work from 7 A.M. to 9 A.M. to bring the children to school and then again from 2 P.M. to 4 P.M. to take them home.

In selecting people for shift-type jobs, it is essential that they are made aware of your company's policies and are amenable to the shift assignments. Most, but not all, companies pay higher rates to workers on the night or midnight shifts. Turnover increases when shifts are arbitrarily changed or changed too often.

In order to accommodate employees who wish to vary the hours they work, many companies have established flexible hour or flextime programs. A great many companies allow employees to select the time they start and end work from a varied menu. Some people may work from 8 to 4; others 9 to 5; still others 10 to 6. All staff is on duty during the greater part of the workday—from 10 A.M. to 4 P.M. This enables people to take care of personal matters such as getting kids off to school before leaving for work, being home after school, or coordinating work schedules with a spouse. A survey by the Society for Human Resources Management noted that in 1998, 55 percent of the surveyed firms offered flextime, up from 42 percent in 1997.

Setting flexible hours is not always feasible. It won't work in situations where all workers are needed at the same time as in most manufacturing operations. It also creates problems when the early arrivers need information or material from people who are scheduled to come in later—holding up work. But in a great number of situations this can be worked out.

Supervisors and team leaders whose members come in and leave at different times have special problems in coordinating their work. Staff meetings, which in companies with traditional hours are usually held in early morning or late afternoon, must be scheduled for mid-day—not always a convenient time as it often interrupts work in progress. The manager has the added problem of communicating with staff members on matters that arise when they are not on duty. Most serious is that the supervisors don't work from 8 to 6. They are not around to lead, guide, and assist members on schedules different from theirs. To deal with this, supervisors should:

- Establish clear-cut policies concerning matters that, based on experience, are likely to develop when you are not around.
- Give staff members authority to make decisions that are needed in your absence.
- Be available by telephone at all times. (Here's where your cell phone comes in handy).
- Vary your shift. (Come in early some days, late others.)

Work-Life Programs

One of the latest tools employers are increasingly turning to are work/life programs that assist employees with balancing the demands of their personal and professional lives. According to human resource consultants Hewitt Associates, employees are concerned about not having enough time to take care of those very important family and personal needs.

The answer is to develop programs that combine the personal needs of employees with the demands of their jobs. More and more companies are introducing work/life programs. It has resulted in greater employee loyalty, higher morale and productivity, and most important, a significant reduction in employee turnover. A survey by *Working Mother* magazine and the Work & Family Connection Inc. reported that 70 percent of surveyed employees at a manufacturing company said they remained with their company because of its work/life benefits. And 60 percent of workers surveyed at another large employer reported that the ability to balance work with personal and family responsibilities was "of great importance" in their decision to stay with the company.

In addition, several studies have noted the link between work/life programs and employee productivity. Hewitt Associates reported that work/life initiatives enable employees to better manage their life responsibilities, and as a result, they can be more focused and productive at work. For example, the Scott Paper Co. reported that work/life programs and other efforts to support employees increased productivity by 35 percent. In our own discussions with employees of our clients, we frequently were told that employees value work/life balance assistance more than money, location and advancement potential.

Successful companies are reaping more than financial rewards from work/life programs. Work/life balance solutions contribute significantly to the characteristics common to *Fortune*'s 100 Best Companies in America by creating a company culture and environment that give greater consideration to their employees' quality of life. Among the companies that have introduced work/life programs are Microsoft, Hewlett-Packard and Charles Schwab.

Employers aren't the only ones becoming more aware of the advantages of tools that enhance their employees' quality of life. A survey by *Fast Company* magazine and Roper Starch Worldwide reported that 89 percent of college-educated, employed adults strongly believe that employers should be mindful of the need to balance their employees' work and personal lives. Companies that recognize this will benefit by having staff members that reward them, through their loyalty and productivity.

The Boss

Over and over again in our surveys, our exit interviews, and in our informal discussions, one of the frequently reported sources of discontent was the boss. Even the word "boss" has a negative connotation. The adjective "bossy" is defined as "commanding, domineering, or overbearing." Sure, there are people who prefer to work for a boss who'll tell them what to do and how to do it, but most creative and productive people resent dominance and rebel against it. How poor leadership affects employees and what can be done to overcome this will be discussed in Chapter 12.

Another complaint about bosses is that they often tolerate mediocre performance. Good, diligent workers resent co-workers

who don't pull their own weight. When two top producers left the
Brooklyn Distribution Center, an industrial tools wholesaler, last
year, we were asked to conduct six-month post-separation interviews. One woman commented that she took her job seriously and
put in long hours and produced over and above what was required.
There were other workers in the department who put out minimum effort. In order to meet the department's quota, she had to
work even harder to make up for what the slackers were not doing.
When she complained to the department head, he shrugged it off
with "That's the best they can do."

The other worker told a similar story. She went out of her way
to produce quality work, even to the point of redoing sloppy work
done by co-workers. She even volunteered to help them become
more efficient, but was not supported by the department head. So
long as everybody showed up for work each day, he was satisfied.

EMPLOYEE LOYALTY

According to several recent studies, employees throughout the
world share a low level of loyalty and commitment and a dwindling
level of faith in their organizations' ethics
and leaders. The studies show that only one-
third of all employees are truly loyal to their
organizations. In addition, only one-third of
worldwide employees believe their organization is highly ethical, and only six in 10 believe their senior leaders are people of high
integrity.

> QUOTES AND QUIPS
>
> "To build trust, you must
> be seen as a collabora-
> tor, not a competitor."
> —*Across the Board*

Sources of Employee Loyalty

The surveys were designed to measure employee perceptions
of their loyalty and commitment to their jobs, and the effect company ethics have on employee loyalty. The survey did not measure employee satisfaction, but rather employee commitment and
loyalty.

The surveys showed that an employee's job performance was directly related to the level of commitment to the company. The research showed that employers everywhere needed to focus on building relationships with their workers so that these employees could feel truly loyal to their organization and believe they are a valued part of the enterprise.

The major areas workers wanted their employers to address are fairness at work, care and concern for employees, and trust in employees. Other workforce factors that influenced employees' commitment to their workplaces were satisfaction with day-to-day activities, and the organization's reputation. Employers need to understand what drives the loyalty and commitment of their employees.

Other findings included:

- Slightly more than half of employees surveyed felt a strong personal attachment to their organizations.

- Slightly more than half of employees surveyed said they believed their employers show them genuine care and concern.

- Fifty percent said they believe their organizations cared about developing people for the long term, not just their current jobs.

- One-third of worldwide employees did not believe their organizations are highly ethical.

- Only six in 10 believe their senior leaders have high personal integrity.

The downsizing that pervaded the economy in the 1980s and 1990s has exacerbated the loss of employee loyalty, and the increase in mergers and acquisitions has diluted the identification employees often had made with their organizations. Loyal workers, experts say, not only express a desire to stay with an employer but also are highly productive and proud of the company and its service principles.

Generating High Levels of Employee Loyalty

It should come as no surprise that there are few things more valuable to an organization than capable employees with a strong sense of loyalty to the firm. IBM was famous for it for years, as was Procter & Gamble and General Motors. More recently, companies like Intel, Nortel and Dell Computer have caught the bug and added it to their lists of key strategic goals for the future.

Webster defines loyalty as *faithfulness to commitments or obligations.* The implication, of course, is that this faithfulness comes from a deep-seated belief in something—in this case, a belief in the mission and vision of the enterprise.

So how can a company, or more precisely, a company executive concerned about morale and turnover rates contribute to the building of loyalty? For answers to this we looked to various research studies, including those conducted as a part of the research for this book. The following is a review of what we believe to be the nine biggest influencers on the building of employee loyalty, listed in their order of importance.

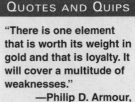

QUOTES AND QUIPS

"There is one element that is worth its weight in gold and that is loyalty. It will cover a multitude of weaknesses."
—Philip D. Armour, Business executive

1. The behavior and reputation of management

Study after study has found that the single most important factor in determining whether or not an employee stays loyal to his or her firm is the credibility and reputation of management. In fact, nearly 80 percent of those interviewed for this and other projects listed it among their top four reasons for deciding either to stay or to leave a company.

2. A clear, well-conceived mission and vision

The second biggest contributor to high levels of worker loyalty is the extent to which the organization develops and promotes a clear, well-conceived mission and vision. This may be surprising to some, given all of the attention paid to mission and vision statements in recent years; however, it's important to keep in mind that the secret lies not in the writing of the statements, but in an ability to communicate their significance and convince others of their importance and validity.

3. A habit of recognizing and rewarding exceptional performance

An overwhelming majority of outstanding organizations with high retention rates and high levels of worker loyalty place a very high premium on recognizing and rewarding outstanding performance. According to some, in addition to its effect on loyalty, this practice also remains one of the two or three most powerful ways of building trust and enthusiasm, topics we talk about in other portions of this book.

4. The reputation of the firm

Numerous surveys of people considered *highly employable* have suggested that they often attach a great deal of importance to the "reputation" enjoyed by a current or potential employer when deciding among competing offers. According to Grant Lehman, an executive recruiter with over twenty-five years of experience, "great people like to work for great firms. I'm often asked by outstanding prospective hires for evidence of a company's commitment to specific causes, or even for a list of recent articles that help shed light on the values of the organization. This rarely happened as recently as ten years ago, and clearly suggests that as opportunities for outstanding people increase, so too does their interest in making selections based on values and reputation."

5. A focus on building pride

Nearly all of the best, most stable companies we've seen over the years have placed a great deal of emphasis on communicating the achievements and positive attributes of the organization. Unlike so many others, they don't leave things like this to the grapevine or to chance. Companies with high levels of worker loyalty all seem to recognize the critical nature of constantly reminding people, if only in subtle ways, why the company is both good and a good place to work. The result, of course, is a kind of organizational pride that can be both quite pervasive and highly motivating.

QUOTES AND QUIPS
"An ounce of loyalty is worth a pound of cleverness."
—Elbert Hubbard, American essayist

6. A sense of long-term viability

The simple fact is that most people will always look for indications of both strength and weakness in their organizations, and use what they find as a way of predicting whether or not the firm remains a good bet for long-term employment and/or advancement. This is particularly true during strong economic times when good jobs are plentiful and good people are more inclined to consider moving from company to company.

One of our clients, a not-too-well-known "old economy" company found it difficult to retain bright young technical staff. These high-in-demand people were tempted by the excitement and growth potential of "new economy" start-ups. To overcome this we recommended an ongoing internal public relations program that reinforced the major advantages of staying with this firm. It included articles in the company paper about the history, reputation, and financial stability of the organization, one-to-one discussions with employees about their career opportunities with the company and discussions of the firm's long-term goals. The result was amazing. Not only did the target group resist the enticements from headhunters, but became so enthusiastic about the company that they became active recruiters for new technical staff.

Another successful approach to building loyalty is that of Nationwide Insurance Company, which offers its 30,000 employees team-building classes, intranets, newsletters, and an anonymous "ethics office" through which they can express themselves and resolve worries and conflicts.

7. Opportunity for growth

Another major contributor to building worker loyalty is the providing of growth opportunities. Recent surveys by the American Society for Training & Development (ASTD) have shown that company-sponsored training and other developmental pursuits is consistently listed among the top four or five biggest motivators of workers between the ages of 25 and 35. This will be discussed in more detail in Chapter 13.

8. Opportunity for promotion

The opportunity for professional advancement is also a very impor-

> **QUOTES AND QUIPS**
>
> **"Think not those faithful who praise all thy words and actions, but those who kindly reprove thy faults."**
>
> **—Socrates**

tant factor in the building and sustaining of worker loyalty. Despite all the emphasis on teamwork, flattened organization charts, and pay-for-performance compensation plans, most people are still very interested in titles, the chance to earn "promotions," and the increases in pay that often accompany them.

9. A commitment to driving out fear and minimizing politics

This final item could just as easily be one of the top two or three in our view. It's just that important. In fact, we know of nothing more destructive to an organizational culture, and indeed, the ability of an organization to attract and retain good people, than a highly politicized, fear-filled work environment. Over the years we've seen companies virtually destroyed because of "management by fear." Threats of job loss were explicit or implied in every assignment. During periods of job shortages, workers would tolerate this environment, but tolerance alone does not breed enthusiasm and commitment. And when the job market opened up, employees left in droves.

PREVENTIVE MAINTENANCE

Supervisors and team leaders should make retaining "A-players" a high priority. It will take months or even years to recover from the loss of a key employee. Here are some suggestions:

- Be alert. If you wait until the dissatisfaction becomes overt, you've waited too long. You must know your staff members well enough to sense problems before they are expressed and take action to resolve them.

- Re-recruit your "A-players." These people are the cornerstone of your team. Don't take them for granted. Make them feel important. Make a point to resell them on the company, the department, and their job. Spend as much time and effort on this as you would in recruiting a new staff member.

- Incorporate your employees into the organizational culture. Make them feel that they are an integral part of the company by giving them opportunity to express their ideas, to participate in decisions affecting their work and most importantly, build up their emotional commitment to their job.

SUM AND SUBSTANCE

- To reduce loss of key people, identify specific problems that an employee may have that might lead to voluntary separation and take steps to alleviate them.

- One of the main reasons good people leave their jobs is a loss of faith in management.

- Another major reason good people give for leaving their jobs is a sense that their efforts and contributions are not appreciated enough.

- Boredom and a sense of having "stagnated" at work is another major reason good people give for resigning.

- 75 percent of the people surveyed during the research for this book said they believed the level of trust in their management had deteriorated over the past two years; and that office politics and employee tensions had increased.

- The compensation package must be, at the least, in line with those of other companies in your industry and community if you want to attract and retain good people. However, just paying more than others will not necessarily result in lower turnover. Money is important, but unless the corporate culture meets the needs of employees, money alone is unlikely to keep them from leaving.

- Most employees today don't expect to stay with the same company all of their lives. They'll change jobs if they feel it will help them meet their career goals.

- Creative benefits packages offer many employees incentive to stay with an organization.

- Flexible hours and setting up programs to enhance the work/life balance is another way to retain good people.

- Job performance is directly related to the level of commitment to the company. Employers need to focus on building relationships with their workers so these employees could feel truly loyal to their organization and believe they are a valued part of the enterprise.

11

Making the Separation Interview Meaningful

Nothing is more frustrating to a supervisor than having a top-producing associate quit. It has often taken months or years to bring that person up to optimum productivity—and now suddenly he or she leaves. Not only does this disrupt the momentum of the team's work, but also it has negative effects on the other members—unless, of course, the person who quit is universally disliked.

WHY EMPLOYEES SAY "I QUIT."

When you ask the person why he or she quit, often the answer will be that it's for personal reasons. Carl decided to go back to college; Vicki's chosen to be a full-time mother; Sam's father's illness requires him to take over his business; Jane's spouse is transferred to another city.

The answer also may indicate a career move: Ben has gone as far as he can in your company; Geri is offered more money by another firm; an opportunity arises in a different field—one in which Tom is particularly interested; Hilary's going into her own business.

But often the reason given is not totally true. Yes, Tom did go to an industry in which he has particular interest, but would he have made that decision if he were obtaining job satisfaction in his current job? Geri is leaving for more money. Sure, she would like more money, but perhaps she wouldn't have even looked for a job if she were not unhappy with the supervisor's management style.

Probing for the Real Reasons

Every time someone quits, it's important to determine the true reason. This isn't easy because it may not even be clear to the person who leaves. It may be deeply imbedded in the culture of the company and subtly has made the person discontent.

QUOTES AND QUIPS

"Speaking or writing without thinking is like shooting without aiming."
—Arnold Glasow, Author

People may feel they are not making the progress they had hoped for, that their salary is too low, that working conditions are unsatisfactory, or that the job has become boring. Some are reluctant to divulge the real reason for deciding to quit. This is particularly true if the real cause of discontent lies with the supervisor or other employees.

When Should the Separation Interview Be Conducted?

Too often companies do not know why they lose good employees. Exit or separation interviews are designed to probe for the real reasons people leave a job and to obtain from the employee information about the job or the company that may cause discontent.

Traditionally, separation interviews are conducted as part of the exit processing. The employee is given the final paycheck, advised of the status of benefits, and the paperwork is completed. He or she may then be asked in a formal or informal way a series of questions to determine the reason for leaving.

There are several serious problems in this procedure. Is this the most appropriate time to obtain this important information? The major objective of the separation interview is to learn, not so much why the employee has quit, but as much as possible about the conditions that caused the employee to make the decision to quit.

But even well-structured interviews may not bring out the pertinent facts if conducted at the time of separation. Employees who leave may be reluctant to tell the whole story at that time. Often they are still too close to the company culture to evaluate it objectively. Sometimes they are concerned that anything negative that they say might be held against them and be reflected in the references the company may be requested to provide. Some people are just reluctant to get into a situation that can become unpleasant.

Some companies have found that conducting interviews with former employees six to eight months after they have left the organization elicits much more meaningful information than the traditional exit interview. The employee has had a chance to reflect on his or her experience with that firm; concern about hurting the feelings of a former supervisor or fear of reprisal has been lessened. In addition, comparison with the new job gives them a sounder basis for judgment.

Over the past few years the authors conducted an informal test of this concept. We took a random sample of employees who had left their jobs during a six- to twelve-month period prior to our test, re-interviewed them and compared what we learned with what had been gleaned from the interview conducted at the time they left.

In addition to the questions asked at the separation interview, we added several questions to amplify the responses and to draw on their experiences after leaving the company. (Examples of good questions to ask will be given later in this chapter.)

Although the original exit interviews had provided helpful information, the post-separation interviews added significant and valuable insights into those aspects of the job environment, corporate culture, and supervisory attitudes that were minimized at the time of separation.

For example, Sarah had stated that she was leaving to spend more time with her children. And she did—for three months. Then Sarah found another job and is now working full time again. When queried, she commented that her creativity and capabilities were never appreciated at the job she left and she felt she would be better off attending to her parental activities. However, after a few months she became bored and now has a job she loves. She commented that if her former employer had utilized her capabilities, she would never have considered leaving.

Another respondent, Peter, had told his former company at the exit interview that his only reason for leaving was financial. He took a job that paid more. At our follow-up interview, he confided that making more money was important, and although he liked the former company, their compensation program was based more on seniority than on performance. "It would have taken me several years to reach my financial goals there." When asked why he didn't bring this up at the exit interview, he responded that it wouldn't have made any difference because the company culture was old-fashioned and they were not amenable to listening to suggestions.

Former employees of one company all told of discontent due to the domination of the organization by an "inner circle" that ran the company as dictators. All feared that if they even mentioned that at the exit interview, it would mitigate against them and their friends who remained with the firm.

Does this mean that exit interviews should be delayed for six months? Not necessarily. A well-conducted separation interview can give the company much insight into how employees view the organization and can even point out critical areas which must be corrected immediately such as violations of various laws. But, to obtain a substantial and profound analysis of what really has precipitated the former employee to even think about leaving the company, a follow-up interview six months after leaving would be well worthwhile.

How to conduct the follow-up interview and what questions should be asked will be discussed later in this chapter.

> QUOTES AND QUIPS
>
> **"The trouble with people is not that they don't know, but that they know so much that ain't so."**
> —Josh Billings,
> American humorist

Questions to Ask at the Initial Separation Interview

We have witnessed a number of exit interviews in which the questions were of such a superficial nature that no significant information was developed. In order to get meaningful information that will enable the company to identify and correct problems that have caused turnover, a well-structured interview must be conducted.

The immediate supervisor of the person who is leaving should *not* conduct this interview. It's best that a more objective individual such as a member of the human resources staff or another manager conduct it.

Just as in an employment or appraisal interview, it is best to start a separation interview by building rapport. The process should begin with a general type of question that will not put the employee on the defensive. The question of why he or she is leaving the company should never be the first one asked. A better start might be: "Tell me about the kind of work you've been doing in your most recent assignment." This will get the conversation going, but will also enable the interviewer to evaluate whether this is the kind of work one might expect to do in that job. One reason people leave jobs is because it was not what they thought they'd be doing. A market researcher might be spending all her time on statistical compilations when she expected to be doing depth analyses.

Here are some important questions that should be asked in a separation interview and some clues as to what should be looked for to interpret the responses.

TACTICAL TIPS
To make the separation interview truly meaningful, use the suggested questions as guidelines. Reframe the questions to meet the specific situation of the person being interviewed. After each response, ask follow-up questions to elicit additional information.

Questions About the Job

What did you like most and least about the job?

Are these job factors or personal factors? The answer provides insight into the job by the pattern of answers obtained from people who leave it.

How do you feel about your compensation?

Many people leave their jobs for another with higher pay. Others feel they should have made more money even though they were being paid the going rate for the work. Taking this into consideration, evaluate the answers to this question in light of the equity of the company's pay scale, the methods used to give pay increases and whether the firm's compensation adjustment system is being properly implemented. This will also enable the interviewer to compare the methods used to give increases with other companies in your area or your industry.

How do you feel about the progress you've made in this company?

A good number of people claim they have left their jobs because of lack of opportunity for advancement. Often this masks the real reasons for leaving. However, it's important to examine what a person might have expected in terms of growth in the company and relate it to the real opportunity for advancement in the job she or he held. This might indicate poor selection or placement practices. Often companies seek people who are overqualified for jobs because they insist that all employees be potential managers. Unfortunately, the opportunity to reach that goal may be much too limited. As a result, the employee becomes impatient or disillusioned and leaves. If failure to make progress shows up often in exit interviews, it may be a signal for the company to reevaluate its hiring standards, training programs and career pathing.

How do you feel about working conditions?

Companies have picked up information from this question about matters that were unimportant in their eyes, but annoyed employees to the point of causing them to leave. Often these are easily correctable.

Questions About Supervision

What did you like most (least) about your supervisor's style of managing?

As many of the problems existing in organizational life are due to problems with supervisors, it's important to probe this factor, particularly if there is a large turnover in that department. It will bring out whether the supervisor is dogmatic, stubborn, or authoritarian, and whether he or she encourages participation. Probe further to learn about how the supervisor dealt with complaints. Some leaders tend to be defensive and take any complaint as a personal affront; others take time out to discuss even the most farfetched grievances. It also helps bring out the good points of each supervisor or team leader so that they can be reinforced when reporting the information back to the leader.

Does your team leader or supervisor tend to favor some employees or act unfairly to others?

Favoritism on one hand and bias on the other are major causes of discontent. The question can also point up blatant areas of cronyism or at the other extreme, prejudice and discrimination. If this bias is based on racial, religious, national origin, gender, or age factors, it might alert you to serious potential legal problems and give the organization a chance to correct them.

Other than your immediate supervisor or team leader, what has been your experience in dealing with other leaders or managers?

This provides an opportunity to get feedback about other persons in leadership positions in the organization from the viewpoint of an employee who is not a direct subordinate. This may give insight into other problems that may cause turnover that is not directly related to the employee's supervisor. For example, the major cause of turnover in one firm was due to the arrogant behavior of the team leader's boss, who vetoed team member's innovative ideas after the team leader had approved them.

> ### TACTICAL TIPS
>
> **The team leader or supervisor of the employee who is leaving cannot conduct an unbiased, objective separation interview. A member of the Human Resources department, another management-level person, or an outside consultant should conduct the interview.**

Additional Questions to Uncover Special Problems

What might have been done differently here?

A frank answer to this question will bring out some of the real reasons he or she was not happy in the job and may give you insight into aspects of the company environment of which you were not aware.

What would have made you stay longer?

When one of my clients asked this of a highly competent technician, he was shocked to learn that the employee had discussed his discontent several times with his supervisor, had been promised the problems would be resolved, and then nothing was ever done.

Questions to Sum Up the Interview

If you could discuss with top management exactly how you feel about this company, what would you tell them?

This open-ended question often results in some interesting insights. Let the person talk freely. Avoid leading questions that might influence the response. Encourage him or her to express real feelings, attitudes, suggestions, problems, fear, and hopes about the organization.

If the applicant has accepted a job with another company, ask:

What does your new job offer you that you were not getting here?

The answer may repeat some of the facts already brought out, but it may also uncover some of the ways the firm failed to meet the person's hopes, goals, or expectations.

If the answers to the above questions have not brought out the true reasons for the employee's leaving, ask specifically:

Why are you leaving at this particular time?

Some of the problems that have come out at the interview may have been in existence for a long time. Some of them have seemed unimportant until now. Find out what precipitated the resignation at this time. Have things become worse? Is there anything that can be recommended to management that will prevent them from becoming even more serious and causing more turnover?

A good separation interview can take an hour or more, but it can provide insight into how employees who have quit really feel about the organization, how these negatives can be overcome, and how the positive aspects of the work environment can be reinforced.

Questions for Short-Term Employees

Inasmuch as a great deal of turnover occurs during the first months of employment, it's especially important to investigate this problem. It may reflect on your hiring practices, your training programs, your orientation process or the possibility that prospective employees are being oversold on the job. Here are some questions to ask people who leave within sixty days after being hired.

When you first started here what impressed you most about the company? In what way did this change? Why?

Most people starting a new job are very enthusiastic and excited about it. Many look upon it as a challenge and an opportunity. Unfortunately, some are disillusioned almost immediately; others remain positive and optimistic for a while, but it doesn't take long for them to face the realities of the situation. Their excitement fades, their optimism turns to pessimism; they believe they made a mistake in accepting the job and choose to quit to move to a more satisfying position. By identifying the factors that caused this, corrections might be made that could prevent early turnover in the future.

How fully was your job explained to you before you accepted it? When you started work? When you were trained to do it?

Each area of explanation should be complete. The human resources department should have given the applicant enough information to assure that he or she understood what he or she was hired to do. The orientation procedure should have given the new employee more detail about the job and the company. The training specialist or supervisor should have taught the employee precisely what had to be done. Many of the causes of discontent stem from failure of the organization to clearly explain the nature of the job and to assure that the new employee fully understands it.

Tell me about the job you held before coming to this company. What aspects of that job did you enjoy doing as compared with what you were assigned to do with our firm?

From the answer to this question, you can determine possible areas of failure in the hiring procedure. If this had been carefully explored in the selection interview, the company might have saved itself the expense, trouble and disruption of hiring a person who would not find job satisfaction in the position offered.

When did you begin to feel that you had made a mistake in taking this job? What happened at that time to cause that feeling?

Often there is one precipitating factor that starts the downward slide in an employee's attitude about the job. It may be the manner in which a supervisor or team leader deals with the new person; it may be a comment by another employee that initiates negative thoughts; it may be a specific assignment. Probe to find this factor. However, often it isn't one thing, but a general feeling of discontent. Try to determine what caused it. Ask:

You commented that you just weren't happy here. Can you tell me what it was about the organization that made you feel discontent?

What you are attempting here is to obtain the employee's take on the corporate culture. This may be the key to general discontent and you must probe carefully and cautiously to get to the root causes. Follow up on every comment. For example:

Employee: "I felt I was looked upon as an outsider. Even though my skills were as good or better than my teammates, they never asked my opinion and cut me short when I made suggestions."

Interviewer: "I can understand your frustration. Did all your teammates do this?"

Employee: "Some of the guys and gals were okay. But the team was really dominated by Chuck L. He's one of those know-it-alls and the other members are in awe of him. They don't dare contradict him, as he gets very sarcastic. They agree with his ideas openly or just keep quiet rather than offend him. After I was squelched a few times, I complained to the team leader, but he seemed afraid to intervene. All he's interested in is avoiding confrontation and getting the work out."

Often the cause is more ambiguous. It's not caused by any one factor but by a general climate. For example, at one company employees left during the first few months because they felt they were always under pressure. At another firm, employees left because it was too bureaucratic. At still another organization, newly hired people felt they were not given enough guidance.

At one high-tech company, the great need was for creative men and women who could take the initiative and work independently on projects. Yet, the culture of the company only gave lip service to this concept. Although told at the interviews that their creativity would be utilized, during the first six months on the job they were kept under very strict control. Innovative ideas were discouraged until "they learned the ropes." Unfortunately, some of the most creative and intelligent individuals became impatient, and when their ideas were ignored, they quit.

As a result of a series of in-depth exit interviews with short-term employees, the company adjusted its policies to fit the individual needs of new people—enabling them to "learn the ropes" more rapidly and to build into their training opportunities to use their creativity during the training.

THE SIX-MONTH POST-SEPARATION INTERVIEW

As noted earlier in this chapter, interviews conducted six months after an employee leaves can often provide very meaningful information. The post-separation interview can be conducted in several ways.

1. By mail: A questionnaire is mailed to all former employees who have voluntarily left the company six months after leaving. Questions are asked similar to those asked at the time of separation. Other questions are added about the ex-employee's attitude about the company at this time. This is the least expensive approach, but it is also the least effective. In the author's test of this method, we received a 12-percent return on letters and most of the responses gave only cursory information. When follow-up calls were made to the respondents, much more valuable information was obtained.

2. By telephone: When interviews were conducted by telephone, using the questions listed below as a guide, the results were excellent.

3. In person. Meeting the ex-employee personally provided the most and best information, but it was time consuming, and expensive. A high percentage of the group we desired to interview was either unwilling or unable to meet with us.

4. Focus groups. Several ex-employees were invited to participate in a focus group. Each group consisted of six to ten former employees who met with the consultants to discuss their experience with and attitude toward their former organization. Respondents were paid an honorarium to participate. In a free-wheeling discussion, guided by a consultant, the participants gave vent to their positive and negative feelings about the organization. Much valuable input was obtained. However, focus groups are only feasible when there is a significantly large population of former employees.

Questions to Ask

Whether the interview is conducted in person or on the telephone, it should begin by thanking the individual for cooperating in the endeavor to identify the good and not-so-good aspects of their experience working for the client company.

Once rapport is established, begin by asking the same questions asked in the previous separation interview. Listen carefully. Compare the responses to those noted on the original interview form. Probe for additional information.

In addition, ask the following questions, fitting them in at appropriate places during the interview:

What are you getting from your present job that you didn't get at our company?

What are some of the things you liked about our company and are not getting in your current job?

From what you have learned in the months since you left our company, what would you suggest to us to make this a better place to work?

Would you consider taking another position in our company if such a position were available? If so, what type of job would interest you?

SUM AND SUBSTANCE

- Every time someone quits, it's important to determine the true reason. This isn't easy because it may not even be clear to the person who leaves. It may be deeply imbedded in the culture of the company and subtly has made the person discontent.

- The major objective of the separation interview is to learn not so much why the employee has quit, but as much as possible about the conditions that caused the employee to make the decision to quit.

- Even a well-structured interview may not bring out the pertinent facts if conducted at the time of separation. Some companies have found that conducting interviews with former employees six to eight months after they have left the organization elicits much more meaningful information than the traditional exit interview.

- Carefully prepare the questions you plan to ask at the separation interview to uncover not just reasons the employee is leaving but to seek the real underlying causes of discontent.

12

Leadership: A Key Factor in Retaining Good People

There seems very little doubt anymore of the direct relationship between the leadership style exhibited most often within an organization and the effectiveness with which that same organization attracts and retains outstanding people.

According to a recent report by the Saratoga Institute, 50 percent of work-life satisfaction is determined by the relationship a worker has with his or her boss. There is no question that the manager's style has a profound effect on retention. Study after study has shown that a person-centered, visionary, value-based approach almost always works better than the often dictatorial, fear-based, heavy-handed strategies of the past.

This was reinforced by a Gallup poll that showed that most workers rate having a caring boss even higher than they value money or fringe benefits. In interviews with two million employees at 700 companies, Gallup found that how long employees stay at a company and how productive they are there, is determined by the relationship with their immediate supervisor. "People join companies and leave managers," said Marcus Buckingham, a senior managing consultant at Gallup and the primary analyst for the study.

When job opportunities are plentiful, people with miserable bosses leave. In fact, they are four times more likely to leave than are people who respect their bosses. According to a survey conducted by Spherion, a staffing and consulting firm in Fort Lauderdale, Florida, and Lou Harris Associates, only 11 percent of employees who rated their supervisor's performance as excellent

said they were likely to look for a job in the next year, while 40 percent of those who rated their supervisor's performance as poor were likely to jump ship.

Too often managers assume that their leadership style is working well when, in fact, it isn't working at all. One of the ways that you can use to measure your leadership status is the following leadership quiz (Figure 12-1). It's a relatively easy way to help focus on some of the key foundations of this very important topic.

The Leadership Quiz is based on over ten years of research and over fifty years of combined training and consulting experience. Why not take out a pen and a piece of paper and jot down your answer to each question? Our guess is you'll be surprised by at least a good part of what you learn.

SIGNS OF LEADERSHIP FAILURE

The relationship between good leadership and a sustained ability to retain top performers seems well-established in both the current literature and among business practitioners. Study after study has shown that one of the two or three most common reasons people give for leaving an organization is a loss of faith in management. Given that, it seems particularly important that well-intentioned managers and executives stay alert to the signs that valuable people may be becoming disenchanted with (here's a twist!) the performance or behavior of their *superiors*. On page 283 is a list of the telltale signs.

Figure 12-1 _____

The Leadership Quiz

Mark "True" or "False" next to each of the following items:

1. The *most common* characteristic among those recognized as outstanding leaders is an ability to inspire trust. _____

2. Good leaders most often emerge from the ranks of good followers. _____

3. Leadership ability seems to be more often acquired than inborn. _____

4. The development and demonstration of leadership skills is *most often* inspired by a passion of some type. _____

5. The development of leadership skills is often inspired by a misfortune, sacrifice, or injustice of some type. _____

6. Most people with outstanding leadership ability consider themselves extroverted. _____

7. More money is being invested in training now than at any other time in U.S. history. _____

8. Working women, on average, tend to exhibit behaviors attributed to good leaders more frequently than working men. _____

9. More often than not, those acknowledged throughout history as great leaders had greatness thrust upon them (by some occurrence). _____

10. The majority of people with outstanding leadership skills have IQs that are well above average. _____

11. Outstanding leaders are most frequently driven by a need to dominate. _____

12. Most great leaders in history emerged from humble beginnings. _____

Figure 12-2 _____

The Answers

Question #1: **TRUE**. It's not unusual to see the bulk of an audience answer this one correctly. The literature has been filled with evidence of the need to restore faith and trust in management for a good long time now. In fact, one recent survey we've seen, a study involving 215 organizations, claimed that a shocking 75% of surveyed executives admitted that they felt trust levels had reduced within their firms during the past two years.

Question #2: **TRUE**. Contrary to what some believe, strong leaders often emerge from the ranks of loyal followers. According to organizational psychologists, such folks understand the importance of followership, and say they always felt that if they worked hard and remained loyal to their superiors that their day would come and they'd be suitably rewarded. "The idea that strong leaders have a history of trouble following others, or serving in anything other than a top role is nonsense," says executive coach Robert McCarty. "I've worked with dozens of outstanding leaders who built their reputations over years and years on the fact they were good soldiers, awaiting the chance to spread their wings and assume positions of greater authority."

Question #3: **TRUE**. While it's true that some people begin demonstrating an ability to lead others at a very early age, most develop such skills over time and in response to leadership-related challenges and opportunities.

Question #4: **TRUE**. According to a portion of the research conducted for this book, 82% of surveyed executives identified as unusually strong leaders said they felt their developing of leadership ability was inspired mostly by the *passion* they felt for a particular issue, cause, or objective. Among the items mentioned most frequently: A desire to excel, a strong desire to "right a wrong" or overcome some injustice, a competitive nature, sibling rivalry, or a deep-felt desire to please one or both parents.

Figure 12-2 _____

The Answers *(continued)*

Question #5: **TRUE**. The answer to this question follows logically from question #4. The difference is the use of the words "misfortune," "sacrifice," and "injustice." Psychologists tell us that most people remain reasonably passive and content with their lives as long as the values and possessions they hold most dear remain unthreatened. When something happens that disrupts or removes one or more of these values, however, the response is often both immediate and extremely strong.

"We see people who had been quiet and compliant suddenly become highly focused and communicative," says clinical psychologist Dr. Raymond Harrison, "any shyness or self-consciousness simply melts away."

One excellent example of this is Carolyn McCarthy from Mineola, New York. A loving homemaker and part-time nurse, Mrs. McCarthy had lived her entire life on Long Island with her family, when on December 7, 1993 her world was shattered by a crazed gunman who shot and killed her husband, and severely injured her son, during an unprovoked rampage on a commuter train from Manhattan. Known as the *Long Island Railroad Massacre,* the horror and rage experienced by Mrs. McCarthy, and many other Long Island families in the weeks and months that followed stirred emotions and an inner strength in Carolyn that she never realized she had. Suddenly she found herself in the middle of one of the largest, most troubling stories in the history of Long Island, an outrage that literally gripped the New York area for months, and was covered in major ways by almost every news organization in the world. She demonstrated tremendous strength and courage during the police investigation, the trial, and the ultimate conviction and sentencing of the killer. There was no telling the number of painful interviews she willingly endured with members of the media, and no doubting, after all was said and done, that through this terrible, terrible ordeal the people of Long Island had been introduced to a very special individual with some very special gifts and abilities to lead.

Figure 12-2 _____

The Answers *(continued)*

In the fall of 1996, Carolyn McCarthy, the self-described quiet house-wife from Mineola, was elected to Congress by the grateful people of Nassau County in one of the most thrilling and impressive shows of bi-lateral support in the history of the state. Her passionate arguments for better gun control laws and the rights of victims continue to resonate in the halls of Congress to this day, and resulted in her being reelected to a second term in 1998, and a third term in November of 2000.

Question #6: **FALSE.** Nearly 65% of surveyed executives said that al-though they were aware others considered them outgoing and gregari-ous, they actually considered themselves *introverted,* not extroverted. It's interesting to note that other informal studies conducted by us over the years have yielded similar results and may suggest that despite out-ward appearances, a high percentage of strong leaders are probably much more reserved and solitary—and less gregarious—than we might suspect.

Question #7: **TRUE.** A number of surveys have placed the estimates at between $60 billion and $100 billion a year, with expectations of con-tinued growth in the range of 5% to 15%, per year, for the foreseeable future.

Question #8: **TRUE.** In fact, a number of recent studies have suggested that working women, on average, demonstrate a *far* better command of key leadership skills than men, and that the gap may be *widening.* Among the abilities tested: listening skills, a values-based management style, consistency in decision-making, the ability to generate and sustain trust, and the ability to inspire and motivate.

Question #9: **TRUE.** Interestingly, it does appear that the majority of those throughout history thought to be truly great leaders demon-strated their abilities during times of great crisis or uncertainty. In the past, some have used this to demonstrate the fact that we all have vast quantities of untapped leadership potential that more often than not lies dormant until stimulated by some (often troubling) event or occurrence.

Figure 12-2 _____

The Answers *(continued)*

Question #10. **FALSE**. Best-selling author Daniel Goleman, among others, has shown quite convincingly in recent years that although important, intelligence has much less to do with success in life, including success as a leader, than many of us previously thought. Dr. Goleman's findings suggest that emotional well-being and emotional maturity play the biggest role, followed by a number of other developmental considerations. The point here is that it's likely many people, including many of us in adult education and training, have placed too much emphasis on standard IQ testing as a predictor of success. The fact is, leaders can be found within a wide range of IQ scores, with some of the very best found toward the bottom of the "normal" ranges, and some of the worst toward the top.

Question #11. **FALSE**. Research has consistently shown that truly great leaders are those most often driven by a desire to *serve* their fellow citizens, employees or communities in some way, not to dominate.

Question #12. **TRUE**. The answer to this question may seem obvious to some, given the fact that, as we know, the overwhelming majority of people born before 1900 lived their lives in comparatively humble, if not poverty-stricken conditions. However, a number of sociologists and social psychologists have theorized recently that some measure of sacrifice growing up, and the discipline that often comes from it, may help stimulate creative abilities in children, as well as greater resilience, and a sustained ambition. According to some, these same qualities tend to be found less frequently in those from extremely affluent and/or privileged families with a reduced need for sacrifice and the preservation of resources.

Although there are many examples of leaders who came from prominent and wealthy families like the Kennedys, Rockefellers and Bushes, a disproportionate number of today's outstanding business and political leaders still emerge from "blue collar" and "first generation" families. These leaders are noted for their strong family values, and for their abilities to overcome challenging problems and other struggles.

1. Reduced upward communications

One of the most reliable signs of a boss in danger of losing his or her credibility is an evident and steady reduction in the feedback, opinions and other communications reaching his/her office. In many cases, this reduction is not as intentional as it is unintentional—but the effects are the same: Despite having the clout, the boss is often in the process of being marginalized and moved "out of the loop" on important issues.

2. Evidence of increasing disregard for authority

This manifestation of worker discontent often takes a very subtle form. In many cases it begins in small, almost imperceptible ways and then grows bolder and more evident. Raised eyebrows in response to something said by the boss, a reluctance to make eye contact, a slight unintentional shake of the head at an important moment, increased tardiness, new or more combative body language, etc. are all frequent indications of early and very subtle signs of rising disregard.

3. Increased evidence of ignoring the superior in order to get things done

Few things are more potentially damaging to a boss-worker relationship—even today in an era of *matrixed* organizations—than even a single instance of intentionally disregarding the chain of command. Yet, this is often one of the first and most commonly occurring indications of problems with a boss. This happened in the technical writing section of an engineering consulting firm. Maxwell S. was a nitpicker. His micromanagement not only frustrated his writers, but frequently caused delay in meeting deadlines. When asked for a decision, he would stall, sometimes for days. Often, in order to get work done, the writers would ignore him and present their work directly to the heads of the departments for which the work was being done. When decisions were needed, they went over Maxwell's head. This led to much discord and unhappiness in the department, low morale and the loss of some good writers.

4. An evident increase in cliques

Although it's difficult to prove statistically, we've often noted that people with a high regard for their managers tend to display a more confident demeanor, and a "one-for-all, all-for-one" type of attitude. Put another way, they seem to be more comfortable interacting as individuals, and as a single member of a large group, than those with "problematic bosses." In this latter case, we've noted evidence of more fracturing of the large group and the developing of "camps" and "cliques." Not surprising, this is often accompanied by reduced communications and increasing tensions. Cliques lead to rivalries in which competition for power supersedes the cooperation needed to accomplish goals.

> **QUOTES AND QUIPS**
>
> "The very essence of leadership is that you have to have vision. It's got to be a vision you articulate clearly and forcefully on every occasion. You can't blow an uncertain trumpet."
> —Theodore Hesburgh,
> Former President,
> Notre Dame University

5. Evidence of a kind of business equivalent of passive-aggressive behavior

We use the expression *passive-aggressive behavior* to describe the kind of malaise that often grips a culture saddled with an incompetent or ineffective boss. In cases like this people often hesitate or refuse to accept responsibility or be held accountable for results, not so much out of deliberate defiance, but rather out of a sense of hopelessness and despondency. In many instances, confused or frustrated employees will alternate between wanting to "fight" or "correct" the problem and simply giving in to the perceived hopelessness of it all. Regardless, evidence of these kinds of emotions and behaviors often indicate a deep-seated disregard for some member or symbol of authority.

6. Evidence of increased documentation and individual recordkeeping

Clearly one of the most disturbing manifestations of life in an increasingly litigious society is the frequency with which people feel a need to document their dealings with others. So often today what used to be sealed with a handshake now requires lawyers and complicated contracts. In many ways, it's a sad commentary on the extent to which trust and honor have been compromised.

Not surprisingly, evidence of increased documenting in the workplace, where filings against employers remain at an all-time high, has also become fairly commonplace. It also should come as no surprise that behaviors like this seem to occur most frequently within organizations with leadership-related and culture-related problems.

7. Increased willingness to openly criticize and/or ridicule the superior in conversations with others

Probably the most flagrant and perhaps most dangerous indication of a growing disregard for a boss or superior involves public criticism and/or ridicule. This tends to occur most frequently in the final stages of a bad working relationship, and almost always results in a separation of some type. The publicizing of criticisms also seems to happen as a result of the natural evolution of more discreet whispering campaigns. In our experience there is very little a boss can do to reverse the momentum of very public criticisms and critiques. It seems that in the overwhelming number of instances we've observed over the years, major personnel changes and shifts in authority inevitably result. An example of this is what happened to Tania D. Tania became so frustrated with her boss's incompetence that she complained about him to everybody in the company. Instead of investigating her complaints and taking steps to correct them, the company fired Tania for being disloyal. By following the hallowed practice of "protecting our own," the company not only didn't resolve the situation that caused the problem—the inadequacy of Tania's manager—but sent a message to its employees that saving the face of a manager was more important than dealing with incompetence.

> **TACTICAL TIP**
>
> To maintain high morale, improve productivity, and lower turnover, managers should encourage their staff members to express their ideas— even if they differ from company practices— without fear of reprisals.

THE CHANGING FUNCTION OF LEADERS

As the dynamics of organizational culture have changed over the past decades, so has the function of the leader. Influenced by technological innovations, the ease and speed of communications and, most important, the attitudes and psychology of the men and women who staff the organizations, the role of the leader has shifted from control by power to coordination and collaboration through persuasion and motivation.

From Vision to Reality

Boyett and Conn, in their best-selling book, *Workplace 2000,* comment that the leaders of the next decade must develop the trust of their staff members. This involves:

- Building confidence through winning. By providing opportunities for achieving a series of small successes, confidence will be developed to meet and conquer any challenge no matter how imposing it may be.

- Reinforcing all successes by meaningful recognition and praise.

- Making work fun.

- Coaching. The leader does not control, order, demand, or criticize. The leader asks people how they will solve their problems, guides them, tolerates their mistakes, and corrects them by added training and coaching. The leader makes sure the staff has the training and resources needed. Together they discuss the general direction to be followed. Then the leader steps back and lets the team member take action. If trouble develops, the leader is available to coach, discuss, and provide additional support.

Employee Involvement—The Key To Effective Leadership

According to the newest study by the University of Southern California's (USC) Marshall School of Business,[1] using data supplied by

---

[1]Miccio, Linda, *Empowering Employees Pays Off,* SHRM, HR News On Line, April 1999.

216 *Fortune* 1000 companies, the researchers rated organizations on the prevalence of employee involvement practices. The researchers then compared the companies' rate of returns on a range of financial indicators. On every one of the indicators—including sales, equity, assets, and stockholder investment—researchers found significantly better returns for companies that were high users of employee involvement.

For instance, in fiscal 1996 the average return on stockholder investment (stock price appreciation minus dividends) was 44 percent among high users of employee involvement efforts, compared with 21 percent among low users. "The difference represents billions of dollars of returns to investors," said study lead researcher Edward Lawler, a professor of management and organization at USC's Marshall School. Lawler noted that employee involvement programs tend to make workers more satisfied with their jobs and less likely to leave them. That's an important finding since many companies are now scrambling to find skilled workers and retain the ones they have.

> QUOTES AND QUIPS
>
> "Leadership is best thought of as a function within the organization rather than the trait of an individual."
> —Edgar H. Schein, Massachusetts Institute of Technology

The challenge of developing leaders for the future

The much reported challenge of locating and retaining top management talent has been exacerbated by a shrinkage in the pool of available managers, escalating costs in recruiting outside talent, and a startling lack of attention to developing leaders from within. As reported in the February 1999 edition of *HR Magazine*,[2] experts are looking more carefully at leadership needs for the 21st century.

William Byham, CEO of Development Dimensions International (DDI), a global HR consulting firm headquartered in Bridgeville, Pennsylvania, says the avoidance of succession planning is a costly time bomb that's been ticking steadily for a decade or more. Byham contends the leadership gap is pervasive and will

---

[2]Byham, William C., "Growing Leaders: Case Studies Grooming Next-Millennium Leaders," *HR Magazine*, February 1999, pp. 46-50.

bedevil the corporate world for decades to come. "We surveyed 150 *Fortune* 500 companies, and the results were sobering," he says. "The average company expects 33 percent turnover at the executive ranks in the next five years, and fully one-third said they're not confident that they will be able to find suitable replacements."

DDI asked 110 managers and executives to estimate first-year costs of filling an executive vacancy. "The average one-year estimated replacement cost is $750,000," Byham says. "That includes finding the new one, training and development costs, and opportunity costs of getting the new hire up to speed."

Three-quarters of corporate officers surveyed for a study by McKinsey and Co., an international management-consulting firm based in New York, said their companies had insufficient talent or were chronically talent-short across the board. This shortage is intensified by the changes in the type of characteristics one seeks in managers today. Leadership is becoming more focused on the psychological needs of human beings. Cindy Hartley, vice president of human resources at Sonoco, concurs. "Today's workforce requires a different kind of leader than 10 years ago, leaders who can inspire people and lead teams are essential. Because of these requirements, the bar has been raised in terms of what we expect."

THE 12 QUALITIES OF TRULY GREAT LEADERS

> QUOTES AND QUIPS
>
> **"We've done more than a million surveys and have found that the old dictator-type of leadership style doesn't work nearly as well as a more caring one. Workers who believe their supervisors care for them perform better, and financial results bear this out."**
>
> **—Don Clifton, Chairman of the Gallup Organisation in London**

During the research for this book and other projects, we've found that while much of the counsel and advice on leadership dispensed by the management "gurus" of the 1980s and 90s is good, there is a tendency to overstate and overcomplicate.

Although it seems fair to say that most outstanding leaders have faced and overcome a multitude of diverse problems in their lives, we've found they also exhibit many similar characteristics and behavior patterns. We call these "The 12 Qualities of Truly Great Leaders."

1. Have enthusiastic followers

Often people in positions of authority can compel subordinates to follow orders by dint of the power of their jobs. But such people are not true leaders. Yes, the orders will be followed but that is all that will happen. True leaders develop confidence and trust in their associates. (Note: They think of them as *associates*—not subordinates.) This engenders a desire not only to follow the lead of the manager, but also to initiate, innovate, and implement ideas of their own that fit into the goals that have been established.

Many business leaders have built up enthusiastic and loyal followers who put in extra hours, sacrifice personal desires and stretch their thinking powers to help achieve the goals set by a leader to whom they relate, respect and admire. When Steve Jobs was asked to return to Apple Computer after the company had suffered a series of major disasters, he agreed to do so with the understanding that he was not looking to take over the company but to just work to bring it back to profitability. He set an example by working day and night to turn the company around. With a leader like that, managers at all levels pitched in and pushed the company forward to achieve its goal—the development and marketing of the highly successful i-Mac computer.

Truly great leaders inspire their people by the example set in their own lives. One of our authors, Frank Ashby, remembers Mike Pizzi as such a person.

Mike Pizzi was the U.S. Marshal of the roughest, most dangerous district in the country—*The Eastern District of New York*, covering Brooklyn, Queens, Staten Island, Nassau and Suffolk Counties. Tough and street-smart, yet funny and with a heart of gold, the winner of countless awards and recognitions, few who knew Mike Pizzi, then or now, would deny he's one of the truly great figures of American twentieth-century law enforcement.

Robert Sabbag, in his book, *Too Tough To Die: Down and Dangerous with the U.S. Marshals*,[3] devotes more space to stories about Mike and references to him than anyone else, and for good reason. Mike was always where the action was, be it nabbing some des-

[3]Sabbag, Robert, *Too Tough To Die: Down and Dangerous with the U.S. Marshals*, New York, Simon & Schuster, 1992.

perate felon single-handedly, late at night, laying a trap for one of the 10 Most Wanted, chatting with the president, or counseling some still-wet-behind-the-ears new deputy.

Mike inspired a sense of duty, loyalty, and commitment in his staff. They would tackle their assignments with enthusiasm and determination, knowing that was what Mike expected of them and they didn't want to disappoint him.

2. Take a constructively discontented view of the world

Good leaders aren't complacent. They're constantly on the alert for innovations that will improve the way work is done, assure continuing customer satisfaction, and increase the profitability of the organization. Their minds are open to new ideas and they welcome suggestions. Even after changes and improvements are made, they still look for even better ways to accomplish their goals. Leaders like this are never fully satisfied. They review practices and procedures on a regular basis to fine-tune them. They do not fall in love with their own ideas, but are open to criticism and innovation.

3. Consider themselves a work-in-progress

Just as effective leaders are constructively discontent about their departments, they are never entirely satisfied with themselves. They attend seminars and self-improvement programs, purchase and listen to motivational tapes, read books and periodicals to keep up not only with the state of the art in their fields, but also to improve their knowledge and understanding in a variety of areas. Great leaders don't limit their talents to their jobs. They take active roles in professional and trade associations not only to keep in touch with new developments but to share their ideas with colleagues from other organizations. They attend and participate in conventions and conferences and develop networks of people to whom they can turn to obtain knowledge or ideas over the years.

4. Excel when the stakes are high

We've all heard the old adage, "Leaders are made not born," and like most adages, there is a great deal of truth in it. However, some people do seem to be born leaders. From early childhood, they take the lead in playing games, are selected as team captains, are elected to student offices and take charge of everything in which they are involved. In some ways (at least according to their proud parents), they always seemed destined for big things in life. However, many of the greatest leaders were not born to greatness, but developed it when placed in leadership positions. History is replete with stories of ordinary men and women who rose to the heights when leadership was needed. Lech Walesa is an example of such a man. In 1980 when the workers at the Lenin Shipyard in Gdansk, Poland, went on strike for better working conditions, the Communist government cracked down on them. Walesa was an electrician in the shipyard and one of the leaders of Solidarity, an independent trade union. He had little education and had never considered himself to be anything more than an artisan. But when leadership was needed, he stepped out to speak up for the workers in defying the authorities. Despite several arrests and imprisonments, his leadership of the strike inspired the Polish people to work to overthrow the Communist regime. In 1983, he was awarded the Nobel Peace Price and in 1990 was elected president of Poland.

5. Great leaders understand people

They know what causes people to act and react the way they do. They recognize the importance of being a motivating factor for people—appealing to the drives and the feelings of others. They take a genuine interest in the people with whom they interact. As Dale Carnegie succinctly pointed out: "You can make more friends in two months by becoming genuinely interested in others than you can in two years by trying to get others interested in you."

6. Expect more from themselves than others

The best leaders we know set high standards for themselves and then work hard to exceed them. They know they are "visible," and take seriously their responsibilities as role models. They are also life-long learners. Like everyone, they make mistakes; and when they do, they view these mistakes as learning experiences and try to turn them into successes.

Coca Cola's late CEO, Roberto Goizueta, demonstrated one of the best examples of this. When he made the decision to change the long-time formula of Coca Cola to "the New Coke," the public's reaction shocked the company. Despite their market research, consumers did not like the New Coke and wanted the old formula back. A man with less integrity would have stuck to his decision and poured advertising dollars into saving his idea, but Goizueta swallowed his pride and brought back the old product under the new name, "Classic Coke." His decision was right. In a short time "New Coke" disappeared from the market as Classic Coke resumed its long established first-place position.

7. Rely on some fixed, unwavering set of convictions or beliefs that serves as their "Guiding Light"

Sir John Templeton, the founder of the Templeton Fund, one of the most profitable mutual funds, adheres to the philosophy that the most successful people are often the most ethically motivated. He says that such people are likely to have the keenest understanding of the importance of morality in business, and can be trusted to give full measure and not cheat their customers. But the most ethical principles, Templeton insists, come from what goes on in the mind. "If you're filling your mind with kind, loving and helpful thoughts, then your decisions and actions will be ethical." Hard work combined with honesty and perseverance is key in the Templeton philosophy. "Individuals who have learned to invest themselves in their work are successful. They have earned what they have. More than simply knowing the value of money, they know their own value."

8. Have both a 'tough hide' and an ability to laugh at themselves

Great leaders have a sense of humor and do not always take themselves seriously. A good example of this is Victor Kiam, now owner and CEO of the Remington Shaver Company. He tells about one of his first jobs, when as a salesman selling Playtex girdles, he came up with what he thought was a great marketing gimmick. Knowing that girdles frequently were hard to clean, he offered a special promotion. Women who brought in their old, worn-out girdles could buy a new, Playtex model at a discount. The plan worked a little too well. So many dirty girdles were turned in at a New York department store that he was nearly arrested for violating health codes.

9. Are not deterred by disappointment, failure, or rejection. They have strong views yet maintain a "visceral equilibrium."

One very successful leader who didn't let failure get him down is Tom Monaghan, who created and grew Domino Pizzas from a one-store pizza parlor to a chain of several thousand home-delivery outlets over a period of about 30 years. In 1989, he decided to sell his hugely successful company and concentrate instead on doing philanthropic work. His plan, however, did not work out. After two and a half years, the company that purchased the chain failed to maintain the momentum that Monaghan had built and in order to save the company, he was forced to come back.

It took much work and persistence to first rebuild and then expand the organization. The dogged determination that enabled Monaghan to rise from a childhood of deprivation, poverty, and abuse to become a great entrepreneur also enabled him to not only return Domino to its original prominence, but to expand it to 6,000 stores—of which 1,100 are in countries other than the United States.

10. Are positive thinkers

The practice of positive thinking increases one's effectiveness tremendously for two reasons. First, it discovers ability which before was locked up, and calls out hitherto unknown resources; and second, it keeps the mind in harmony by killing fear, worry, and anxiety, which are the enemies of our success and our efficiency. It puts the mind in a condition to succeed. It sharpens the faculties, and makes them keener. Because it gives a new outlook on life, it turns one about so that he or she faces toward the goal, toward certainty, toward assurance, instead of toward doubt, fear, and uncertainty.

Michael Jordan attributes much of his success to positive thinking. In basketball as in all aspects of life, it is easy to become discouraged when things are not going well. Jordan writes: "Some people get frozen by *fear of failure*—by thinking about the possibility of a negative result. They might be afraid of looking bad or being embarrassed. I realized that if I was going to achieve anything in life, I had to be aggressive. I had to get out there and go for it. I don't believe you can achieve anything by being passive. I know fear is an obstacle for some people, but to me it's an illusion. Once I'm in the game, I'm not thinking about anything except what I'm trying to accomplish."

Whether leading a sports team or a business team, the leader who thinks positively will convey that attitude to the entire team. It will pay off with renewed enthusiasm and commitment to achieve the desired goals.

11. Focus on getting things done

We've all come across people in management positions, who appear to have all the attributes of a good leader, but somehow never quite succeed. Somewhere along the line, they have missed the boat. Why does this happen?

A few years ago we had the opportunity to study this first hand. One of our clients had hired a regional sales manager, about whom they were extremely enthusiastic. He had come to them highly recommended. During the selection process, he had impressed the interviewers with his thorough knowledge of their markets, his innovative ideas on how to increase business and his charming personality. During the first several months on the job, he developed a creative and comprehensive marketing program. He spent weeks fine-tuning the program, writing materials, and creating graphics for it. This led to his making several impressive presentations to management and to the sales force. And that's where it ended. He never was able to actually get out and make the program work. In our investigation of the problem, we learned that in his previous job, he was a staff marketer, who had never had line responsibility. In that capacity he was excellent, but he did not have that key trait of leadership—getting things done.

12. Understand the power of the informal organization

Many people have developed a deep distrust of bosses or managers—often due to their experience with current or past managers. They turn to the informal leaders—fellow workers who have gained their respect and whose opinions and actions they admire and emulate. The effective leader recognizes the influence these men and women have in the acceptance of new ideas among their followers.

Barbara W., the supervisor of a department of 15 sewing machine operators, was commended by her boss for running a highly productive unit. At a staff meeting, her boss commented that her department was always the first to accept new ideas, adapt to changes in operation methods and seemed to exhibit the highest morale. He asked Barbara to share with the other supervisors her "secret of success." Her response was one word: "Rachel." Rachel, she explained, was one of her best operators. She'd been with the company for 13 years and was a mother figure to the younger women in the department. They brought her all of their problems and accepted her advice whether the situation was job-related or personal. When Barbara took over the supervisor's job a few years ago, she recognized the important role Rachel played and carefully moved to gain her support. Over the years she discussed with Rachel problems she had with any of the workers, changes that were to be made in the work, and together determined how to deal with them. The result was a long-term, smooth and successfully run department.

In most companies there is an informal structure parallel to the formal organization. Effective leaders work within that structure

---

QUOTES AND QUIPS

"Contrary to the opinion of many people, leaders are not born. Leaders are made, and they are made by effort and hard work."
—Vince Lombardi,
Football coach

rather than trying to defy it. They identify and cultivate the informal leaders and together they work toward the achievement of their goals.

INNOVATIONS IN LEADERSHIP DEVELOPMENT

The challenge of providing leaders for the future is both quantitative and qualitative. There is an urgent need to be ready to fill the vacancies that inevitably will occur. More important, however, is the challenge of selecting men and women with the personality traits that make for successful leaders in the 21st century, and to develop training programs that will hone their leadership skills.

In January 1998, the ASTD together with the American Productivity and Quality Center, James Kouzes, Chairman of TPG Learning Systems and Professor Robert M. Fulmer of the College of William and Mary conducted a study to identify and examine innovations and key areas in present-day leadership development. They made a depth study of thirty-five organizations recognized as having strong, innovative leadership development processes.[4] Let's look at some of the highlights of this study:

- Leadership development does not stand alone. It must be aligned to overall corporate strategy.

- Senior level executives with extensive line experience must be involved in the leadership development program. Combining their experience and expertise with persons experienced in human resources, corporate education, and academia, creates a business and educational mix that results in a program based on sound theory and vital business achievements.

- A model of leadership competencies is developed which is consistent throughout the organization and reflects the values of the organization.

---

[4]Fulmer, Robert, and Wagner, Stacey, "Leadership: Lessons From The Best," *Training & Development*, March 1999, pp.29-32. Full report: *Leadership Development: Building Executive Talent* can be obtained from ASTD Service 1-800-NAT-ASTD.

- Best-practice organizations develop their own leaders rather than recruit them from other companies.

- Action, not knowledge, is the goal of best-practice leadership development. The program not only provides leaders with knowledge and information, but also equips them with the necessary skills, qualities, and techniques to apply their knowledge in a variety of situations. By having participants solve actual business problems, the learning experience is tailored to the organization's and learner's development.

- The leadership development process is linked to the organization's succession planning. Leadership development becomes important in maintaining a steady flow of information throughout the organization to ensure that its top talent is tracked and continues to grow.

- The leadership development process is a symbiotic tool of effective leadership. To succeed it requires top-level support. Conversely, the success of the program engenders continued high-level support.

- Successful programs are being continuously assessed. Although the study showed companies used a variety of assessment methods, all assessed results on a regular basis, reflected on the results, made adaptations, and kept listening and learning.

THE 8 WAYS TO HASTEN THE DEVELOPMENT OF LEADERSHIP ABILITY

We're often asked advice about the best ways to speed the development of the qualities and characteristics most commonly observed in terrific leaders. It's not an easy question to answer because people are different, and no one strategy seems to work best for everyone.

Having said that, our research has suggested that there are some unusually good ways to increase the likelihood of developing solid leadership skills quickly. Here they are:

1. Master the Fundamentals

It's amazing how many otherwise smart people still believe in a magic pill, or the existence of some super quick and super easy way to build leaders. Despite what a management and training guru may say on occasion, those one-day and two-day workshops promising all kinds of terrific results only provide superficial coverage of a complex matter. People need time to develop new habits, and they need to begin the process by first understanding the critical importance of getting back to the basics: the creating of a sound value system, the building of self-confidence, the improving of interpersonal skills, learning to deal with excessive stress and worry, the maintaining of positive attitudes, etc. When these things are tackled first, people dramatically increase the likelihood of preparing themselves for true emergence as a leader. When they aren't, the job is much, much harder, if not impossible.

One of the best ways to begin mastering the fundamentals of good leadership is to sit down and do an assessment of your strengths and weaknesses in each of several areas. This kind of careful self-reflection can be very beneficial for a number of reasons, especially when combined with the results of 360-degree assessments or other third-party evaluations.

To gain insight into your own strengths and weaknesses as a leader, consider conducting your own 360-degree evaluation. Make a list of your strengths as a leader on one side of a sheet of paper, and then list the things you consider in need of improvement on the other side. Then invite three or four people who know you well (spouse, parents, siblings, children, close friends) to do the same, with you as the subject. Once all of the feedback is collected, match it against your own perceptions of your strengths and weaknesses. Chances are you'll be surprised—if not stunned—by the dissimilarity of at least some of the findings. But you are sure to learn things about yourself that you may not have realized.

2. Get Focused on the Right Objective—Become an Outstanding Person First, Then an Outstanding Leader

This second item is closely related to the first. In the overwhelming majority of cases we've seen, world-class leaders emerge from the ranks of world-class people—people with the right motives, a genuine concern for others, a spirit of cooperation, and an ego in check. It's not at all unusual to find people considered terrific leaders by their peers to be highly involved in their communities. They are

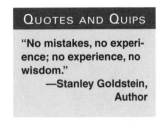

QUOTES AND QUIPS

"No mistakes, no experience; no experience, no wisdom."
—Stanley Goldstein, Author

often known for having quietly and without a lot of fanfare reached out to others less fortunate.

True leadership is hard to fake. People sense when someone is less than genuine or less than sincere in his or her efforts to motivate or inspire others. They can just feel it, and it's often not long before sentiments begin to change. In fact, history is replete with examples of people who were considered great inspiring leaders who never aspired to lead. They were simply fine upstanding people, who couldn't help but be recognized for the good works they had done. They ended up inspiring others, not out of any interest in being noticed or recognized, but simply as a result of the attention naturally attracted by the outstanding example they set for others. These include people like Albert Schweitzer, a doctor, philosopher, and theologian, who devoted his life to caring for desperately sick people in Africa and was awarded the Nobel Peace Prize in 1952; Mother Theresa, whose work with the poor people of India has been acclaimed by world leaders; and Elie Wiesel, another Nobelist, who overcame the tortures of the concentration camps to inspire people of all nations and faiths in their fight against bigotry and despotism.

QUOTES AND QUIPS

"When the best leader's work is done, the people say, 'We did it ourselves.'"
—Lao Tzu, Chinese Philosopher

Such leaders are not necessarily world-renowned. We find them in every community and often in business organizations—men and women who combine their intelligence and diligence with integrity and concern for others. Seek out such people. They can be the core of leadership for the future of your organization.

3. Get Involved in Something Bigger than Yourself— Something for Which You Feel a Genuine Passion

One of the best ways to speed the development of leadership ability is to get involved in a cause or important project with implications or potential benefits far beyond the usual. Some examples of this might be managing an important fundraiser, organizing an important event or gathering, working on a political campaign, championing an important social issue, or running for the local school board.

Over the years we've seen hundreds—maybe even thousands— of otherwise "average" people suddenly catch fire and begin demonstrating great volumes of leadership skill simply as a result of the enthusiasm they felt for a cause or other major endeavor. The great thing about this way of hastening the development of leadership skill is that opportunities like this surround us every day. We may not always see them, but they're there—in the newspapers we read, the things we hear on the radio and on television, and in the things people talk about. Of course, the key to it all is taking the plunge, actually getting involved in something that fires up your passions and at the same time helps accomplish something important.

The passion that one shows often has little to do with the work one is doing. It may stem from some other aspect of life, which can often be transferred to the work place. Cliff W., a sales rep for one of our clients, loved to write. As a young man he wrote poetry and tried his hand at short stories. After he settled into his career, he used this talent to write articles about the industry in which he worked and sold them to the trade and professional journals in that field. His boss read one of his articles and was impressed with its quality. He recognized that Cliff's writing skills plus his understanding of customers' needs from his experience in dealing with them, would make him a valuable asset to the marketing department. And indeed, it was a good move. Today Cliff heads up a product division and is slated for higher positions.

Estelle A.'s passion was drama. She was an active member of the community theater and often played starring roles. When her boss saw one of her performances, she wondered how these talents could be channeled into Estelle's work for the company. A few months later, several executives were invited to participate in an international conference. Estelle was asked to coach them in their presentations. All of the participants did exceptionally well. This led to Estelle's promotion to a position in public relations, and now, several years later, she heads the public relations department.

4. Fill Your Head with Important Things

Great leaders share their knowledge with others. One of our authors, Frank Ashby, recalls how he learned about concentrating on the important things from his former boss, Dr. Paul Mackey. He commented: "In those days Paul was the vice president of instruction for Dale Carnegie & Associates, Inc. It was a big job, and one that carried with it the responsibility of being not only one of the country's top adult educators, but also the model of how an instructor licensed by Dale Carnegie was expected to look, teach and behave. We would carpool to and from our homes to the office—an hour's ride each way. I learned much during those rides. I'd listen carefully between sips of coffee to Paul's musings on any number of topics. I remember being amazed by the range and depth of his understanding of what seemed like an infinite number of subjects. Yes, Paul Mackey was, and still is, a student of the world."

> QUOTES AND QUIPS
>
> "To most men experience is like the stern lights of a ship, which illuminate only the track it has passed."
> —Samuel Taylor Coleridge, English poet and essayist

"One story he was fond of telling in those days was about his mother. Paul's father died when he was a very young boy, and his mother had to struggle hard for years to keep the family together and put enough food on the table. Like every mother she dreamed of a better life for her children, and, as Paul tells it, she would constantly drill into them the importance of not only learning, but of learning things that were *important*—things that would serve them well in the future.

"It seems to us that the distinction Paul's mother made between learning and the learning of important things is as relevant today as ever. All of us are bombarded with messages and information about all sorts of things every day. Unfortunately, much of it has little long-term value. I remember one of my friends in junior high school, Jimmy R., who was, at best, an average student, but who could recite from memory the team, position, batting average and the number of home runs for darn near every baseball player in the major leagues! Jimmy remembered these things because he was interested in them, like many boys his age. However, because he spent most of his time, even as he got older, reading sports magazines and watching baseball on television, he never quite developed the well-grounded and well-rounded view he needed of more pertinent issues."

5. View Yourself as a Work in Progress. Be Unsatisfied with Yourself, but Not Dissatisfied

Another great way to speed the development of leadership ability is to start looking at yourself as a work-in-progress. The fact is we're all constantly evolving. We learn new things every day, and assimilate those new bits of information into what has become, over time, our core beliefs and core perceptions of the world. In our opinion, one of the greatest barriers to the development of leadership skill is the fact that most of us are creatures of habit. We develop routines and ways of doing things over time that, consciously or not, keep us from considering new ways of doing things that might make us more effective.

Some of the best leaders we've seen and studied over the years take precisely the opposite position. They see themselves as good, but imperfect; competent, but needing to improve in important areas; experienced, but still uninformed about a great many things. And it's this *unsatisfied* feeling that in many cases provides the impetus for continued growth and development as a person, and as a leader.

Harry G. exemplifies a person who was always open to self-improvement. When his company began marketing its products in South America, Harry realized that although most of its customers could speak some English, it would be to his advantage to be able to converse with them in Spanish. His friends and colleagues scoffed at the idea of a man in his fifties acquiring a new language, but this didn't discourage Harry. He enrolled in an immersion course in Spanish and in a short time was able to converse easily in this newly acquired language. But Harry was still not satisfied. To perfect his new skill, he joined an inter-American cultural organization where he met with nationals from several Spanish-speaking countries. By using this as an opportunity to converse with them in Spanish, he was able to perfect his pronunciation and understanding. This gave him a competitive advantage when he visited his customers, and was a significant factor in building up his business in that market.

Today, in order to keep up with the technology, everybody must acquire computer skills. Only a few years ago, executives depended on computer specialists to do the computer work and then fill them in on results. This is no longer practical. Most every executive now has a personal computer and must learn to use it in order to make timely decisions. Managers who failed to recognize this or who were complacent about their job knowledge have fallen by the wayside. To thrive—even survive today, one must develop a sense of constructive discontent. There's no place for complacency or lassitude in today's dynamic business world. You must keep learning, keep acquiring new skills, and above all, be open to making changes that will advance your company and your career.

6. Conquer Your Attitude

The current literature, especially in psychology, is loaded with new evidence of the key role our daily thoughts and perceptions play in our ability to grow and develop new skills. Ralph Nichols of Detroit, Michigan, is one of the most successful business people licensed to sell the Dale Carnegie program. He puts it simply when he says that "attitude is everything."

> **TACTICAL TIPS**
>
> **Always keep in mind that perception is reality in the mind of the perceiver.**

Attitude really is everything, because we are all, above all else, a product of what we think. People who wake up in the morning with negative thoughts in their heads will almost assuredly be less enthusiastic and less productive than those who wake up with a positive, optimistic outlook on their day.

One of the best ways to develop confidence and a more positive attitude is to stay ever more conscious of the things for which we should be grateful—the things going well for us. Consider making a list of these things and carrying it with you in your wallet or purse. Then, at least three times a day take out the list and remind yourself of all of the reasons you have to be grateful and optimistic. Research has shown that this kind of ongoing reinforcement really does help in the strengthening of attitudes by releasing hormones that raise our spirits and increase our sense of control over our lives.

The fact is, we'd be hard pressed to think of a terrific leader who isn't in command of his or her attitude. We'd also be hard pressed to think of a truly great leader with any staying power who didn't have a genuinely optimistic, happy, enthusiastic way of looking at things.

The good news in all this is that like many other things, our attitudes are controllable. We can learn to think in more positive ways, and train ourselves to live with more optimism and more enthusiasm. There are lots of terrific books out today with advice on how to go about this, many of which draw heavily from the original works of folks like Norman Vincent Peale, Napoleon Hill, and Dale Carnegie.

7. Create Conditions in Your Life that Support Your Development as a Person, and as a Leader

One of the most interesting observations we've made over the years about truly great leaders is that they almost always create environments that nurture and encourage ongoing success. Put another way, they work toward creating conditions within their personal and professional lives that increase the likelihood of whatever kind of success they're pursuing actually happening.

A part of doing this successfully obviously involves the people with whom you surround yourself. For example, if you're interested in losing a few pounds, you might be wise to surround yourself with others who have changed their eating and exercise habits. If you're anxious to quit smoking, it might be smart to start spending more time with ex-smokers or non-smokers.

The key point here is that success begets success, and in order to create conditions that increase the likelihood of favorable things happening, it's critical we stack the odds in our favor. That's what some of the best leaders we've known do routinely. The same strategy will work just as well for those who aspire to be great.

Even the most successful people will experience disappointments and failures. It's very easy to lose one's confidence when your decisions turn out to be wrong or unforeseen hurdles derail your progress. This is when turning to the experience of other successful people helps. Every one of them has had failures and has overcome them. Remember that even Babe Ruth, who broke all records for hitting home runs, also broke all records for striking out. Steven Jobs was forced out of his position as CEO of Apple

Computers, but came back a few years later and revived a company that many had given up on. Stories of rebounds from failure abound in all aspects of life including politics, sports, the arts, science, and business.

8. Decide to Be Happy

This last way of hastening the development of leadership ability may seem so obvious and trite that it's not worth spending much time on. In fact, just the opposite is true. When asked about how he developed and maintained such a positive outlook on things, despite often being surrounded by complicated problems and personal attacks from his political enemies, former president Ronald Reagan was reportedly fond of smiling that famous smile of his and responding, "Beats me, I just wake up happy."

The truth is, many people do just wake up happy. Research has shown that in many cases people with this quality show higher levels of particular body chemicals that literally lift their spirits each day and help them maintain a stable, optimistic equilibrium.

For the majority of others, making a deliberate, *conscious* decision to be happy works almost as well. The fact is, we all have a long list of things to be grateful for and happy about, and no doubt a long list of concerns and potential problems. As Winston Churchill reportedly once said during the darkest days of World War II, "Every one of us has every reason to be both hopelessly depressed and deliriously happy every day now. Depressed about the horrors we've seen and might see again, and happy that we're still among the living and with at least some of those we love. Every day when we rise to start the day we have a choice to make— whether to wither under the tremendous sadness and problems that surround us, or to be grateful and heartened for the blessings we have left. For the sake of my body, and my country, I chose to be grateful and heartened."

It wouldn't surprise us if some of the most resilient, most effective of today's leaders quietly wished they had more of Reagan's

QUOTES AND QUIPS

"Most people are about as happy as they make up their minds to be."
        —Abraham Lincoln

chemistry, and made a point of following Churchill's advice. The simple fact is that actions follow thoughts, and if we accept the notion that we can improve our actions by improving our thoughts, it makes sense that we should start our day by simply making a conscious decision to be happy and optimistic.

Sure, there are times when we do feel frustrated and lost. Earlier in this chapter we suggested that one way of helping yourself when you feel this way is contemplating the experiences of others who overcame failure and defeat. Another way we have found very helpful is to focus on your own successes. Failure breeds failure. Success breeds success. Even if the most recent project didn't work as you had hoped, it doesn't mean you are a failure. You were successful over and over again in the past. Focus on those successes rather than dwelling on the recent failure.

One way of doing this is keeping a "success file." Here's how it works:

Every time you get a letter of appreciation from your boss, a customer or anybody else, file it in your success file. Every time you accomplish something about which you are particularly proud, write yourself a note describing what it was and place it in the success file. Now, when things go wrong and you're depressed or frustrated, and you feel you're a failure, take out that success file. Reread those letters and memos. This is your proof that you have the capability and are a special person. You did it before and you can do it again.

> **TACTICAL TIP**
>
> Encourage your employees to set up their own success files. Help by writing notes to them praising their accomplishments and suggest they place them in their success files. Remind them when they have failures or disappointments that you have confidence in them. Why? The proof is in that file. They did it before; they can do it again.

TRAIN MANAGERS TO BE LEADERS

To assure that managers, team leaders and others who have authority over employees become and remain true leaders, every company should have an ongoing program of training for leadership. This includes, but is not limited to seminars, individual coaching, and special programs. Yes, such programs are important and are integral to reaching the goal, but they must be reinforced with day-to-day attention to each manager's leadership style. To accomplish this, we recommend the following process:

Five-Step Leadership Development Commitment

1. Indoctrination

Every new manager should be given comprehensive training in the techniques of interpersonal relations. They should have a clear concept of what is expected of them as managers. This includes the company's human resources policies, the psychology of developing a cooperative, collaborative environment, techniques of interpersonal relations, and specific factors that may be applicable to their jobs.

2. Implementation

During the first several weeks on the job, assign a mentor who will guide the new manager and review his or her activities on a daily basis. This will be supplemented with recommendations for added training, reading, or coaching in specific areas. Over time these reviews will be reduced to weekly or even monthly meetings with the mentor.

3. Measurement

Periodic 360-degree assessments should be used to measure how well the new manager is doing. Regular feedback should be provided so that he or she knows at the earliest point what is going well and where improvement is needed.

4. Reward

Performance as a leader should be rewarded. This can be in the form of bonuses for maintaining a high retention rate, reduction in grievances, increase in employee suggestions, or improvement in morale as indicated by the assessments. These factors should play an important role in the manager's performance review and salary increments.

5. Enforcement

Managers who do not live up to the standards set should be given every opportunity to improve. However, if this rehabilitation fails, the manager should be removed. Poor leadership cannot be tolerated. Long term employees who have been promoted to management and fail should be given the opportunity to return to a non-managerial position in the company. Some companies keep transferring mediocre leaders from one department to another in the hope they'll be more effective dealing with different employees. This rarely works. This is one area in which companies must be firm.

An employee's immediate supervisor or manager is vital to that person's satisfaction with his or her job. Our research and observation bears out that reinforcing leadership skills significantly improves the rate of retention and is a key factor in winning the war for talent.

SUM AND SUBSTANCE

- Too often managers assume that their leadership style is working well when, in fact, it isn't working at all. Don't be complacent about how well you believe you lead.

- As the dynamics of organizational culture have changed over the past decades, so has the function of the leader. Influenced by technological innovations, the ease and speed of communications and, most important, the attitudes and psychology of the men and women who staff the organizations, the role of the leader has shifted from control by power to coordination and collaboration through persuasion and motivation.

- The average one-year estimated replacement cost for a manager who leaves the organization is $750,000. That includes recruiting and selecting, training and coaching, and the loss of productivity until the new manager gets up to speed.

- Great leaders:
    1. Have enthusiastic followers.

2. Take a constructively discontented view of the world.

3. Consider themselves a work-in-progress.

4. Excel when the stakes are high.

5. Demonstrate a good understanding of people.

6. Expect more from themselves than they do from others.

7. Rely on some fixed, unwavering set of convictions or beliefs that serves as their guiding light.

8. Have both a 'tough hide' and an ability to laugh at themselves.

9. Are not deterred by failure or rejection.

10. Are positive thinkers.

11. Focus on getting things done.

12. Understand the power of the informal organization.

- 8 Ways to Hasten the Development of Leadership Ability are:

  1. Master the fundamentals.

  2. Become an outstanding person first, and then an outstanding leader.

  3. Get involved in something bigger than yourself—something for which you feel a genuine passion.

  4. Fill your head with important things.

  5. View yourself as a work-in-progress. Be unsatisfied with yourself, but not dissatisfied.

  6. Conquer your attitude.

  7. Create conditions in your life that support your development as a person, and as a leader.

  8. Decide to be happy.

- An employee's immediate supervisor or manager is vital to that person's satisfaction with his or her job. Our research and observation bears out that reinforcing leadership skills significantly improves the rate of retention and is a key factor in winning the war for talent.

13

Training Well

According to the annual industry survey reported in *Training* magazine in October, 2000, a whopping $54 billion was spent in the United States on corporate training in the 1999-2000 period. Although it's difficult to compare the findings this year to those from the past (due to some changes in the way the magazine makes its estimates), it's generally felt that a far greater percentage of organizations increased their investment in employee training and development during the period surveyed.

The evolution of investments in training by companies large and small in America has made for some fascinating reading during the past ten years or so. Once thought of as a luxury, and even a costly "necessary evil" by many executives, the importance of helping employees continually improve their skills and stay current with changes in technology—and just *change* in general—has given birth to one of the fastest growing industries on the planet. According to *Training:*

- $19.3 billion of the $54 billion went to outside training providers.
- $34.7 billion was invested in training staff salaries.
- 99 percent of all companies in America teach employees to use computer applications.
- 35 percent of U.S. companies pay to teach some employees remedial math/arithmetic.
- 55 percent of all computer-delivered training is devoted to teaching computer skills.

The three training-related topics offered most frequently by companies are new employee orientation, leadership development and sexual harassment. Executive development accounts for about 13 percent of all training. About 40 percent of all training received by employees is designed by outside sources, but only 31 percent is actually delivered by outside sources, 73 percent of all corporate training is delivered by an instructor; 13 percent is delivered by a computer.

Properly developed training programs can have a dramatic, lasting, invigorating effect on a business, and show an enormous return on investment as individuals increase their current skills and develop new ones. This results in an increase in innovative ideas, more creative approaches to solving problems, and is a major factor in the retention of your "A-players." In addition to training in specific occupational and professional areas, training in the soft skills—leadership, communications, and interpersonal relations—provides tools and techniques that lead to closer and more meaningful relations with co-workers, subordinates, supervisors, customers, vendors, and the public.

THE SKILL DEVELOPMENT PROCESS

A good part of the authors' work has been devoted to the design and development of training programs. Over the years we have synthesized a highly successful formula that has been implemented in the training endeavors of not only the clients with whom we have been directly involved, but in many other organizations. It consists of a four-step procedure intended not just to dispense content, but to actually change behavior.

The four steps are described on the next page.

1. The Attitude Conditioning of Learners

Unless the training participants are properly oriented so that they're receptive to learning, the chances of success are minimal. Not only must minds be open to receive and accept new information and ideas, but also they must become excited about it. To accomplish this, a thorough orientation of training participants becomes an essential prelude to the actual learning. The following steps should be included:

Participants should be given a clear picture of what's involved

This includes an overview of what will be taught, the reasons for its importance and a preview of the techniques and methods that will be applied. For example, if workshops, interactive team projects, or brainstorming sessions will be used, let participants know about this in advance. Get them interested and excited about using these training tools.

Participants should understand how they would benefit from the training

Demonstrate how it will enhance their careers, make the work easier, and allow them to work smarter rather than harder.

Participants should be reminded that they participated in determining their own training needs

Their input weighed significantly in the design of the program as it stemmed from the O-MRI in which they were important participants.

Get the participants excited about what will be learned and the satisfaction they will get from participating fully in the training process

Motivate them to be active participants. Let them know that learning can be fun.

Demonstrate to the participants that they can change, grow, and improve

Describe how the change process has succeeded in the past. If possible, use current examples from the organization. Supplement this by describing similar successes in other firms.

Be enthusiastic about the entire process

By your enthusiasm and that of others in management, make everyone desirous—even anxious—to begin.

2. Presentation and Demonstration of Content

It has long been established that the key to successful training is active involvement and participation of the entire group. Real learning begins when all participants are drawn into the process. Unless the members of the group are fully involved in the training, only superficial knowledge can be obtained. Active participation through case studies, role-plays, simulations, working assignments, and similar exercises make the material come alive—leading to better learning and long-lasting retention. Demonstrations of what is being taught in the classroom and on the job give learners meaningful exposure to how the material they are learning applies to their actual work. All members of the group should be encouraged to engage in discussions, debates, disagreements, and deliberations. Dissenters should be encouraged to express their opinions. Only when doubts are resolved can full consensus be reached and the new learning be absorbed and accepted.

The trainer must resist the temptation to be a preacher-teacher. He or she should assume the role of facilitator, helping the

---

TACTICAL TIPS

The Success Development Process consists of four steps:
1. Participants must be conditioned to accept that training will involve change in their behavior.
2. Content of training should be presented and demonstrated in an interesting, participative and dynamic manner.
3. Participants must practice what has been learned.
4. The training must be followed up and the new behavior reinforced.

trainees through the process, not spoon-feeding information to them, but enabling them to examine, evaluate, think about, and truly learn the new material. The best trainers are active listeners and observers who are alert to the actions and reactions of the trainees, and skilled at getting input and providing feedback.

3. Practice

The classroom training is just the first step in the learning process. Unless class members try what they have learned on the job, it cannot be determined if the learning has taken hold. We cannot wait until after the training has been completed to measure this. Errors and misunderstanding must be corrected immediately before they become bad habits; successes must be acknowledged immediately to give the program participant positive reinforcement.

One way to do this is to start each session with a reporting period at which everyone reports on how the lessons from the previous session were applied and what resulted. Recently we were conducting a sales training program for a client in which some new approaches to selling the firm's service were introduced. Participants were asked to use at least one of the techniques learned in the first session during the week between the first and the second session and to report on how it worked. When the reports were given, the entire class critiqued each participant's experience. All of us benefited. The reporter received feedback on his or her performance and all class members learned from the experiences of each of the participants. The facilitator learned what areas had been successful in providing learning and how the training could be made even more effective.

4. Follow-Up and Reinforcement

We have often come across organizations that bemoan the failure of their training programs, complaining that all of the money they spent was wasted because after a short time, participants reverted to their old habits. The complaint, valid as it may be, is usually not the fault of the training program, but the lack of proper follow-up. Just as a muscle will atrophy if not exercised, knowledge and skills will be lost if not used.

To overcome this, follow-up programs should be incorporated into the training plan. The first meeting is usually 30 days after the completion of the training sessions. This meeting, designed in an exciting and motivational format, reinforces and remotivates participants. Included are reports of progress, opportunities to ask questions and discuss problems that have arisen on the job and motivational exercises so that everybody leaves with the enthusiasm to assure continued commitment. Subsequent meetings are spaced 30 to 60 days apart for as long as desirable.

It's essential that representatives of top management show their support for the program. By word and deed, they should let all involved know that the application of the new skills, and the changes in attitudes and culture based on the training, are paying off in their impact on productivity, progress, and profits.

MENTORING

Mentors are valuable resources in developing the skills of their protégés—and equally important in orienting them to the organizational culture. Most organizations don't have a formal program to encourage mentoring. Some managers want to share their knowledge and experience with newcomers; others take a special liking to a new employee and become his or her mentor; some young people take the initiative and ask managers they admire to become their mentors.

A formal mentoring program that systematically identifies and trains managers on the techniques and subtleties of the art of mentoring and then pairs up mentors and protégés is more effective than a haphazard process. This not only assures that younger employees will obtain mentoring, but gives the opportunity to managers to participate in the program.

COACHING

Trainers must not only utilize the most effective techniques of instructing, but must also be good coaches. A coach has the ability to recognize each trainee's strengths and limitations and work with each to maximize his or her potential.

Some of the qualities that good coaches possess are:

- They are expert motivators. They bring out the best in others.
- They instill self-confidence by reinforcing the strengths of the team members and their determination to succeed.
- They provide the tools, the plans, and the techniques that will enable people to achieve their individual goals and the goals of the team.
- They're role models. They practice what they preach.

Coaches do not have to be skilled in every aspect of the jobs they supervise. Some workers on a job may be better performers than their supervisor. The ability of the coach lies not in his or her ability to excel in every aspect of a job but in bringing out the best in team members.

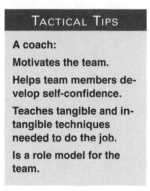

TACTICAL TIPS

A coach:

Motivates the team.

Helps team members develop self-confidence.

Teaches tangible and intangible techniques needed to do the job.

Is a role model for the team.

Executive Coaching

In many companies, coaching has been restricted to helping workers become more effective in their jobs or in preparing junior employees to move up to more responsible positions. In recent years companies have found that even senior members of their staffs can benefit from coaching. Often the characteristics that helped a person move up the ladder are different from the characteristics needed to succeed as a managing executive.

According to a survey of chief executive officers, 45 percent said senior level executives need coaching in new management skills and techniques.

In another survey of human resource executives, poor communication skills were regarded as the number one problem in how managers *manage* people. Poor interpersonal skills was cited as the number one problem in how managers *relate to people.*

In addition, the surveyed CEOs revealed the skills they most want to develop in members of their executive teams: team building, strategic thinking, leadership, the ability to motivate others, entrepreneurship and well-roundedness. Executive coaching is one way of developing these special skills in individuals.

We have found that the following are the ten most common skill deficits where coaching was indicated:

1. *Management:* Assuring that assignments are clearly presented, holding employees accountable, providing direction and support, facilitating consensus, and providing mentoring, trust, recognition and rewards.

2. *Empathic Listening:* Talking less and paying more attention when others talk. In addition, asking the right questions, not interrupting too much, showing enthusiasm and emotion, balancing seriousness with humor, good body language and smiling.

3. *Collaboration:* Developing relationships with associates within and outside of the team, treating people consistently, building alliances, networking, maintaining a win-win attitude and mingling with others.

4. *Conflict Resolution:* Developing constructive approaches to confronting others as conflicts arise; and giving clear, direct feedback in a nonaggressive fashion that demonstrates respect and support.

5. *Positive Attitudes:* Giving consideration to other viewpoints with an open mind, demonstrating enthusiasm, focusing on positive solutions rather than negative problems, and presenting opposing views with a win-win approach.

6. *Self-Confidence:* Being willing to take reasonable risks without being overwhelmed by fear of failure and without becoming defensive; taking tough stands in a decisive, forceful way.

7. *Being Respectful:* Letting others know that they can make a valuable contribution, demonstrating a true respect for other's viewpoints without appearing to be condescending or arrogant.

8. *Strategic Leadership:* Viewing the business from a big-picture, long-term perspective; building strategic plans; articulating ways to implement these plans; and developing strategic initiatives.

9. *Establishing Priorities:* Managing time effectively, setting reasonable standards, letting others know what is expected of them, and holding them accountable without micromanaging them.

10. *Upward Communication:* Keeping upper managers advised of the status of your activities, knowing their priorities, selling your concepts to your bosses when you know when you are right, promoting the accomplishments of all the members of your team.

Techniques of Coaching

As part of our research for this book, we interviewed Edward G. Verlander, a management consultant who not only is a successful executive coach, but also has trained numer-

---

QUOTES AND QUIPS

"The question often arises, can people ever really change? But if we think about it for a moment, everyone knows someone who has changed significantly and sometimes quickly. History and literature are replete with examples from Moses and the burning bush to Ebenezer Scrooge. The more relevant question is, why do some people change and under what circumstances? Fortunately, modern psychological research is beginning to provide some major answers."
—Raymond P. Harrison, Ph.D., executive Transformetrics

ous executive coaches. He suggests the following key action steps be taken to assure successful coaching.

Step 1: State the purpose of the discussion

Why: Make sure the person being coached fully understands the reason for the coaching. When that person has requested coaching, the purpose of the discussion will already be clear. When you initiate the process, you must make it clear why you have done so. By stating the purpose of the discussion right at the beginning, you help the other person to focus on your input and to be more receptive.

How: Be sure you understand your purpose before you start the process. Remember, an important feedback principle is to focus on the person's actions, not on their personality. State that you would like to give the person some feedback about something you have observed in his or her performance.

Step 2: Describe specifically what you have observed

Why: When you start off by describing specific observations, you help the other person understand exactly what you mean. There are three important ideas here: 1) be specific; 2) focus on direct observations rather than opinions and rumors; and 3) balance positive and negative observations.

First, very general feedback may be more confusing than helpful. By being specific you help the other person really understand your point. Second, it is important to separate what you have actually observed from your opinions or what others have told you. If you begin with an opinion, it can turn people off or make them defensive.

How: When giving feedback, avoid generalities, be specific. Avoid irritators such as "yes, but," "you usually," "you always," or "you never." *Stress both positive and negative observations.* Have a specific event or action in mind and be able to say when and where it happened, who was involved and what the results were. Stick to what you personally observed and do not try to speak for others. Remember that third-hand information is not feedback—it's gossip. State the positive things first, then the areas that need improvement.

Step 3: Describe the impact and action of what you have observed

Why: When you describe your reactions to their behavior, people understand the impact their behavior has had on you and others. Your personal reactions can provide useful information for your co-workers. This helps people understand how others perceive them and the impact of their behavior that may be causing problems. It serves to get their attention, when needed.

How: After you have described the facts, offer your reactions to those facts. Make sure you identify those reactions as your personal point of view. Tell how the other person's actions make you feel. Give examples of how you and others are affected. Be sure to link your reactions to getting the job done.

Step 4: Search for solutions and offer helpful ideas

Why: After you describe the impact and offer your personal viewpoint, employees need to know what to do with this information. You can help them by suggesting constructive ideas. When giving corrective and developmental feedback, it is important to include helpful ideas for improving things. Offering ideas shows that your intention is to be friendly, constructive and a good colleague.

How: Start a dialogue. Ask questions and offer ways to fix the problem. Make sure your suggestions are things he or she can do. Give practical examples. Also, offer your ideas tactfully, not as commands. You could state improvements as: *"The next time you try that, I'd suggest you do the following..."* or *"Have you thought of doing it this way?"*

Step 5: State expectations and show encouragement

Why: To make sure that the future is better than the past. After you have had a good discussion about the ways to solve a problem, the new behaviors that will help the person do better the next time around, and you've both agreed on a course of action, it is important to say something that makes it clear you want to see those changes and improvements.

How: Review the major points/actions/changes you have discussed. If you have given positive feedback, emphasize the main strengths you have observed. For corrective feedback, stress the main things you expect the person to do differently. Say something that encourages the person to make those changes, and reiterate your confidence in that person's ability to accomplish them.

In addition, if Step 4 (solution discussion) has been long and involved, it would be advantageous to summarize the entire feedback session in Step 5. By summarizing the discussion, you clarify what was said and agreed to. It also will quickly identify areas of misunderstandings, so that they can be corrected immediately. At this time, take the opportunity to show your support for the man or woman you've been coaching. End the feedback discussion on a positive note and maintain a constructive, positive relationship.

Transformational Coaching

It is often the most seasoned and successful executives who have the most difficulty in making the change. They have a vested interest in maintaining their past success patterns and often have strong personalities which make it difficult for them to change their behavior. In addition, they have built up a reputation within the organization of being tough, often abrasive leaders and small incremental changes in their management style is likely to be either ignored or considered a minor aberration of their usual style. It tends to be unnoticed and therefore not reinforced. This leads to their reverting to their old behavior and no real progress is made.

In an interview with Dr. Raymond Harrison of Executive Transformetrics, he enumerated eight principles to make executive coaching more effective:

Principle #1: Capitalize on "teaching moments"

There are certain times in the lives of all executives when you have their attention about management style issues. These may be times of triumph, disappointment, personal crises, leaps in levels of responsibility, demotions, etc. These periods of heightened emotionality and vigilance are also opportunities for learning because as these people flounder to regain balance, they will also be receptive to new ideas and suggestions from others.

Principle #2: Organizations arrive at impressions about people as a result of "critical events"

Many executives have reputations that precede them, which were founded on specific events observed by others. The key question is "how do we know what we *think* we know about the executive?" In most cases it can be traced to some specific events that led to the creation of the perception. People come to conclusions about another person as a result of specific interactions with them or observations of them interacting with others.

Principle #3: Memory for critical events is notoriously faulty

A fundamental technique of most executive coaching interventions is that you talk to the executive about problematic things that have happened in the past, what might have been done differently, and what needs to happen differently in the future.

Some of the basic problems with this approach are that people often lie, have selective memories, distort the recollection, or subconsciously create events that never happened.

The practical implication is that it isn't sufficient just to get critical events about an executive's behavior, but it is necessary to get descriptions of the events from several sources. We call this the

Roshomon technique in tribute to the ancient Japanese story of the same name about a robbery and attack told from multiple perspectives. Hearing a specific event described from the perspective of several participants and observers gives it more depth and reality, causing the executive to deal with the collective perceptions.

Principle #4: Practice to mastery

Practice to mastery refers to learning an activity not just to the point of competence, but to the point where the behavior can be produced easily and automatically. Think of learning to drive a stick-shift car. Once it is mastered, you do not think about shifting gears, it occurs virtually automatically.

When an activity is practiced and learned to the point of mastery, it is also more likely that *transfer of training* will occur. For example, if one masters a four-speed transmission, he or she can usually master a five-speed easily. Practice to mastery facilitates transfer of training to related situations that cannot be anticipated by the executives or their coaches. A good example of this is that if one fully masters the techniques of giving employees accurate, specific, and constructive performance feedback, it will be much easier to use the same techniques with a subordinate who seeks career guidance.

> **TACTICAL TIPS**
>
> Activities must be over-learned and practiced to the point where the individual can reproduce them easily. Once learned, they must be put into practice *immediately* in the workplace. Failure to practice will lead to regression to the former ways.

Principle #5: Behavior drives attitudes

Changes in ideas, assumptions and attitudes as well as emotions and motivations are critical if lasting change is to occur. Direct methods of verbal persuasion are often useless. Psychologists understand that what happens as a person is being harangued to behave in a particular way is that they react to the threat of diminished personal choice with silent counter arguments, leading them to come out of the experience even more entrenched in their positions than before.

So how can one change attitudes? Surprisingly, direct methods of verbal persuasion have often been shown to be worse than useless. Studies in smoking cessation, for instance, have shown that when subjects are given lectures or films about the evils of nicotine, they are even less likely to stop than groups receiving no treatment at all. Psychologists now understand that what happens as people are being harangued to behave in a particular way is that they react to the threat of diminished personal choice with silent counter arguments, resulting in their coming out of the experience more entrenched in their positions than before.

Attitude change must *follow* behavioral change. In the example of smoking cessation noted above, it was discovered that interventions like asking subjects to role-play picking up a cigarette and putting it away, or to role-play the refusal of an offer of a cigarette resulted in a greater likelihood of subjects giving up smoking. Research in this field has shown that changes in ideas, attitudes, and values will result in long-lasting behavioral change, but this is likely to be preceded first by actual changes in behavior.

Principle #6: Stakeholder analysis and action planning

Executives do not just work alone; they are constantly interacting with others: superiors, peers, subordinates, customers, etc. Analyzing who the key stakeholders are and developing productive relationships with them is essential for success.

Once this key constituency has been determined for the executive being coached, initiatives need to be taken with each stakeholder.

Principle #7: Measure what you want to change

Feedback about one's performance is critical to any kind of ongoing learning. An essential aspect of feedback is that if it is to be helpful, it must be fairly immediate, allowing for quick corrections. Whatever methodology is used, selection of the specific behaviors needed for change is essential. The executive who resists the culture change because of fear of losing power over others needs to identify specific critical events with peers that have contributed to their negative perception of him. With the help of the coach, that person must devise new behaviors that will begin to challenge those perceptions, followed by timely and accurate feedback.

Principle #8: Reward what has been changed

People need reinforcement for the changes they make. A systematic reward program best accomplishes this. This may take the form of tangible rewards—bonuses, salary increases, profit sharing, etc.— or intangible rewards such as special recognition. However, to make this effective, the reward must tie in specifically with the things that are changed in the management behavior of the executive. It starts with a clear discussion between the executive and his or her boss outlining the behavioral goals and how and when they should be attained. Then the behavior should be monitored, deviations pointed out, corrections made and followed through. Unless the executive involved truly changes, no reward should be given — and indeed, failure to change should be considered a serious negative factor in that person's next performance review.

> QUOTES AND QUIPS
>
> "When teaching adults:
> - Encourage independence. Adults want control over how they learn.
> - Link learning to daily work life. Minimize theory; emphasize practicality.
> - Focus on the learner, not the lesson."
>   —Malcolm Knowles, Educator and author

If these steps are implemented, not only will the individual involved have a very good chance of making a dramatic and rapid change in behavior, but also a powerful message will have been sent to the entire organization about what is really required for executive success.

MEASURING THE EFFECTIVENESS OF TRAINING

Are the time, energy and money spent in training really worthwhile? Until relatively recently there were few tools available to enable organizations to evaluate the effectiveness of their training activities.

Over the past few years much research has been done in this area. Because training is so important in retaining personnel, it seems logical that evaluating it is a critical factor in establishing a culture conducive to retention.

Over the years, many senior executives have been skeptical about the value of training because they could not quantify the results. Attempts to measure the effectiveness of training programs were generally done superficially, usually by asking each participant to fill out a questionnaire reflecting his or her reaction to the program.

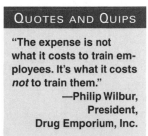

QUOTES AND QUIPS

"The expense is not what it costs to train employees. It's what it costs *not* to train them."
—Philip Wilbur, President, Drug Emporium, Inc.

Donald L. Kirkpatrick, now professor emeritus at the University of Wisconsin, first proposed a model for measuring training programs in 1959. This model was recently revised and updated in his book, *Evaluating Training Programs: The Four Levels*[1]:

The four levels described by Kirkpatrick are:

Level 1: Using the traditional trainee evaluation forms

Although not very sophisticated, immediate feedback by class members serves the function of determining their reaction to the program including such important aspects as the trainee's feelings about course content, instructor effectiveness and whether the course met trainee's expectations.

Level 2: Determination of what the trainee learned

Just as schools have always tested students as to what they learned in class, this level may take the form of a written or oral examination, or a demonstration of skills acquired.

Level 3: Evaluation of behavioral changes and application of learning on the job

This can be a significant tool in determining the value of training. Has what the trainees have been taught been applied on the job? This is easy to measure in training in such areas as reduction in number of rejects, increase in productivity, etc. However, it is

---

[1]Kirkpatrick, Donald L., *Evaluating Training Programs: The Four Levels*, San Francisco, Berrett-Koehler, 1994.

much more difficult to measure in the soft skills. Some examples of how this is accomplished will be discussed later in this chapter.

Level 4: Tying training to organizational impact

Did the training result in a measurable improvement in business results? This level focuses on the actual results the program achieves in the organization when the program objectives have been met successfully.

To these four levels, Dr. Jack J. Phillips, a leading consultant in training program evaluation, has added a level.

Level 5: ROI —Return on Investment

This focuses its attention on whether the monetary value of the results exceeds the cost of the program. This may be the most valuable measurement and it will be discussed in depth later in this chapter.

Implementing the Kirkpatrick-Phillips Model

Level 1 evaluations are used by most organizations. They are usually obtained by getting feedback from participants through questionnaires and evaluation reports immediately or shortly after the completion of a training program. *Level 2* evaluations (what has been learned) can be accomplished by written or oral tests right after the program.

Techniques to implement Levels 3 and 4 have been more difficult to develop and apply. Let's look at how this has been accomplished in some companies.

Level 3: Application. Probably the best example of measuring the application of new skills is that developed by Motorola University. Motorola created its university in the 1980s to institute continuous learning as an integral part of its company culture, as described in more detail later in this chapter. To assure its success, they developed a Level 3 evaluation program. According to Karen Neuhengen, Senior Training Evaluation Specialist at Motorola University, the first step was to determine the specific behaviors that represent a soft skill such as leadership and then track the changes in behavior the trainees exhibited.

One of the techniques used is the 360-degree evaluation. Surveys were sent to trainees, their bosses, and their subordinates, in which the trainees were rated on the frequency in which they displayed those behaviors that relate to leadership. This was followed by quarterly discussions between trainees and their bosses to reinforce the principles of the leadership programs. Their primary concern was whether the courses result in the behavior changes that they have been designed to develop.

The Motorola evaluation program has been adopted by several other organizations including the Ford Motor Co., Texaco Refining and Market, Inc., Caterpillar Construction and Mining, Goodyear Tire and Rubber Co., and the Internal Revenue Service.

Level 4: Tying training to organizational impact. A few years ago 26 companies joined in a task force to develop a means of Level 4 evaluation. The result: TVS—Training Valuation System. It starts with an in-depth situation analysis and concludes with the dollar value added to an operation by training or other factors. Through this approach, specific, current and potential values can be identified before training is conducted. It then measures the value obtained after training. If the training fails to produce the anticipated results, it helps to determine why.

A good example of this is Alberta General Telephone, Ltd. of Edmonton, Canada. After this company decided to save training expenses by shortening the entry-level training program for customer service representatives from two weeks to one, they tracked the effect of the decision.

By using the TVS model and performance measures already in place, it was found that reps who completed two weeks of training were able to complete a call in an average of 11.4 minutes. Those completing only one week of training took 14.5 minutes.

> ## QUOTES AND QUIPS
>
> "Most organizations conduct evaluations to measure satisfaction; few conduct evaluations on ROI level. Both are desirable. Evidence shows that if measurements aren't taken at each level, it's difficult to show that any improvement can be attributed to the training."
> —Dr. Jack J. Phillips, President, Jack Phillips Center for Research

The extra time required to complete calls cost the company more than $50,000 in lost productivity in the first six weeks. In addition, the cost of lost quality due to increased errors, increased collectibles and service-order errors brought the added cost to $100,000. Management quickly decided to restore the two-week training programs.[2]

Level 5—A New Approach: Measuring Return On Investment

With the increase in the amount of money being spent on training, questions have been raised as to whether this expenditure is really justified. Until recently there were no studies available concerning this critical area.

In 1994, the American Society for Training and Development (ASTD) published the first of a series of articles describing specific company experience in measuring ROI.[3] The author, Dr. Jack J. Phillips, describes the process as follows:

Two common formulas for calculating return on investment are the benefit cost ratio (BCR) and ROI. To find the BCR you divide the total benefits by the cost. In the ROI formula, the costs are subtracted from the total benefits to produce the net benefits, which are then divided by the costs.

For example, a literacy skills training program at Magnavox produced benefits of $321,600 with a cost of $38,233. The BCR is 8.4. For every $1 invested, $8.4 in benefits were returned. The net benefits are $321,600 - $38,233 = $283,367. The ROI is $283,367 divided by $38,233 x 100 = 741 percent. Using the ROI formula, for every $1 invested in the program, there was a return of $7.4 in benefits.

Typically, the benefits are annual, the amount saved or gained in the year after training is completed. The benefits may continue

---

[2]Fitz-ens, Jac, "Yes, You Can Weigh Training Values," *Training*, July 1994, pp. 54-58.
[3]Phillips, Jack J. "ROI: The Search for Better Practices," *Training and Development*, Feb. 1996, pp. 42-47.

after the first year, but the effect begins to diminish. In a conservative approach, long-term benefits are omitted from calculations. In the total cost of a program, the development cost is usually front-loaded and prorated over the first year of implementation. Or, you can prorate development costs over the projected life of the program.

The basic steps in measuring ROI[4] include:

1. Collection of data. The information that is needed in order to measure effectiveness include:

   Hard data: These include:

   > Production output (units produced, forms processed, etc.)

   > Quality (scrap, waste, rejects, returns, etc.)

   > Equipment downtime

   > Employee overtime

   > Training time

   > Costs (overhead, sales expense, accident costs, etc.)

   Soft data: These include:

   > Employee absenteeism, turnover, tardiness, etc.

   > Employee grievances, discrimination charges, job satisfaction, loyalty, etc.

   > Employee development (promotion, training programs attended, performance rating, skills acquired, etc.)

2. Isolate the effect of training from other factors that may have contributed to the results. This includes:

   Changes in the overall economy

   Changes in the industry

   Changes in management

   Installation of new equipment

---

[4]Phillips, Jack J. "ROI: The Search for Better Practices," *Training and Development,* Feb. 1996, pp. 60-61.

Installation of new processes

Significant changes in personnel

3. Convert results into monetary benefits.

Phillips suggests five steps for converting data into monetary values:

Step 1: Focus on a single unit. For hard data, identify a particular unit of improvement in output (such as products, services, and sales), quality (often measured in terms of errors, rework and product defects or rejects), or time (to complete a project or respond to a customer order). A single unit of soft data can be one employee grievance, one case of employee turnover or a one-point change in the customer-service index.

Step 2: Determine the value for each unit. Place a value on the unit identified in step 1. That's easy for measures of production, quality, time, and cost. Most organizations record the value of one unit of production or the cost of a product defect. But the cost of one employee absence, for example, is difficult to pinpoint.

Step 3. Calculate the change in performance. Determine the performance change after factoring out other potential influences on the training results. This change is the output performance, measured as hard or soft data that is directly attributed to training.

Step 4. Obtain an annual amount. The industry standard for an annual performance change is equal to the total change in performance during one year. Actual benefits may vary over the course of a year or extend past one year.

Step 5. Determine the annual value. The annual value of improvement equals the annual performance change multiplied by the unit value. Compare the product of this equation to the cost of the program, using the formula: ROI = net annual value of improvement − program cost.[5]

---

[5]Phillips, Jack J. "How Much is Training Worth?" *Training and Development,* April 1996, p. 22.

As you can see, the making of ROI evaluations takes considerable time and money. The ASTD study found that it was not feasible or necessary to subject every program to level 5 evaluations. Many organizations required all of their training programs to be evaluated at level 1 and 40 to 70 percent of the training activities at level 2. Both of these levels are relatively easy and inexpensive to utilize. Level 3 (on-the-job application) takes more time and expense to perform and was used on only 30 to 50 percent of programs. Only 10 percent of programs were evaluated at Level 4 (business results) and only 5 percent at Level 5 (ROI), as both of these processes require significant resources and budgets.

EXAMPLES OF GOOD TRAINING PROGRAMS

Many companies have highly successful training activities. Among such organizations are:

Walt Disney World Resorts

Disney University is not a campus but a process for training all employees of this enterprise. Jayne Parker, Director of Training and Development for Disney University commented: "Our training exercises reinforce the basic foundation of what Disney is and what makes us different as an organization. The first thing we want our people to understand is the culture of Disney and our values. That way, all employees, regardless of the positions they hold can communicate them to guests through their work."

The first week includes a workshop called "Traditions," in which, using multi-media techniques, the participants are given an overview of Disney history and culture and the vision of the organization. The facilitators for the sessions are a variety of cast members (the generic term for all employees of Disney theme parks, whether they get into costumes or not). Professional facilitators lead only technical and executive sessions. The cast members share with the trainees their own interactions with guests (the Disney term for customers).

What makes this program really unique is that the trainees mingle among the visiting crowds at the parks to observe and study cast members in action. Parker says, "We are witnessing people who are experiencing their one fantasy day of the year... Our training helps each of us understand that, whether we are in costume, at a desk or back in the laundry, we are all here to help serve the guest, which is our business." The result: The attrition rate at Disney is only 15 percent compared with 60 percent for the rest of the hospitality industry.[6]

Saturn Co.

To manufacture the Saturn, General Motors created an entirely new organizational structure. The use of teams is the key to this structure. An important facet of the training program for all employees is Saturn University whose function is to teach employees to operate as continuously learning, fully independent work teams.

The first part of the program involves training or retraining in quality, finance, and other areas. This is done in traditional classroom format. Gary High, manager of resources development, states: "Teams learn from day one where they fit in the overall process. They know who are their upstream suppliers in production, and who are the customers of their production. They also learn what the ramifications are if their customer expects one hundred parts, but receives only ninety-five. ...They must understand the consequences of that."

Once the basic training is completed, the teams become responsible for their own development. High noted: "As a team they're running a business. They manage their own budgets, order their own materials and gauge their own educational progress."

Each employee is responsible for creating his or her own training and development plan. It may be brushing up on current skills or acquiring new skills. It can include attending seminars, complet-

---

[6]Carey, Robert. "Five Top Training Corporations," *Successful Meetings*, Feb. 1995, pp. 58-59.

ing computer-based training programs, even teaching a training session or cross-training a team member.

Half of all training is in the soft skills. High says: "People make a difference here—not technology. These are highly intelligent, motivated people doing their jobs every day, and we have to support them and provide a nurturing environment."

Saturn guarantees that each employee will receive a minimum of 92 training hours while on the job; however, the average for most workers is 170. Gary High says: "Our definition of a leader is someone who teaches." The best example of Saturn's commitment to education is that all executives, including the CEO, teach at Saturn University.

Allstate Insurance Company

The Senior Management Team at Allstate Insurance Company, the nation's largest publicly held personal lines insurance company, laid the groundwork in 1996 to maximize business results through the creation and implementation of a long-term, systemic leadership development process. According to Trina Stephens, president of Human Resource Dynamics, Inc. in Boiling Springs, North Carolina, "the process consists of a four-phase cycle of Assessment, Feedback, Development Planning, and Development."

"A 360-degree feedback instrument was created and became the core of assessment and development efforts for all leaders in the company. The preliminary results as to the success of the program were compiled by correlating data from the 360-degree feedback instrument with an existing tool, *The Quarterly Leadership Measurement Survey*. The findings indicate there is a relationship between leadership behavior and superior business results and that certain behaviors create more impact than others. Allstate is using this data to more aggressively develop its near-term and future leaders."

What helps make the Allstate example so powerful is the fact that the company went to such lengths not only to generate baseline data on the behavior-related effectiveness of executives, but also found credible ways to link the demonstrating of certain behaviors to the bottom-line performance of the organization. According to measurement expert Ron Stone of Jack Phillips Center for Research, "that's one of the big reasons Allstate has had so much success over the years retaining its best people. It knows what it needs and expects in executive behavior and has found ways to measure the impact certain leadership-related behaviors have on the performance and profitability of the firm. It really is an excellent model."

GTE

A few years ago, GTE, which has since merged with Bell Atlantic and formed a new company called Verizon, was the fourth largest telephone company in the United States. The company served both commercial and residential customers, and had previously undergone a merger, a major reorganization, and substantial downsizing. Proposed changes in government regulations were in the offing. Employees at all levels were experiencing the effect of these changes with no end in sight.

An employee opinion survey in 1996 showed that satisfaction ratings of hourly employees on a broad range of workplace issues were falling. To correct this, GTE formed a Culture Council made up of employees from a cross-section of the firm. Its function was to seek ways to share information, encourage employee involvement, demonstrate leadership commitment, and reward achievement.

The first step involved benchmarking successful culture changes in other organizations. The Council studied the practices of these firms, taking into account the differences in their work environments and that of GTE. From this they developed the Culture

Initiative, a comprehensive culture change program consisting of the following elements:

- Coaches' clinics. These one-day meetings were geared for frontline supervisors for information sharing, problem solving, skills development and training.

- Jump starters. Structured meetings in which cross-functional, multi-level teams raised and resolved issues.

- Continuous process improvement. A process to improve cost, quality, and time measures for nine key business processes.

- Employee zealots. This program introduced the principles of *appreciative inquiry*. This is a method of studying what gives life to an organization to enhance its vitality and effectiveness rather than emphasizing what's wrong with it.

Using this approach enables an organization to discover the best of its past and present and to design its future. It involves a detailed, four-part process:

1. Discovering. Understanding and appreciating the "as-is" situation.
2. Dreaming. Imagining what might be.
3. Designing. Determining what should be.
4. Delivering Results. Creating what will be.

All of these were fueled by a training course for frontline employees to learn about GTE's business, recent industry developments, and the utilization of the principles of appreciative inquiry as it applies to day-to-day work.

One of the early results of this program is that GTE has a renewed recognition of the importance of employee understanding and support of the company's business direction. A performance measure now is in place that tracks how well employees understand the business direction and how well they think information is shared within the company. In just one year's time (1996-1997) employee's support for GTE's business direction jumped 50 percent and their perception that information is shared openly rose nearly 140 percent.

One example of the result of the training was increased employee participation and innovations. This was demonstrated in the work of the collections process team. In one year (1996), the team improved GTE's credit verification process, resulting in the collection of $3 million. They streamlined the payment process saving $7 to 8 million annually, and they developed a new way to automate the insufficient funds process, saving $4 million.

As a large company with more than 60,000 employees, GTE could commit significant resources to its Culture Initiative—$4.2 million in 1997. But any organization can adopt these elements:

- Creating cross-functional teams to identify internal and external factors affecting the organization's culture.

- Using benchmarking to discover the best problem-solving techniques used by other organizations—such as training, continuous process involvement, and including all employees in a positive way in performance management systems.

- Establishing a common set of principles to bring all employees into the change process.

GTE's program was recognized in 1997 as one of the winners of the American Society for Training & Development's "Excellence in Practice" award.[7]

In 2000, when GTE merged with Bell Atlantic to form Verizon, the people responsible for coordinating the human resources aspects of the merger studied what was accomplished in 1996 and 1997. What they learn from this experience will be a major influence on the steps taken to integrate the cultures of both parties in the new organization.

QUOTES AND QUIPS

"Be not afraid of growing slowly, be afraid only of standing still."
—Chinese Proverb

---

[7]Cheney, Scott and Jarrett, Lisa L. "Up-front Excellence for Sustainable Competitive Advantage." *Training and Development,* June 1998, pp. 45-46.

SUM AND SUBSTANCE

- As corporate cultures change, employees will often be required to handle more and more functions and tasks. The only way this can be accomplished is through total commitment to training and development at all levels.

- The Success Development Process consists of four steps:

  1. Trainees must be conditioned to accept that training will involve change in their behavior.

  2. Content of training should be presented and demonstrated in an interesting and dynamic manner.

  3. Trainees must practice what has been learned in the class and on the job.

  4. Training must be followed up and new behavior reinforced.

- Trainers must not only utilize the most effective techniques of instructing, but must also be good coaches. A coach has the ability to recognize each person's strengths and limitations and work with each to maximize his or her potential.

- Mentors are valuable resources in developing the skills of their protégés—and equally important in orienting them to the corporate culture.

- It is often the most seasoned and successful executives who have the most difficulty in making the change. They frequently have a vested interest in maintaining their past success patterns and often have strong personalities which make it difficult for them to change their behavior. An effective way to deal with this is "transformational coaching."

- A company's training investment is most likely to pay off best when training is held accountable for results, used only when it is the appropriate tool, and linked to the company strategy.

- The Kirkpatrick-Phillips Five Levels of Measuring training are:

  Level 1: Using the traditional trainee evaluation forms. Although not very sophisticated, immediate feedback by class members helps determine their reaction to the program, including such important aspects as the trainee's feelings about course content, instructor effectiveness, and whether the course met expectations.

Level 2: Determination of what the trainee learned. Just as schools have always tested students as to what they learned in class, this level may take the form of a written or oral examination, or a demonstration of skills acquired.

Level 3: Evaluation of application of learning to the job. This can be a significant tool in determining the value of training. Has what the trainees have been taught been applied on the job?

Level 4: Estimating impact. Did the training result in a measurable improvement in business results?

Level 5: ROI—Return on Investment. This focuses its attention on whether the monetary value of the results exceeds the cost of the program.

Ongoing, well organized, and carefully implemented training programs keep employees at the cutting edge of effectiveness and are a major contributor to reducing overall turnover and especially in retaining your best employees.

14

Sowing the Seeds for Continued Success

The war for talent is not likely to abate for many years to come. The need for highly trained personnel will continue to increase as the technology becomes more complex. Not only will companies compete for young, knowledgeable workers just entering the world of work, but also there will be increased efforts to "steal" experienced specialists away from their current jobs.

This poses two major challenges to companies who plan to thrive in the next decades: (1) What can they do to develop the talents they need so there will be an ongoing supply of qualified candidates for their expanding job requirements, and (2) How can they make their organizations the type of workplace that is conducive to attracting and retaining "A-players."

BUILDING A CORE OF TALENTS

Meeting the first challenge—developing an ever-growing supply of people with the needed talents—can only be accomplished by the combined efforts of companies, government, and local communities. It starts in the schools from the primary grades on.

The first step is to develop an interest in the basic tools needed for future careers as early as in the elementary schools. More innovative approaches to teaching mathematics and science at the earliest levels will stimulate many children's interest in pursuing these fields. This early interest, once kindled, can be cultivated and enhanced as the children move into middle and high schools.

Here is where companies like yours can be of great help. Many schools don't have the funds for laboratory equipment, up-to-date computers, and even appropriate textbooks and library resources. Financial aid to the schools in your district to remedy these lacks will go a long way to build up that future source of talent.

In addition, you and other companies in the community can arrange for some staff members to work with the teachers as guest lecturers or demonstrators, and to work with the students as mentors. Not only will this provide practical know-how to amplify what the students are learning in the class, but will make the company visible to the students, who, after all, are potential employees.

This is not a new idea. Some companies have been doing this for years. If there's a shortage of certain types of skills needed by a company, it can request the high school or community college to develop courses to train students in those skills. For example, when a chemical company in western Pennsylvania suffered a shortage of lab technicians, it worked with the local schools to create a series of courses to train students in the needed skills. The company donated the necessary equipment to the schools, and recommended two staff members to teach the courses. Once the program was established, the schools trained dozens of students who were hired by the company.

QUOTES AND QUIPS

"Progress comes from the intelligent use of experience."
—Elbert Hubbard
American essayist

Community Colleges and Local Universities

Community colleges usually offer courses that are designed to serve the industries in their communities. For example, in South Carolina, where many textile companies are located, community colleges offer courses in various aspects of technologies needed in that industry. In Wichita, Kansas, home of Lear Jet, Cessna and a Boeing plant, community colleges train students in aviation-based programs. One innovative company in Milwaukee came up with an idea that really paid off. They offered the graduates of the community college, whom they hired, tuition refund programs to continue their studies at the evening sessions of local four-year colleges.

Community colleges are not the only training facilities that a company may use. Many universities have continuing education divisions, which offer certificate programs in special areas. Some years ago the Employment Agency Association of New York decided that a formal program to train employment agency interviewers would be valuable. A representative of the association contacted New York University's School of Continuing Education. The association and the school worked together to develop a program that met the needs of the association and the standards of the university.

Internships

One of the most effective ways of aiding students in acquiring the skills you need is setting up an internship program. Such programs are established so that students can work part time at the company while pursuing their studies. Although some companies employ high school students as interns, most offer internships at community colleges, trade schools and four-year colleges. Internships not only give the students practical experience, but also enable the company to feed back to the school suggestions on the effectiveness of the courses and what, if any, changes might be made to improve the students' training. Another advantage of student

TACTICAL TIPS

Looking for interns? You can advertise for them on the Internet at little or no cost. Log in at one of these sites: *www.intern-shipprograms.com*; *www.jobweb.org*, or *www.studentsearch.com*.

internships is that the company can observe the interns and identify those whom they may want to hire once they complete the program.

Lifelong Learning

"What I learned in school was obsolete by the time I graduated." Have you heard that plaint? Unfortunately, it's true. Modern technology is so dynamic that it's very difficult to keep up with it. Does this mean that the education one gets in school has been a waste of time? Of course not. Everything one learns becomes the base upon which new learning is built. But, it does bring another challenge to management. Companies now have the added responsibility to assure that their employees keep up with the state of the art in their fields.

Practitioners of most professions make a point to continually study the latest developments in their specialties. They enroll in seminars, read professional journals, take on-line programs and attend meetings of professional associations to accomplish this. Companies must require all employees to be just as diligent in keeping up with developments in their areas of expertise.

A growing trend in progressive companies today is to appoint a senior executive as Chief Learning Officer (CLO) to be responsible for providing ongoing training of employees in whatever areas are pertinent to their jobs and their continuing growth. We predict that as companies recognize the contribution ongoing learning makes to higher productivity and greater retention of "A-players," the status of the CLO will equal that of other senior executives.

As pointed out in Chapter 13 there are a variety of training and development techniques that companies can use. As the approach to training becomes more sophisticated, companies will turn more and more to outside training specialists to bring the appropriate types of training to their employees. We predict that much more of the basic types of training will be provided through on-line sources. New software programs are being designed, implemented, and tested every day and will enable companies to train in operational skills more rapidly, efficiently, and more cost effectively. In addition, new approaches are being developed for training in the more complex areas such as management development, leadership, communications, interpersonal relations, and other soft skills. We see increased use of specially designed programs based on depth analyses of a company's unique needs. Such programs are best constructed and conducted by professional training consultants.

Another area that many companies have found extremely valuable in keeping current employees on top of their jobs and preparing them for future growth has been executive coaching (see Chapter 13]. We predict that such programs will become an essential tool that successful companies will use over the next decade.

ATTRACTING AND RETAINING "A-PLAYERS"

Meeting the first challenge, assuring an adequate supply of talent, is both a community and a company responsibility. Meeting the second challenge, attracting and retaining talented employees, rests entirely on the company. Here you are on your own, indeed, you are competing with companies, not only in your own industry, but also in the entire community or even on a national or global level for these hard-to-find and harder-to-keep men and women.

Attracting and Hiring Staff

Remember those 22 mistakes companies make in hiring? (See Chapter 4.) To sow the seeds of success for the next decade, not only will companies take steps to avoid those errors, but also will become proactive in bringing "A-players" into their ranks.

As pointed out in Chapter 4, company recruiters will be surfing the Internet on a 24/7 basis. They will be visiting Web sites of competitors to identify their top producers and attempt to entice them away. They'll be reviewing the constant flow of listings on the Internet referral services such as *Monster.com, Careerpath.com,* and others, and will be on the lookout for the talents needed by their firms. Internet recruiting will probably be the major source for staffing within the next few years. According to research by Hunt-Scanlon Associates, Stamford, Connecticut, the budgets for Internet recruiting will increase from its 1999 total of $250 million to almost $8 billion dollars by 2005. Farsighted recruiters are gearing their organizations to make the most of this growing medium.

Another major activity of the successful recruiter is the use of current employees to refer people they know using creative incentives. For example, in addition to giving bonuses to employees who

refer candidates who are hired, one company conducted a quarterly lottery for all employees who made recommendations—not only of people who were hired, but also of any candidate that reached the stage of a first interview. Lottery prizes included large screen TVs, computers and similar high-ticket items. This resulted in an increase in referrals and employment of some really great candidates.

Compensation packages and perks will continue to be major factors in attracting people, and companies must keep up with what is being offered by other firms competing for the same type of personnel. Innovative perks may attract certain people, but these alone will not be the main reason people will join a firm.

By far the most effective way of attracting, and indeed retaining, "A-players" is determining what that person seeks in his or her job and creating a position that will integrate those needs with the objectives and goals of the company. Tough job? You bet! Attracting people depends on the reputation a company has for having a culture in which the needs of the employee and the goals of the company are congruent. What attracts good people is much the same as what keeps good people from leaving.

Retaining "A-players"

It's hard to find "A-players" and even harder to keep them. New firms spring up every day and in their desperation to build a staff, they entice our best people with higher salaries, hiring bonuses, stock options, wild perks and many promises. This starts a cycle in which the companies that lose those staff members need to replace them and go after people in other companies. It's a never-ending circus. What can any one company do to hold on to their best people?

Counteroffers—more money, a promotion, more perks, a better assignment—do help somewhat. We've discussed all of these throughout this book. But money and benefits alone don't solve the problem. As we pointed out, the key is the company culture, the corporate way of life. The organizational culture must be one that encourages innovation, reduces bureaucracy, emphasizes collaboration, and is flexible enough to change when change is warranted.

What do people want? Although individuals do differ in what they seek from their jobs, management experts, psychologists and focus groups all agree that most men and women crave recognition, a climate in which they can develop their skills and the opportunity to do work that they feel is meaningful. Here are some examples of seeds that you can sow now that will allow you to reap benefits over the years.

A proactive approach to promotion

As noted in Chapter 4, more and more successful companies are taking an active role in helping talented employees move ahead in their careers.

Diane M. was fortunate to work for such a company. When Cozy Cushions hired Diane, she was assigned to the marketing department as an administrative assistant to the Brand Manager for institutional sales.

As Cozy Cushions had developed a long-term plan for expansion, all managers were requested to keep alert for employees who demonstrated potential for advancement. They were designated as 'HIPOs' meaning high potential personnel. It didn't take Diane's boss, Kevin L., long to recognize that she fit the designation. Not only did she perform her work in an exemplary manner, she also contributed creative ideas for dealing with complex problems.

The Human Resources department carefully monitored the progress of people, who like Diane, had been targeted as 'HIPOs'. An HR representative met with those employee's from time to time to discuss their goals and to work with them toward accomplishing those goals.

Although Diane was happy in her job and wanted to move up the marketing ladder, she was open-minded about other opportunities within the company that might be interesting and rewarding. The

H.R. manager reviewed her record and noted that her MBA was in marketing; but her undergraduate college major was in Spanish. When queried about this, she commented that as an undergrad she planned to be a high school teacher of Spanish, but changed her mind as a result of part-time and summer jobs in sales and marketing.

"How fluent is your Spanish now?" he asked.

"Not too bad," she responded, "with a refresher I could become fluent pretty rapidly."

The HR manager then told her about the company's plans to enter the international market. With her background and accomplishments in marketing, plus her knowledge of Spanish, he suggested that she might find this an exciting challenge.

The result: Diane took an immersion course in Spanish and a series of seminars in International Marketing. She was sent on two extensive trips to Latin American countries to work with Cozy's representatives in those countries.

Today, four years later, Diane is the Director of Latin-American marketing for the company. But this is not the end of her training. She is now studying Chinese to prepare for the company's entrance into that up-and-coming market.

WORK-LIFE CONSIDERATIONS

As pointed out in Chapter 10, one of the latest tools employers are increasingly turning to are work/life programs that assist employees with balancing the demands of their personal and professional lives. New technology tools have neither eased the workload nor shortened the workday for many workers, and more and more of them are looking for ways to achieve a better work/life balance, according to a new survey conducted by CareerPath.com. The survey questioned 1,862 Americans from various professions about their work lives. The resulting report, "Balancing Work and Life," concludes that most workers want a job that offers good pay and flexible hours and that will allow them to take care of personal concerns. Forty-nine percent of respondents said that they have deliberately sought out a flexible work schedule, and 74 percent said they would like to work from home. This trend is especially prevalent in white-collar workers between the ages of 20 and 39, who make up the core of our future managers. Family time topped the list of workplace priorities for 82 percent of the men and 85 percent of the women.

What can companies do to meet the demand of workers for a better balance between their jobs and their home life? Here are some suggestions based on what some companies have found successful:

More Effective Use of Available Technology

A tremendous amount of time is consumed in most companies at meetings. Staff members are called into the home office to discuss a variety of matters at regular meetings and special conferences. This not only reduces the amount of time they can use for more productive work, but also in many cases requires them to travel at night or over weekends to attend the meetings. More and more companies are using telephone conference calls to replace face-to-face meetings. By using the Internet to supplement the phone call with visual information such as tables, graphs, diagrams and photos, many meetings can be eliminated and travel minimized. Even employees who are at home or not at their desks can be reached and can participate. This gives the staff member additional time to accomplish creative work or, if they wish, to spend with their families or engage in other personal interests.

Telecommuting

Over the past few years there has been a significant increase in the number of people working out of their homes. Some teams have members who do most of their work at home; even more have members who work at home part of the time. This has been made possible by the use of telecommuting.

Companies have discovered that it's often advantageous to let employees telecommute: It frees up office space for other people. It enables a company to use the services of experienced workers who may not be able to come to the office regularly. These workers include parents with young children, people who can't leave their homes because they care for elderly or ill relatives, people with a temporary or permanent disability, and others who just prefer to work, at least some of the time, from their homes. The computer and modem have enabled companies to communicate in real time with anyone at another location who also has a computer. Documents, drawings, and statistical tables can be transmitted electronically to one person or to dozens of people simultaneously.

Not every type of job is suitable for telecommuting. Many jobs require constant interaction with others on the job or the use of expensive or complex equipment that cannot be provided for home use. However, with a little imagination, jobs that seem to be limited to the office often can be redesigned so that they can be done at home.

Making telecommuting effective

Managers and consultants who have worked with companies that use telecommuters suggest that the key to success for both telecommuters and companies is a well-designed plan for orienting and training all people who are either hired as telecommuters or have transferred to that type of work. This plan should be followed by ongoing interaction between the manager and the telecommuter. Here are some suggestions:

- Set specific hours for working, and stick to them.
- Although some telecommuters are paid on an hourly basis and must keep time logs, most work in salaried jobs in which their work is measured not by hours worked but by their achievement of key results areas. Some jobs require telecommuters to be available at the telephone or at the computer during normal business hours; in others, the specific hours worked aren't important as long as the work is done. However, the manager should always know when the employee can be contacted.
- Set priorities so that both manager and employee are always aware of deadlines and progress on each assignment. Keep a to-do list current at all times. List new assignments and deadlines,

check off work completed, keep a record of what data or materials are needed from other staff members, and what is needed from the telecommuter.

- Managers should be aware of progress on each assignment and be alert to problems as soon as they arise.
- Help should be available and willingly provided.

Keeping telecommuters in the loop

No matter where the team member is located, he or she is still a part of the team and must never be forgotten by the manager or associates at the base facility. Keeping in touch on a regular basis is not limited to passing work back and forth. Telecommuters must be fully integrated into team activities. Here are some suggestions:

1. All area telecommuters should be treated as full members of the group, not as second-class citizens. They're continually informed about all the same things that employees in the home office are told. Because employees who work at home often miss out on the chit chat that goes on in most office environments, some companies send telecommuters a weekly chatty newsletter that includes tidbits about what's going on in its employees' lives.

2. The manager should take a personal interest in each telecommuter. Telephone them at least once a week just to chat about how things are going. If a telecommuter does something special, make a congratulatory call. Send him or her a birthday card or an e-mail greeting, and on special occasions, such as weddings, births, or special anniversaries, send flowers or a snack basket to the telecommuter's home.

3. Meetings are held periodically so that employees who are situated in various locations can regularly meet face to face. To supplement the annual convention that one of our clients holds for its salespeople, quarterly regional meetings are held. Sales reps at these meetings can meet reps from other areas in a more intimate environment than the convention provides. It gives them an opportunity to exchange ideas, get to know their

colleagues as real people, and build up the team's esprit de corps.

4. Sharing of ideas among staff members, whether they work at home or in a company facility, should be expedited. The exchange of ideas isn't limited to meetings. All staff members should be encouraged to communicate with each other by phone, fax, and e-mail. They share with each other their experiences, techniques, and advice about handling problems.

5. The manager should maintain personal contact with all staff members. His or her schedule should include visits to telecommuters to discuss special problems, or just to say "hello."

Secrets of success

As part of our research in preparing this book, we asked several team leaders who work with telecommuters the secrets of their success. Here are some of the responses:

- "I keep the telecommuters informed of all team activities, even those in which they're not directly involved."

- "I invite them to come to the office for business meetings and training programs."

- "As all our home-working members live within commuting distance of the office, I encourage them to participate in such extracurricular activities as bowling leagues, softball teams, and family picnics."

- "Our company puts all home-workers on the distribution list for all the same materials they would receive if they were in-house employees."

- "I require that they visit the office regularly—not just for discussion of their own work but also for in-person discussions about team activities and to give them an opportunity to interact with other team members."

- "I make a point to be easily accessible by telephone. I return voice mail or other messages promptly. I encourage other members to phone telecommuters periodically just to show a personal interest and to give them the opportunity to exchange ideas about overall activities—not just specific work assignments."

TACTICAL TIPS

Members working in remote locations often feel left out of the team's business. Keep them informed of what's going on in the home office and in other regions. Let them share in celebrations and participate in successes.

- "Our members are connected through an intranet program that enables us to have instant messages sent by any team member to any or all others. As our telecommuters are at their monitors most of the time, it's faster and less time-consuming than telephoning."

- "We have a birthday party at one meeting each month for all members who have a birthday that month. E-mail greetings are also sent on the actual birthday."

Working at home isn't for everyone

Be aware of the many potential problems of working at home. One home-based computer programmer complained that her friends and neighbors barged in for friendly chats or to ask her to accept deliveries, be available for service people, and even watch their children. She had to make clear to them that she was an at-home worker, not a lady of leisure. Being assertive cost her some "friends," but it was essential.

Another at-home worker soon found that the freedom of working at home, setting his own time schedule, and avoiding rush hour traffic didn't make up for the social life of the workplace. He missed the interaction of daily contact with colleagues, the gossip around the water cooler, and even the daily parrying with his boss. He chose to return to the office.

Betty B. was thrilled when her request to work at home was agreed to. She was a well-disciplined, self-sufficient person, and she knew that even with two toddlers at home, she could accomplish a great deal. And she did.

Two years later, when her team leader moved up to a higher management position, Betty wasn't even considered for the promotion. When she complained, she was told that the job required being in the home office all of the time and as a telecommuter, she couldn't do it.

Betty agreed that being the team leader would mean giving up working at home, but her gripe was that she wasn't even given the opportunity to make the choice. She learned one of the hard lessons of being a telecommuter. Make sure that prospective telecommuters are fully aware of the negative as well as the positive aspects of working at home. Have them try it for a trial period before agreeing to a permanent arrangement.

Although there are some leadership jobs that can be done by telecommuting, most cannot. Career-oriented people should keep this in mind when opting for working at home. People who work at home one or two days a week are more likely to be considered for promotion than those who work exclusively at home.

Job Sharing

Another way to contribute to the need to resolve the conflict between work and home is job sharing. According to a recent survey by the Society For Human Resources Management (SHRM) 23 percent of companies surveyed employed people working in job sharing positions.

Here's how it works. Two people share one job. For example, at a public utility company, Thelma and Louise are customer service reps. They both perform analogous functions, but due to family responsibilities can only work on a part-time basis. They arrange with the company to share the job. Thelma will work from 8 A.M. to noon; Louise from 1 P.M. to 5 P.M.

At a savings and loan association, Ben and Jerry are loan officers. Ben and his wife decided to share the duties of caring for their newborn son. Jerry is attending law school and needs time for his studies. They arrange to share a job. Ben works Mondays and Wednesdays; Jerry, Tuesdays and Thursdays and each works alternate Fridays. The salaries for their jobs are divided between the workers, and the benefits are adjusted according to their company's policy.

The advantage of job sharing is that an experienced worker is always on duty to perform the work. The downside is that there may be a loss of continuity, and as the perspective of each person may differ somewhat, a loss of consistency. Both of these problems can be overcome with good training and by arranging for frequent meetings in person or electronically between the job sharers. Most firms that have instituted job sharing have been satisfied with the results.

Outsourcing

Another trend we see is the growing use of outside organizations or freelance specialists to handle various aspects of the work that were normally done in-house.

This allows the company to get the work done less expensively but also frees company management to concentrate on the areas in which it is most competent. Let's look at an example from a manufacturer of valves, one of the companies contacted in our research.

Robert L. had been in the traffic department of his firm for 17 years. He had moved up to the number two position in the department and reported to the vice president for distribution. One day he heard a rumor that the company was planning to eliminate the traffic department and subcontract it to an outside source. Panicked, Robert confronted his boss, who verified that the company was seriously considering that option. "But what will happen to me?" Robert asked.

His boss responded that the move was at least a year away and asked him to consider being the subcontractor. Because Robert knew as much about traffic as anyone in the company, the boss suggested that the company would become Robert's first customer and that he was then likely to get additional customers. The boss also suggested that Robert continue in his present job during the transition period but begin the process of developing his new company on his own time. In this way, he could keep things moving smoothly during the transition and be ready to begin functioning as a subcontractor immediately when the new system went into effect.

Companies planning to outsource are often happy to assist one of their own employees in becoming a subcontractor. They can then work with someone they know and trust and who knows their special problems. This process offers to ambitious men and women a career opportunity the company cannot provide internally. By changing the status of these "A-players" from employee to contractor, instead of losing them completely, the company retains their services and contributions to the organization.

Other companies in our survey, that had undergone reorganization and downsizing, retained some of their valuable contributors by using them as freelancers or consultants. This served a dual purpose. The company was able to take advantage of their expertise without keeping them on their permanent payroll, and the individual was given the opportunity to build a consulting practice over time, with the former employer as the first client.

Being an independent entrepreneur isn't for everyone. Risks are involved: The independent business owner has to raise capital, lease workspace, purchase equipment, and perhaps hire staff members. And there's always a risk that it won't work out. Being one's own boss may sound appealing, but it often involves longer hours and harder work than being employed by a company. In addition, health plans, pension plans, insurance, and other benefits must be provided by oneself. People who feel more comfortable under a corporate umbrella may find it difficult to adapt to being in business for themselves.

The Flexible Work Force

Another way that companies are using to reduce turnover is to maintain as small a permanent staff as feasible. The trend toward smaller permanent staffs started in the 1980s and is becoming standard practice in large companies. Why pay wages, benefits, and perks to people who are only needed at peak periods? There are three major sources for obtaining such employees:

1. *On-call workers.* These are a list of employees who have been trained by the company in the requisite skills. They often are former employees who have been downsized or have retired. They are called in when the need arises. This is a common practice in seasonal businesses. The advantage is that you have a pool of skilled workers who are available, and easily identified and contacted. The limitation, of course, is that good workers can often find more steady employment and are not there when needed.

2. *Contract workers.* There are firms whose chief business is to sell the services of their employees to other companies. For example, the engineering field abounds with "job shops," which perform engineering functions for companies who don't have or need a full-time engineering team. A construction company needs civil, mechanical, and electrical engineers to work on the design of a project—a four- or five-month job. They contract the assignment to a job shop that will either do the engineering at their own premises or send a team of engineers to work on the project at the offices of the construction company. When the job is finished, the engineers move on to another assignment.

   In recent years companies have "leased" employees from a variety of contract shops for all kinds of jobs ranging from cleaning up after a flood or hurricane to filling rush orders to providing computer technology. The client companies save the time, trouble, and expense of recruiting personnel not only for jobs that are of short duration, but also sometimes for entire operations. Such firms have very few permanent staff members and lease all but their key managers.

3. *Temp Services.* Unlike the contractors discussed above, temp services provide personnel to work at company premises usually for a short time. For example, they are used to replace employees who are on sick leave or on vacation—an assignment that may last from one or two days to several months. Temps are hired to handle special projects or to deal with rush orders. Temps are not put on the payroll. The company pays the temp service a fee for each employee, and the temp service pays the

workers. Although the fee is higher than the amount they would pay a regular employee, it is cost effective because the company pays no benefits to temps and eliminates the high cost of recruiting for a short-duration job. Because temps are already trained in office skills, the only training they need is to learn the specifics of the work assignment.

Over the past few years there has been an increase in using temps in managerial and professional jobs. Companies have hired temporary managers to head up a company during a transitional period. For example, when the president of a small firm in Long Island, New York, died last year, his heir-apparent was his 25-year-old son. The Board of Directors, realizing that the young man was not prepared to take over the job, hired an experienced manager from a temp service to run the business and train the son.

According to the National Association of Temporary and Staffing Services (NATSS) one of the fasting growing demands for temps has been in the professional segment, such as accounting, law, sales, and management.

ONGOING CULTURAL ASSESSMENT

In this dynamic world, we must expect things to change. What works today may not work tomorrow. What makes our employees happy, productive, and loyal next year may differ from what motivates them this year. Companies must make it a practice to reassess the state of its culture on a regular basis.

Among the factors that lead to changes in the attitudes of employees is the average age level of the workforce, the increase in the number of knowledge-workers in proportion to the total workforce, the technologies used by the company and the priorities of top management.

These changes can be measured by making periodic Organization MRIs (O-MRIs) as described in Chapter 3. For companies that have been relatively stable, a complete O-MRI should be undertaken every five years. For companies where significant changes have occurred, a full O-MRI should be undertaken no later than six months after the changes have been implemented.

Top management should carefully study the results of the O-MRI and action should be instituted as soon as possible to adapt to the findings. For example, six months after one of our clients acquired a smaller competitor, we conducted an O-MRI with the employees of the parent firm and the one they acquired. We identified several areas in which the cultures of the two organizations clashed. This enabled management to set up special training programs to close the gaps between the two groups. The programs were successful in integrating them into a cohesive working team.

Benchmarking

Some firms have been more successful than others in maintaining their "A-players." All of us can learn from them. Will they share their "secrets?" Surprisingly, most will. True, some companies hold tight to what they consider proprietary information, but most are happy to talk about their successes. In the 1990s when the Total Quality Management (TQM) concept was at its height, many companies that had been cited for excellence in quality assurance made a practice of encouraging other firms to visit them to observe their TQM procedures. Indeed, one of the requirements for winners of the Malcolm Baldrige awards—given to companies that were cited for the high quality of their products and services—was that they share the methods that contributed to their success.

Seek out companies that have successful records of retaining their best people. This practice, known as "benchmarking," lets you learn what these firms are doing. What has worked for them may very well work for you. Don't just look at what your competitors are doing. Retention of personnel is not restricted to just your industry, it's a universal problem.

For example, one of our clients, a medium-sized automobile dealership, had read how Sears Roebuck dealt with work-life concerns of its employees. The owner phoned a senior Human Resources executive at Sears' regional headquarters in his area and was invited to visit them. He learned that Sears made regular surveys on employee attitudes concerning workload, stress, work-life balance and other facets of their job satisfaction. He also was invited to sit in on some of their training sessions that dealt with working on some of the problems identified in the surveys. He was introduced to the manager, who was responsible for coordinating the work-life balance. She encouraged him to phone her at any time for information or advice. Even though his dealership was minute compared to the giant retail chain, he was able to adapt several ideas that he learned from that visit to his operation.

The ultimate responsibility in winning the war for talent lies with the top management of the organization. The CEO and the executive team must be fully behind the efforts to change the corporate culture so that an atmosphere of collaboration between management and its employees is created.

The seeds for success in retaining "A-players" will begin to sprout when individuals who work for the organization feel that they are respected, that their talents are being utilized, that they are full participants in the work they perform, that their compensation and benefits are equitable, and that they are able to reach their own goals as they work toward reaching the organization's goals.

These seeds are sown by top management, cultivated by middle level managers, supervisors and team leaders, and will result in a harvest of high morale, low turnover, high productivity and, ideally, an ever increasing bottom line.

SUM AND SUBSTANCE

- Developing an ever-growing supply of people with the needed talents can only be accomplished by the combined efforts of companies, government, and local communities.

- One of the most effective ways of aiding students in acquiring the skills you need is setting up an internship program.

- The key to retaining top people lies in the company culture, the corporate way of life. This culture must be one that encourages innovation, reduces bureaucracy, emphasizes collaboration, and is flexible enough to change when change is warranted.

- By far the most effective way of attracting, and indeed, retaining "A-players" is determining what that person seeks in his or her job and creating a position that will integrate those needs with the objectives and goals of the company.

- One of the latest tools employers are increasingly turning to are work/life programs that assist employees with balancing the demands of their personal and professional lives.

- Some of the approaches in which companies have been successful in reducing turnover include:

  Career pathing. Enabling "A-players" to identify, train for, and be promoted to positions which enable them to reach their career goals within the company.

  Telecommuting. Arranging for employees to work at home part or all of the time.

  Job sharing. Splitting one job between two workers, so each has adequate time off work to meet personal requirements without loss of productivity.

  Assigning work to consultants and freelancers. Assuring that the company can utilize the best available sources without having to hire them as employees.

- Seek out companies that have successful records of retaining their best people. This practice, known as "benchmarking," lets you learn what these firms are doing. What has worked for them may very well work for you. Don't just look at what your competitors are doing. Retention of personnel is not restricted to just your industry, it's a universal problem.

- In this dynamic world, we must expect things to change. What works today may not work tomorrow. What will make our employees happy, productive, and loyal next year may differ from what motivates them this year. A company must make it a practice to reassess the state of its culture on a regular basis.

Appendix

SOURCES OF ARTICLES
ON RECRUITING AND RETENTION

Managers, team leaders, and others who deal with people problems must keep up with what's going on in the human resources arena. The best way to be on the cutting edge of change is to read regularly several of the magazines and newsletters that cover these matters.

Almost every industry and profession has periodicals devoted to its fields, and most of them have occasional articles on retention and recruiting. This is an excellent source of information.

Here is a list of some of the better general publications that either specialize in or have significant coverage of human resources matters.

Across the Board
    The Conference Board
    845 Third Ave.
    New York, NY 10022
    Phone: 212-339-0345
    Fax: 212-980-7014
    Web site: www.conference-board.org

Business Week
    1221 Ave. of the Americas
    New York, NY 10020
    Phone: 800-635-1200
    Fax: 609-426-5434
    Web site: www.businessweek.com

Forbes
    60 Fifth Ave.
    New York, NY 10011
    Phone: 800-888-9896
    Fax: 212-206-5118
    Web site: www.forbes.com

Fortune
    Time-Life Building
    Rockefeller Center
    New York, NY 10020
    Phone: 800-621-8000
    Fax: 212-522-7682
    Web site: www.fortune.com

Harvard Business Review
60 Harvard Way
Boston, MA 02163
Phone: 800-274-3214
Fax: 617-475-9933
Web site: www.hbsp.harvard.edu

HR Magazine
Society for Human Resources
   Management
1800 Duke St.
Alexandria, VA 22314
Phone: 703-548-3440
Fax: 703-836-0367
Web site: www.shrm.org

INC.
477 Madison Ave.
New York, NY 10022
Phone: 212-326-2600
Fax: 212-321-2615
Web site:www.inc..com

Management Review
American Management
   Association
Box 319
Saranac Lake, NY 12983-0319
Phone: 800-262-9699
Fax: 518-891-3653
Web site: www.amanet.org

Manager's Edge
Briefings Publishing Co.
1101 King Street
Alexandria, VA 22314
Phone: 703-548-3800
Fax: 703-684-2136
Web site: www.briefings.com

Nations Business
711 Third Ave.
New York, NY 10017
Phone: 212-692-2215
e-mail: editor@nbmag.com

Success in Recruiting and Retaining
National Institute of Business
   Management
PO Box 9206
McLean, VA 22102-0206
Phone 800-543-2049
Fax: 703-905-8040
e-mail customer@nibm.net

Training
50 South 9th St.
Minneapolis, MN 55402
Phone: 612-333-0471
Fax: 612-333-6526
Web site:
www.trainingsupersite.com

Training and Development
American Society for Training and
   Development
1640 King Street
Alexandria, VA 22314
Phone: 703-683-8100
Fax: 703-683-9203
Web site: www.astd.org

Workforce
245 Fischer Ave.
Costa Mesa, CA 92626
Phone: 714-751-1883
Fax: 714-751-4106
Web site: www.workforce.com

Working Woman
135 West 50 St.
New York, NY 10020
Phone: 800-234-9765
Fax: 212-445-6186
e-mail: wwmagazine@aol.com

HELPFUL WEB SITES

Human Resources Information

For information about equal employment laws: www.eeoc.gov
For statistics on jobs, try the U.S. Dept. of Labor: www.bls.gov
For information about Americans with Disabilities Act (ADA):
www.janweb.icdi.wvu.edu

Helpful Associations

American Management Association:	www.amanet.org
American Psychological Association:	www.apa.org
American Society for Training and Development:	www.astd.org
American Staffing Association:	www.staffingtoday.net
International Foundation of Employee Benefits Plans	(e-mail: pr@ifebp.org)
National Association of Personnel Services:	www.napsweb.org
Society for Human Resources Management:	www.shrm.org
H.R. News on Line:	www.shrm.org/hrnews
Pro2Net:	www.hrpro2net.com/x19137.xml
Industry Week Magazine:	www.industryweek.com

Job Listings

To advertise your open jobs or to search for applicants who may qualify for your jobs, use the following Web sites:

www.monster.com	www.hotJobs.com
www.careerpath.com	www.dice.com
www.careerMosaic.com	www.careerBuilder.com
www.headHunter.net	www.nationJob.com
www.jobSearch.org	www.jobs.com

Index

"A-players", attracting, 345-46

360-degree assessments, 55-57, 66-67, 329

Abilities
as leaders, 297-307
to do the job, 123-26
to take criticism, 137
to work in a team, 137-38

Active listening, 161, 162

Advancement opportunities, 5-7

Applicants, *see* Candidates

Appreciation, for employees, 12-13, 241-42

Appreciative inquiry, 337

Aptitude tests, 167

Assessment of attitudes, 46-52

Attitude
of leaders, 304-05
of learners, 313

Authority, disregard for, 283

Benchmarking, 359-60

Biases in hiring, 99-100

Boredom on job, 242

Boss mentality, 4-5

Bureaucracy, 251

Bypassed employees, 223-24

Candidates
"dream," 88-89
ability to perform, 123-26

intangible qualities, 170-73
pre-screening, 112-26
pre-screening, 92-94
qualifications, 81, 84-85
reasons for rejecting, 85-87
special characteristics, 139-40
unqualified, 88, 94

Career goals, 138

Career path
applicant's, 124-25
lack of, 5-7
of new hire, 233-34
stagnant, 248-49

Career pathing, 6-7, 109-10, 347-48

Casual dress, 200

Certified Public Accountant (CPA), 88-89

Chief Learning Officer (CLO), 344

Chronological resumes, 115-16

Climate of understanding, 2-19

Club memberships, 198

Coaches, qualities of, 317

Coaching, 7, 317-26
techniques, 319-22

Colleges, 342-43

Communication skills, poor, 17

Communication
in interviews, 158-62
lack of, 283
listening skills, 159-62

with telecommuters, 351-52

Community, and corporate culture, 29-31

Compensation package
competing, 244
flexible, 247-48
in offer, 179-80
perks, 197-202

Compensation, 190-93
adequate, 42
correcting inequities, 43
inequities in, 3-4, 195-96

Concierge service, 201

Conduct, and corporate culture, 32-34

Constructive discontent, 290

Corporate culture
assessing, 46-52
changing, 22-23
formation of, 28-32
negative, 2
perceptions of, 47-48
reassessing, 358-60
signs of excellence, 34-41
and technology, 21-22
unofficial, 23-32

Corporate image, 29

Corporate Way of Life, 2, 46

Counteroffers, 183-84
to new hires, 102

Creativity, 38-39

Critical few objectives (CFOs), 211-14

Culture of excellence, 41
Customs, 24, 28-29

Deceptive hiring prac-
tices, 228
Dependability, of employ-
ees, 17-18
Development programs, in
schools, 341-45
Duties, clarifying, 178

Education requirements,
86, 88-89
Education
partnerships with, 341-
42
see also Training pro-
grams
Educational background
exaggerating, 121-22
questions, 133-34
Employee loyalty, 255-60
generating, 257-60
Employee retention, 346-
58
Employee surveys, 54, 62-
63
Employees
complaints about, 13-20
and future of the firm,
245-46
reasons for losing, 239-
55
short-term, 271-73
perceptions, 47-48
Employment offer, 176-80
Employment testing, 166-
69
Enterprise contracts, 27-
28
Environment
and new hires, 210-11
unsatisfactory, 250-53
Equal Opportunity Em-
ployment Law, 130
Evaluating training pro-
grams, 326-33
Executive coaching, 317-
319, 322-26
Exercise rooms, 200
Exit interview, 264-71
follow-up, 273-75

questions to ask, 266-
70
timing of, 264-66
Expectations, 41
clarifying, 179
too high, 227
Experience requirements,
86-87
Experience
exaggerating, 122
questions on, 135-36

Fear of failure, 294
Fear-based management
style, 4-5
First impressions, 215-17
Flexible hours, 181-82,
199, 251-53
Flexible work force, 356-58
Flextime, see Flexible
hours
Focus groups, 53
peer-based, 63-65
Fraud on resume, 121-23
Freelance help, 355-56
Functional resumes, 116-18

Golden Rule, 44
Government, and corpo-
rate culture, 31

Hands-off management,
226-27
Help wanted ads, 91-92
High potential,
people with, 347
Hiring bonuses, 180
Hiring decision
intangible factors, 170-
73
intuition, 176
team factors, 174-75
use of testing, 166-69
Hiring from within, 102-
10
Hiring mistakes, 87-102
biases, 165-66
common, 175-76
emphasis on appear-
ance, 165
Hiring
deception in, 228
reasons for, 76-78

Holistic diagnosis, 49
Incentive programs, 188-
89
financial, 191
Induction, 230-35
see also On-boarding
Informal organization, 24-
32
power of, 295
Information gathering, 52-
57
Initiative, lack of, 16-17,
18-19
Innovation, 38-39
Intelligence tests, 166-67
Internal transfers, 102-10
see also Promotions
Internships, 343
Interview summary sheet,
151-52
Interview
common mistakes, 153-
58
communication prob-
lems, 158-62
concluding, 145, 147-48
first, 129-30
key questions, 131-40
preparation for, 112-26,
128-29; see also Re-
sumes
putting applicant at
ease, 142-43
separation, 264-71
structured, 141-42
taking notes during,
149-50
unlawful questions, 95-
96
with employees, 54-55
with informal leaders,
65-66

Job analysis, 76-81
Job description, 78, 82-83,
100
for new hire, 220-21
gathering information,
80-81
mismatching candidate
to, 100
worker interview, 79
worksheet, 82-83

Job offer, 176-80; *see also*
Offer of employment
Job opening, analyzing,
76-81
Job posting, 106
Job Results Description,
222-23
Job sharing, 354-56
Judging applicants, 164-66
intangible factors, 170-
73

Key manager assessments,
55-57
Kirkpatrick-Phillips Model
of training evaluation,
328-30
Knock-out factors, 113-14

Labor, 27-28
Leaders
future, 287-88, 296-97
informal, 65-66
qualities of, 288-96
Leadership
changing functions of,
286-88
development of, 296-
307
development program,
307-310
employee involvement
in, 286-87
failure of, 277-85
informal, 24-26
quiz, 278-82
role models, 39-40
Lifelong learning, 343-45
Listening skills, 159-62
Loss of employees, 239-55
Loss of leadership, 277-85
Loyalty, 255-60

Management style
autocratic, 10
dislike of, 254-55
and employee retention,
276-77
on exit interview, 268-
69
fear-based, 4-5
great leadership, 288-96
hands-off, 226-27

and loyalty, 257
self-centered, 9-10
value-based, 37-38
Management
assessing, 55-57
faith in, 239-40
support of, 60-61
see also Leadership
Managers, complaints
about, 3-13
Master, Business Adminis-
tration, 88-89
Memberships, perks, 198
Mentoring fatigue syn-
drome, 217
Mentoring, 316
Mentors, assigning to new
hire, 214-15, 219
Military style of manage-
ment, 10
Mission statement, 46
Money, 188-89
see also Salary; Com-
pensation package;
Satisfiers vs. motiva-
tors
Motivators, 187-88, 189-90
Multi-level assessments,
55-57

Negativity, in corporate
culture, 2
New hires
induction of, 230-35
jealousy of, 228-30
orientation, 208, 226
support for, 217-18,
224-25
see also On-boarding

Objectives, for new hires,
211-14, 220
Offer of employment,
176-80
compensation package,
178-80
duties and expectations,
178-79
obstacles, 180-84
On-boarding, 208-30
critical few objectives,
211-14
first impressions, 215-17

plans, 209-10
successful practices,
219-25
worst practices, 225-30
Organizational MRI (O-
MRI), 48-50
procedure, 59-74
worksheets, 69-74
Orientation, 207-35
see also On-boarding
Orientation, 207-35
Outsourcing, 355-56

Performance tests, 167-
68
Performance
poor, 8
superior, 11-12
Perks, 197-202
Personal development,
297-307
Personal referrals, 90-91
Personality tests, 168-69
Physical qualifications,
133
Politics in workplace,
243-44
Poor communication, *see*
Communication
Positive thinking, 293
Post-separation interview,
273-75
Practices, unsatisfactory,
250-53
Pragmatism, 28-29
Pre-screening candidates,
92-94, 112-26
Pride, 35-36
Problem-solving teams, 59
Professional standards, 41
Profit sharing, 41, 192
Promises, broken, 8
Promotions from within,
90, 102-10
pros and cons, 103-04

Questions, for applicant,
131-40, 143-44
non-directive, 145-46

Recruiting
cost of, 76
deceptive, 228

Reference checks, 97-98
Reinforcement theory, 12
Rejection, of resume, 120-21
Reports, on Organizational MRI, 68
Requirements for employment
see Job description;
Specifications
education, 86, 88-89
experience, 86-87
Respect, for employees, 10
Resumes, 112-26
between the lines, 114-15
evaluating, 119-23
misleading, 92-94
styles of, 115-18
Retention of "A-players", 346-58
Retention, *see* Turnover
Retirement of colleague, 247
Retreats, 57, 67-68
Return on investment
evaluations, 330-33
Rewards, for superior work, 11-12
Role models, 39-40
Root problems, assessment, 50-51

Salary negotiations, 180-83, 193-97
Salary, 101-02
and employee retention, 187-88
for new hires, 195-96
Satisfiers vs. motivators, 187-90
Self-employment, 122
Separation interview, 264-71
Short-term employees, 271-73

Situational questions, 144-45
Skill development, 312-17
Socializing, 15-16
Specifications, job, 78, 81, 84-85, 100
trivial, 89-90
Stability, candidate's, 125-26
State of the art equipment, 251
Stock options, 193, 196-97
Structured interview, 94-95, 141-42
Success Development Process, 314
Success, celebration of, 43-44
Surveys, 54
Survival of the Fittest, 226-27

Talent, resources for, 341-45
Teams, problem-solving, 59
Telecommuting, 349-353
Temporary staff, 356-58
Terms of employment, 101
Testing, pre-employment, 166-69
Town meetings, 58
Trainee evaluations, 327
Training programs, 311-26
Allstate Insurance, 335-36
GTE, 336-38
measuring, 326-33
Saturn Company, 334-35
Walt Disney World Resorts, 333-34
Transformational coaching, 322-26
Trust, earning, 51-51
Turnover
exit interview, 264-71
preventive maintenance, 261

reasons for, 239-55
reasons for, feeling bored, 242
reasons for, feeling exploited, 245
Turnover, reasons for, feeling unappreciated, 241-42

Unions, 27-28
Unlawful interview questions, 95-96
Unqualified candidates, 88, 94
Unstructured interview, 94-95

Vacancy
notice of, 87-88
reasons for, 76-78, 239-55
see also Job opening
Value-based management style, 37-38

Way of Life, *see* Corporate Culture
White Space management, 232-33
Work environment, unsatisfactory, 250-53
Work habits, poor, 13-16
Working at home, 353-54
see also Telecommuting
Work-Life programs, 202-04, 253-54, 348-58
Worksheets
Final Selection Spreadsheet, 177
Interview Summary, 151-52
Job Results Description, 222-23
The Leadership Quiz, 278-82
Workshops, to gain trust, 51